RESERVOIRS

A Assabet Reservoir
B Lake Cochituate
C Fort Meadow
D Millham Reservoir
E Sudbury Reservoir
F Sudbury No. 1
G Sudbury No. 2
H Sudbury No. 3

A Conscious Stillness

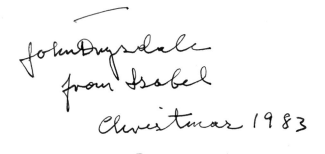

Ann H. Zwinger

John Drysdale
from Isobel
Christmas 1983

Maps and drawings by Ann Zwinger
Photographs by Edwin Way Teale

1817

HARPER & ROW, PUBLISHERS, New York

Cambridge, Philadelphia, San Francisco,
London, Mexico City, São Paulo, Sydney

A Conscious Stillness

Two Naturalists on Thoreau's Rivers

Ann Zwinger and
Edwin Way Teale

FIRST EDITION

Designer: C. Linda Dingler

Library of Congress Cataloging in Publication Data

Zwinger, Ann, date
   A conscious stillness.
    1. River ecology—Massachusetts—Concord region. 2. Concord region (Mass.)—History. 3. Thoreau, Henry David, 1817–1862—Homes and haunts—Massachusetts—Concord region.
   I. Teale, Edwin Way, 1899–1980. II. Title.
QH105.M4Z84   974.4′4   81–48153
ISBN 0–06–015002–5   AACR2

82 83 84 85 86 10 9 8 7 6 5 4 3 2 1

With love,
for Nellie and Edwin

Contents

*The stillness was intense and almost conscious,
as if it were a natural Sabbath, and we fancied
that the morning was the evening of a celestial
day. The air was so elastic and crystalline that
it had the same effect on the landscape that a
glass has on a picture, to give it an ideal
remoteness and perfection.*

HENRY DAVID THOREAU,
*A Week on the Concord
and Merrimack Rivers,* 1849

Preface

"I am also happy to report," Edwin wrote, "that my annual dawn canoe ride up the river was especially fine this year—stealing through mist curling up from the stream and then, after sunrise, passing under the arch of a bridge where the ripples reflected the rays upward to form running lines of light all across the curve of the masonry."

That letter dated July 12, 1976, described a canoe trip with Walter Harding on the occasion of the annual Thoreau Society Meeting in Concord, Massachusetts. To me, miles away in Colorado, it offered an enticement I can't explain. Partly, I think, it was the irresistible pull of a river. Partly, Edwin's letter reminded me of the kind of canoeing I grew up with. And partly it was Edwin's engaging enthusiasm that lured me to see those "running lines of light."

In any case, the letter was the beginning. And out of that, the gentle nature writer of more than thirty books and a naturalist from Colorado who loves rivers came to a decision to write a book about the Assabet and the Sudbury, which join to make the Concord, Thoreau's and Hawthorne's and Emerson's and history's river. In the concept was an implied parallel: two writers who grew up in Indiana and went their separate ways, met in later years to write about two rivers that begin close together, diverge, become quite different and meet again. As Edwin characterized us:

All three of us, Nellie, Ann and I, had roots in Indiana. In time, Nellie and I had moved east, and Ann and her husband, Herman, a retired Air Force lieutenant colonel, had moved west. Ann and I had each grown up beside midwestern streams. By different paths, Ann and I had arrived at the same combination of intense interest, emotional response, a feeling of oneness with our surroundings in the out-of-doors. Like the two rivers, following their separate ways to reach a meeting point at Egg Rock, we had come by widely separate routes to arrive at this common ground.

There was other "common ground" as well. From 1959 until his death, Edwin and his wife, Nellie, lived an idyllic existence at Trail Wood. And I do most of my work at our place in the mountains. In both places there are winding paths and quiet woods, spring flowers and a needed quiet. Edwin wrote:

> We [have] both found some special foothold upon the earth, some plot of ground to which we [are] deeply attached: I, at Trail Wood, our sanctuary-farm among the hills of northeastern Connecticut; [you, Ann] at Constant Friendship, 8,500 feet above sea level in the Front Range of the Rockies. For us, Constant Friendship and Trail Wood are like little islands of simpler life in a sea of ever-increasing complexities. There we can strip away so much that is really unneeded. There we can untangle ourselves from the sticky webs that hold us fast elsewhere. . . .

Our original outline, based largely on Edwin's conception, called for three parts, covering first the Sudbury, then the Assabet, and finishing with a section on the Concord River. The first two were to include what fascinated us—the history, geology, the flora and fauna, written in tandem, so to speak. The last section was to be more philosophical, dwelling on viewpoints. I also saw it as becoming somewhat biographical about one of this country's most loved and respected authors. Sadly, we were never able to complete the last section.

Before Edwin's death, we had canoed or walked most of each other's rivers at one time or another, together or separately, and had canoed the part of the Concord we wished to cover. Even when I canoed stretches of the Assabet that Edwin, because of doctor's orders, could not, he was there on the bridge as I careered under, leaning over the railing, shouting a word of encouragement lost in the rush of the water. And when Edwin went on an expedition with some other companion—after all, he lived close by and he and Nellie used to "run up to Concord" frequently—he would share the trips in long detailed letters filled with the delights of discovery.

The days Edwin and I had together on the rivers were the kind that one goes back to in memory as what a day should be, always capped with dinner, Edwin and Nellie and I, and when he could be there, my husband, Herman. In spite of the fact that, as his notes reveal, he often slept very poorly when traveling, Edwin was the most amiable and cheerful of companions. He had the energy and the spring in his step that was youthfulness incarnate. Perhaps he himself was aware of it, for he wrote:

> Here is something to ponder on: To what extent is the secret of a long and happy life never quite growing up, never becoming completely adult, settled down and no longer continually surprised and diverted by things as are the young. Keeping a youthful interest is rare as people become more staid with the years. Certainly I have never felt completely grown up. And, no doubt, that is the way I have appeared to others!

It was the enthusiasm which lighted his face and his words that endeared him to everyone who spent time with him. One Sunday we paddled seven miles on the Concord River in an unremitting rain. Warm in my rain suit, I watched the bubbles dance on the water surface as the raindrops hit, basking happily in the moisture like a mushroom, the rain a real treat for this desiccated Westerner. Suddenly I thought: Good Lord, this must be *miserable* for Edwin! Just at that moment, a voice from the stern said, "Oh, *isn't* this fun!" And within the week a letter came to Colorado: "I will never forget all that multitude of great shining bubbles on the surface of the river when we paddled down the Concord in the rain.... I kept thinking that there was nowhere else in the world I would rather be. There was nothing else I would rather be doing. This was what I had looked forward to for so long." Many times he entered in his notes phrases like "a golden day" or "What fun, what fun!" A marvelous companion indeed.

Edwin was a tenacious researcher with terrier-like persistency. "In the delights of research, I develop a kind of prospector's fever: the next book I skim through, the next person I talk to, the next thing I see, may produce a nugget or at least high-grade ore." (We probably both, given our druthers, would have preferred being holed up in the "Basement Cage" of the Concord Free Public Library doing research to writing.) When he finally pinpointed a fact, he was triumphant. And in his notes, after a day of interviewing, there was always a word about how empathetic he had found someone, or "another wonderful day!" and how pleased he was to have spent time with someone so generous and giving of his knowledge. In spite of the isolated life he led, Edwin loved people and they responded in kind.

At Trail Wood, Edwin methodically filed blue notebooks of letters, journals typed and handsomely bound, and posted his month's schedule, typed out on yellow paper, precisely framed and underlined in different colors, neat and orderly, as he planned and executed his life. His home provided the isolation and protection he needed, and he was able to maintain a distance there in order to accomplish the work he wished to accomplish. While completing final editing on his last book, *A Walk Through the Year*, he wrote me:

> This is the kind of life I am leading: I get up every morning between five and five-thirty, walk the fifth of a mile down the lane and back for the morning paper, have breakfast, consisting of a cup of Sanka and a toasted English muffin, and am at work by six or a little after. I am feeling well, living intensely, making good progress, and am happy. I am sure most of the people living on the face of the earth would feel sorry for me and think the life I lead extremely dull. But not for me. It is the life of all lives for me. This is what I am trying to do. . . . But what is the use of explaining? If the book is a success, it will explain itself. If it isn't, it won't matter. I suspect I am living in a time of your 'expanded time.' [Edwin never forgot Herman's comment, "Ann has jellybeans in her hourglass."] But in the back of my mind there is always the question: What if expanded time is not enough? I saw a headline in *The New York Times* the other day: "Time is no longer running out. It is gone."
>
> Can you make use of bits and pieces and fragments of time? Some people can, some cannot. I am lucky to be able to salvage something out of fragmented time. But, of course, there is no substitute for sustained, uninterrupted stretches of work. You have so many more responsibilities and obligations and

contacts to interrupt you. We live a pretty quiet life here. People do drive down the lane, strangers that want to visit. But I have developed a pretty smooth routine in giving visitors about three minutes and then turning them loose on the paths to see things for themselves. None, so far, has fallen into the pond or become lost in the woods.

In truth, it is difficult for me to write just "Edwin," for their relationship was so close that I always think of "EdwinandNellie." Married just after college, they enjoyed a companionship that most people cannot even conceptualize, let alone realize. It is perfectly expressed in Edwin's dedication to Nellie in *A Walk Through the Year*—the most loving and lovely tribute I've ever read.

Amused by a reviewer of one of his books who commented that Edwin never missed anything, but if he did, Nellie caught it, Edwin wrote that the reviewer

> was at least half right—the latter half. I have never known anyone else who was quite as observant of little things as she is. It is always fun to talk about what we have seen after we have been in the woods. This includes little sounds, little sights, little actions. Also she is especially good at seeing relationships and the workings of cause and effect. That is a quality that would be invaluable somewhere, perhaps in a research library.

All during their married life Nellie read out loud; he once wrote:

> We are reading *Don Quixote* again. Whenever we are desperate, seemingly at the end of our rope, unable to cope with overwhelming misfortunes, it is *Don Quixote* that saves our sanity and keeps us from having some kind of nervous breakdown. It happened the first time in 1927, that dreadful year at Furnessville when my father was dying and did die, when David [their son] had an abscess in his ear and the doctor thought the ear drum was ruptured, when Nellie had acute appendicitis and I was taken to the hospital with a high fever and blood poisoning and when we were running out of money and I lost my job. Then, every evening, we would go to bed and Nellie would read in *Don Quixote*. For us it is the greatest book ever written, such a wonderful combination of the ridiculous and the noble, the wise and the absurd. We came to love Don Quixote in a special way that has never left us. As chapter follows

chapter, he and Sancho Panza become more real than the light or the room around us. We were completely taken out of ourselves. For a little time we could forget our troubles. The endless squirrel cage of worries, of problems too big for us to solve, could be left behind.

Nellie had an ear for the cadences of his prose and read all his manuscripts out loud to him. It was an indispensable part of preparation. It had to be "right" to his ear, and together they listened for melody, for flow; Edwin described the scene as she read the final version of *A Walk Through the Year* in May of 1977:

> You would never recognize me these days, Ann. Nellie is reading aloud the long revised manuscript. And I have turned overnight from that gentle, lovable character, the author, into a flinty-eyed, mean-spirited, carping, gloating, nitpicking, never-give-anybody-the-benefit-of-the-doubt critic. We still have a little fire in the fireplace. While Nellie reads, I sit at a folding table with a long red record book before me jotting down with a Parker's wick pen scathing denunciations and sarcastic comments on the inadequacies of the author. I am tearing him to shreds and jumping up and down on him.

Nellie read most of this book out loud to me, and I learned what Edwin was talking about and how unbelievably helpful it was: one hears things one cannot see. Those were precious hours for me.

Nellie and I discovered early on that we both love to pour over botany books. She has a knowledge of birds and flowers that complemented Edwin's. When I asked what an unfamiliar plant was, Edwin *always* said, "Let's take it back to Nellie—*she'll* know!" And out came the well-thumbed volumes of Britton and Brown's *An Illustrated Flora of the Northern United States and Canada*, and then came the answer, delivered with Nellie's crinkly-eyed smile that lights up the dark. And there were those days, when the paddling had been arduous, when I though that on *this* book Nellie had all the fun.

Edwin's wide reading made me envious. His recall of detail was superb, his breadth of knowledge was marvelous. In addition, he had made it a point to meet all contemporary nature writers, an impressive list—"I have known, and have been on a friendly basis with, all the major nature writers from Henry Beston and Donald Culross Peattie to Rachel Carson and Joseph Wood Krutch and Loren Eiseley and Hal Borland." He compiled *Green Treasury,* a rich selection from several centuries of nature writing.

He introduced me to writers I had not read, most particularly W. H. Hudson. And Trollope—there was always a tiny English edition from Edwin and Nellie to go home in my briefcase.

We spent hours absorbed in conversations that cut across time and place and experience, involved in what nature writers write about. We both found in the natural world a world that made sense, in which sunrise and moonset and the turning of the seasons could be counted on to measure our lives. Edwin described it quite accurately when he wrote that neither of us had been "driven to nature because we could not hold our own in society. We have gone because we found nature supplied something that meets a special, often hard-to-explain need, something we miss everywhere else. A deep and close relationship with nature seems essential to our lives."

For canoeing, Edwin and I worked out an amiable arrangement—Edwin in the stern, I in the bow—which suited us both. Being in the stern is being confined in a supervisory world of steering and responsibility. With his characteristic good humor, Edwin, who had been reading a book on canoeing, wrote that "the paddler in the stern is the one in authority, the captain of the boat, who should be looked up to with respect and even reverence. And here, all this time, I thought he was only the one who weighed the most!"

To me, whoever sits in the stern sits in an always populated space; I can't abide being in the stern with a back forever in front of me. In the bow, even though my woolgathering can never be done surreptitiously, I can see more. I like being at the edge of a world that ends two feet in front of me. I want to see the rock ahead that I'm likely to hit, the riffle to perk down, the ruffles of white water.

And Edwin said he couldn't abide the bow. And I think perhaps where each of us sat was indicative of how we saw the world.

Like all co-anything, while we shared a devotion to craft and pleasure in working together on this book, Edwin and I had our differences. My commitment to the Assabet came early on. I was enchanted by the beauty in its lower reaches: the clear golden water, the huge oaks and maples and hemlocks bending over it, the soft clarity of the light, its smallness and intimacy. There were touches of wildness—brief, it's true, but there nevertheless. In its upper reaches it is a river more connected to the economics of the area, with the changes that brings to a river, and that interested me *very* much.

So I suggested that I do the Assabet, Edwin the Sudbury, and both of us the Concord. Edwin entered in his notes: "Ann, who has fallen in love with the Assabet River, on the basis of seeing only the last few miles, has the idea I may take the Sudbury and she the Assabet. I am less than enthusiastic about it but we can talk it all over via letter." He opined that we ought to have good discussions, "an Indiana lawyer's daughter and an Indiana state's championship debater.... I am good at giving in when I am convinced by arguments. But I can feel my ears shooting up and I became a mule when presented with an ultimatum."

In short, Edwin demurred. Edwin had had in mind a kind of "canoe conversations" book:

> We can "earmark" conversations we might have had along the way and then work them up later. We will make note of links to ideas in what we see as we paddle down the streams. Let's not "flood the carburetor" by trying to do too much. It will all come back if we have a good time. (When I was editing an edition of *Walden*, I once checked back where material came from in the journals and it was surprising what a large proportion of the book appeared in the journal entries made *after* Thoreau had left the pond.) We can do the same. Anything we think of at any time before our book goes in is fair material to include.

He was a quietly stubborn person and held to his original intent that this was to be an interwoven book. Since I also incline to stubbornness on occasion, we reached an impasse that was solved by a *deus ex machina*: Edwin's doctor decreed "*No* white water!" which prevented him from canoeing what, if not true white water, were the more lively reaches of the Assabet. He wrote afterwards:

> So I will have to make a 180-degree turn there and we will have to consider what that will mean to our plans for the book. If you are the only one to make the most exciting part of the trip down the Assabet—while Nellie and I watch you go by from successive bridges—it surely will shift the balance of the

collaboration. Under these conditions, we may have to go back and think about the unthinkable. We may have to organize the book as you proposed so long ago and I opposed so stoutly—you taking the Assabet while I take the Sudbury. I am getting dizzy making 180-degree turns! I still see all the same old objections but we can try to find ways around them.

Whether the book could be finished at all after Edwin's death in October 1980 was predicated upon whether there was enough material in his hand to make a balanced work. Thanks to Nellie Donovan Teale and the Teales' close friend and executor, W. Clark Stocking, all the work Edwin had done was searched for and found, and thanks to John McDonald, head of the library at the University of Connecticut (where Edwin's papers now reside), all were xeroxed for use. The editors at Harper & Row with whom I am fortunate enough to work, Buz Wyeth and Corona Machemer, and I felt, after months of sifting through Edwin's reworked text and chapters he had virtually completed, some 200 single-spaced pages of notes (when we have used Edwin's notes in the text, they are bracketed), over 250 pages of letters (Edwin was an indefatigable letter writer), plus 100 pages of "Canoe Conversations," that there was indeed sufficient material.

We were aided immeasurably because Edwin was a fastidious writer; he once told me that he was the only author at Dodd, Mead—with whom he had had a long and felicitous relationship—whose book they began setting into type before the final chapters were in, such was their confidence in the perfection of the completed work.

In the chapters for this book, each in its own labeled envelope, were often from three to a dozen retypings of a single page. And each chapter manuscript was dated, page by page: "Completed at 4:45 P.M., on December 31, 1979—seven hours and fifteen minutes before the year ends and the new year begins."

Not that writing came easy:

But I feel a little better since the last day of 1979. At 5:30 P.M. on New Year's Eve I finished getting the first chapter down on paper. It had been like climbing up the face of a cliff an inch at a time, using a rope. But it is ridiculous how relieved I felt. I was on my way!

He did not write in sequence but from a sense that the research was done and thus a certain chapter was ready to be written; because he did not write until he was mentally ready to do so, the chapters simply bloomed onto the page. But he felt about writing first drafts as I do: I'd rather clean closets first. And perhaps he hit upon the reason:

> I think the reason we dread the first draft of a book so much is not only that it is a time of endless decisions—what to put in, what to leave out, how to begin, how to end, etc. etc.—but it is the time when the book we dreamed of writing, the book that has been floating in the air, so to speak, has to be confined by words on paper. Immediately there are intimations that the book is beginning to be less than we hoped it would be. The reason the revision is so much fun is that little by little, day after day, we feel we are lifting the book back nearer the original goal.

But working on revisions wasn't that easy either, especially when he was interrupted and had to start all over again:

> These are my "Earthworm Days" when I am plowing back and forth through the paragraphs, loosening up lumpy or soggy sentences and enriching the book by inserting new facts and ideas as the earthworm enriches the soil by pulling pieces of leaves underground. Or, to put it another way, I am occupied these days folding over my manuscript in the sense that Thoreau meant when he wrote to Ralph Waldo Emerson: "In writing conversation should be folded many times thick."

Edwin was the quintessential note-taker. That immediate recording of what he say gave his work accuracy and freshness, and reading his notes, written in terse phrases, often in present tense, gives one the pleasure of seeing his intelligent and receptive understanding of the natural world about him. When I complimented him upon the excellent and thorough notes he took, he wrote back:

> Speaking of journal-keeping, William Beebe once told me of something that Ernest Thompson Seton said to him. I have thought of it innumerable times since. Seton advised Beebe to stop, when he was making notes in the jungle about something he planned to write about later, and imagine himself back at his desk at home, asking himself what else he would like to know. I have often done this and been thankful for the addi-

tional specific sights and sounds and smells recorded that helped bring the scene to life later on.

He also typed up his notes faithfully, and this is a sincere tribute from one nature writer to another: transcribing field notes is one of those tedious workaday tasks I am hard pressed to get done, and I was in awe of Edwin's dedication and accomplishment. Each page of those notes was likewise dated and titled and numbered. Edwin *always* knew where he was.

In working from his notes I am also in awe of his typing; he almost never made the kind of transpositions that one ordinarily makes and his pages are generally without error. But he had one maddening trait: he put no spaces after periods or commas, and typed right to both margins of the page. When I mentioned this to him several times, he finally asked Nellie, "What *is* she talking about?" And Nellie replied sensibly, "Because it makes it easier to read!" To which Edwin replied, "Never underestimate the power of *two* women five feet tall." Well, he tried valiantly for a while but couldn't resist a little good-humored nudge:

> Ann, do you notice all the double spaces after periods in this letter? I wonder if you have considered all the works of wisdom, words of wit, words of advice, words of praise that might have been included in this letter if all available space had been used?"

And his notes and letters soon reverted to the comfortable form he was used to.

In writing, Edwin preferred the objectivity of the past tense, I like the immediacy of the present. "Do we want to put part, or most, or all, of the narrative in the present tense?" Edwin wrote, back at the beginning in 1976, "or do we want to put it all in the past tense?" Somehow we never got around to discussing it—there were always so many *other* things to talk about. So the tenses as each of us wrote have been retained; perhaps they, too, are indicative of our ways of looking at the world.

In an odd way, and one that gives me a secret smile, I think the book as it now stands is closer to Edwin's original concept of "canoe conversations" than I ever imagined it would be. And it goes along much as Edwin and I went along in the canoe, from one river to the other, exchanging information about times and places that we had discovered, attuned to the progress of the rivers, enjoying them to the fullest. The intercutting of Edwin's text (mostly on the Sudbury) with mine (primarily on the Assabet), weaving as Buz Wyeth suggested, I think would have pleased Edwin very much.

I can hear him say, in a typical Edwinism, "Now it's the *real rabbit!*" which he explained once in a letter:

> When the French sculptor Rodin was a poor art student he lived at a cheap boardinghouse where the one big meal of the week consisted of rabbit stew. To fill up the boarders as cheaply as possible the rabbit was prepared with an immense amount of gravy. All the rest of his life, Rodin divided people and events into two classes. People of real character and events of lasting significance were "the real rabbit"; people intent merely on show and events of passing value were "the gravy."

So bless you, Edwin, for a long and rewarding conversation—on the river and on paper, for graciousness under pressure, for putting up with an outspoken companion whose ideas were often not yours, for listening, for enjoying the rivers, for providing continuity and accomplishment. Although you and I agreed at the beginning that this book would be dedicated to the central characters in our own scripts, Nellie and Herman, I hope Herman will forgive me if it is dedicated, as it should be, to Nellie and Edwin.

Ann Zwinger

Constant Friendship
January 12, 1982

A Conscious Stillness

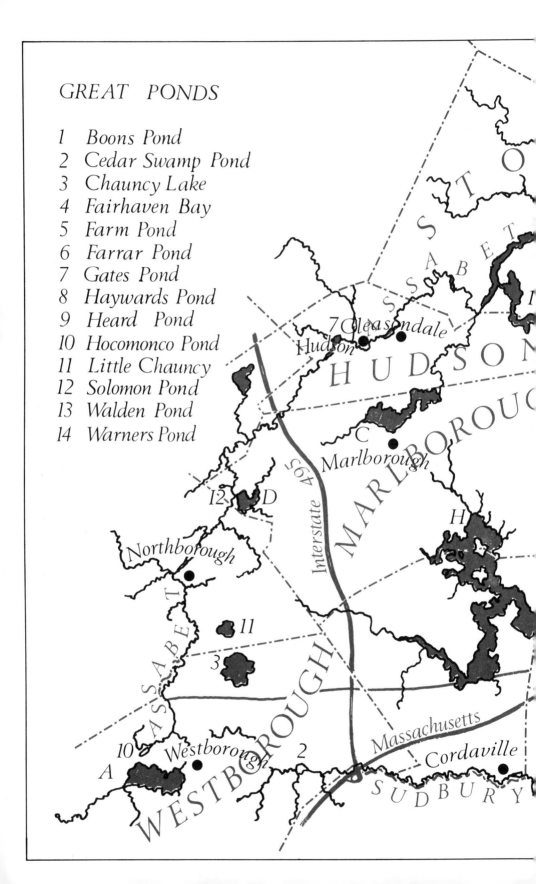

GREAT PONDS

1 Boons Pond
2 Cedar Swamp Pond
3 Chauncy Lake
4 Fairhaven Bay
5 Farm Pond
6 Farrar Pond
7 Gates Pond
8 Haywards Pond
9 Heard Pond
10 Hocomonco Pond
11 Little Chauncy
12 Solomon Pond
13 Walden Pond
14 Warners Pond

RESERVOIRS

A Assabet Reservoir
B Lake Cochituate
C Fort Meadow
D Millham Reservoir
E Sudbury Reservoir
F Sudbury No. 1
G Sudbury No. 2
H Sudbury No. 3

We are favored in having two rivers flowing into one, whose banks afford different kinds of scenery, the streams being of different charac-ters; one [the Sudbury] a dark, muddy, dead stream, full of animal and vegetable life, with broad meadows and black dwarf willows and weeds, the other [the Assabet] comparatively *pebbly and swift, with more abrupt banks and narrower meadows. To the latter I go to see the ripple, and the varied bottom with its stones and sands and shadows; to the former for the influence of its dark water resting on invisible mud, and for its reflections.*

HENRY DAVID THOREAU,
Journals, July 5, 1862

1

EWJ We left the singing of meadowlarks and the smell of
fresh-cut grass behind us that June morning when we
lifted from the runway at Hanscom Field and climbed to the
height of a mile above the Great Meadows along the Concord River. The blue-and-white Cessna Skyhawk tilted into a sweeping
curve to the left. It swung our gaze in an immense arc from the
distant gray blocks of Boston's highest buildings to the shine of
the Merrimack winding through Lowell. Then, as we straightened
out, it became centered on the scene below.

The winter snow had melted. White had become green. The
spring freshets had carried off the meltwater, and now the rivers
far below us wound through a summer landscape and the great
fan-shaped watershed spread away below the plane.

Appearing just ahead, its streets and stores and houses and
white steeples all in miniature, lay the historic town of Concord. It
huddled along the banks of the Sudbury, spilled across the Assabet, trailed away downstream on either side of the Concord River.
In its midst lay Egg Rock, an outcropping of some of the most
ancient stone of the region, the prow of a point of land. Here we
glimpsed "the meeting of the waters" where the Sudbury, winding up from the south, and the Assabet, curving in from the west,
meet and joint to form the larger Concord.

Beyond, extending away to the south and west, sharply imprinted in the sunshine close at hand, dimming into a hazy soft

1

focus toward the far-off horizon, stretched a vast expanse of fields and woods, towns and villages, streams and farms, with its network of interconnecting roadways—three hundred and more square miles that comprise the watershed of the rivers.

Looking ahead, we let our gaze wander across this land, following the irregular courses of the two upper streams, seeing them bulge outward from their joining point, eventually to turn inward, to narrow, and almost to touch at their separate places of origin, less than five miles apart on opposite sides of the same Massachusetts town, Westborough. On a map, they suggest an immense pair of calipers, Egg Rock forming the base and hinge.

Beside me, in the four-place cabin of the Skyhawk, Steve Rosenthal, our pilot, eased back the throttle, and we slid in a long descent to an elevation of a thousand feet for a closer view.

The two seats behind us held Nellie, my wife, who has been part of all my wanderings through the natural history of America, and Ann Zwinger, of Colorado Springs, whose books on the Rocky Mountain region, *Beyond the Aspen Grove, Land Above the Trees*, and *Wind in the Rock*, have been additions to the best in modern nature writing. We had met when she had received the John Burroughs Memorial Association Medal for *Run, River, Run*, her account of following the wild Green River from its source in the Wind River Range of Wyoming through Utah to its juncture with the Colorado. At the time, I had suggested that after her experiences with the mighty rivers of the West, she might enjoy exploring quieter streams of special interest that flow through the Thoreau country of eastern Massachusetts. This overview of the three rivers was a prelude to that adventure.

Steve swung to the left of Egg Rock and we began tracing, upstream, the wide brown flow of the wandering Sudbury River. Below us, it and the Main Street in Concord ran side by side. We curved above it into the south along that portion of the stream whose features added so many entries to Thoreau's multivolumed *Journal*—Sunset Reach, Money-Digger's Hill, Bittern Cliff, Hollowell Farm, and that lake-like widening of the river, Fairhaven Bay.

Beyond Lee's Bridge, we looked down on a river flowing in lazy serpentines through a land bordered by wide green floodplains. Broad river meadows dominated the far landscape, pushing back the houses and the roads on either side. Here, mile after mile, the Sudbury cuts its track through the green of wild sedges

2

and grasses, endlessly winding along what was once the length of a prehistoric body of water, Lake Sudbury, which, at the end of the Ice Age, stretched almost from just south of Concord to just north of Framingham.

We circled for a time over Pantry Brook, which enters the river from the west, noting how it wanders far inland, a shining thread of water draining some miniature valley or tapping some saturated depression. The "pantry" part of the name of the brook and the valley arose from the immense flocks of waterfowl it attracted in the fall, the tons of wild cranberries it supplied and the valuable hay that grew along the borders of the shallow valley in pioneer times.

Just beyond, where the river takes a wider swing, we enclosed Weir Hill in another spiral in the air. There, before the sailing of the *Mayflower*, the Indians stretched their weir where the river shallows, to harvest fish in the spring.

Wayland Meadows, Sudbury Meadows, Sedge Meadows. They expanded and contracted beside the river. Sherman's Bridge, the Causeway Bridge, the Route 20 Bridge—these landmarks along the river appeared ahead and drifted past beneath our wings. Between Weir Hill and the wooden pilings supporting Sherman's Bridge, we found ourselves looking down on the commencement of more abrupt and erratic swings to the right and left, a spectacular feature of this portion of the river. Ahead, on either side of the vivid green in the widening valley, rose the white steeples of churches in the two earliest towns in the region, Wayland close to the eastern bank, Sudbury on higher ground further removed from the western bank. Between the two, where the Causeway Bridge supports the connecting highway, the lowland spreads out to a width of nearly a mile. Here, in Colonial times, extended those prized tracts of wild hay, dense and high, that formed the famous river meadows of Wayland and Sudbury.

The brown serpent that dragged its coils between the lush, wet meadows, the sediment-filled river, abruptly narrowed as we neared the landmark of landmarks along its course. We tilted into a revolving turn above it, the ruins of an old stone bridge that stood out in the sunshine like some weathered remnant of a Roman aqueduct. It only partially spans the river. The western end was destroyed in 1955, following the devastating flood that accompanied Hurricane Diane. All across the shallows above it, from

3

bank to bank, the water was in sinuous motion, alive with the endless waving of the freshwater eelgrass.

Just upstream, the celebrated Ox-Bow of the Sudbury throws its wide loop toward the east. The shadow of our plane drifted across it and over Pod Meadow, which arches as a green pea pod along the top of the Ox-Bow's loop. Then we were over a narrowing, twisting upstream river with multiplying buildings pressing it close, and, in their midst, hemmed in by houses and factories, the Saxonville Falls, the Great Falls of the Sudbury.

Smoke and haze increased. Ahead, mile after mile, the maze of Framingham, the largest city on the Sudbury. Toy houses crisscrossed in lines and curves and curlicues below us. Dots of brilliant turquoise, round and square and oval, stood out in the cityscape, each a modern status symbol, a backyard swimming pool. Tiny rectangles of yellow, drawn out into long lines, were school buses parked in storage fields. And spanning it all, the waters of the river, here stilled in the shining expanses of a chain of reservoirs originally built to supply water to Boston.

As we headed west, leaving Framingham, we could see a freight train, nearly a mile long, laboring over the rails of the Penn Central below. The river, a smaller, swifter stream now, in the early miles of its flow, wriggled beside the double track of the right-of-way, now drawing near, now swerving away, hurrying toward the east. The shine of its water appeared and disappeared among the trees.

We traced it upstream through Ashland, through Cordaville, through Southville. Ahead of us, in the distance, the town of Westborough took shape, and closer at hand, the rich green of the saturated bowl of Cedar Swamp. At its edge the railroad and the emerging river pass side by side under the same high bridge, and twin superhighways, angling toward each other, carry a millrace of traffic to and through their meeting place.

In wide circles we swept over the lowland where the Sudbury River begins its flow. Then we swung with the railroad west again—through Westborough, the one hundredth town incorporated in Massachusetts, and the birthplace of Eli Whitney, inventor of the cotton gin. Hardly more than two miles from the swamp that produces the Sudbury, we came to the lowland on the other side of Westborough that is the beginning place of the Assabet. The double tracks of the railroad skirt the edges of both swamps, the tiny crossties looking from the air like neat parallel rows of surgical stitches.

The second time Cedar Swamp lay below us, we crisscrossed it, descended for a closer look, noted how the brown water of the pond was ringed with a stippling of floating lily pads, traced the course of wandering threads of water, now a brilliant light green with a covering of duckweed, the meanderings of the small tributary watercourses that angle in to lose their identity in the dark, heart-shaped body of water called Cedar Swamp Pond. From its lower, more pointed end, with small incessant changes of direction, the beginning Sudbury, that river of innumerable bends, cuts east across the swamp, beginning the journey that will carry it to Egg Rock and its confluence with the Assabet.

AHZ   I cannot believe all this green. Nor all this civilization imposed upon it. As far as I can see beneath the airplane's wing are towns and highways and reservoirs, a table display set up with green-sponge trees, metal-strip streams, the straight lines of parking lots and tennis courts, a confetti of car rectangles and roofs roofs roofs, culminating in the vertical rectangles of Boston thirty miles away.

Even though I went to college here, taught art history here, met and married my husband here, I now feel alien. Alien to this verdure, this heat and humidity, this well-worn landscape whose horizons are blurred with haze. It's even another language: I'm learning to say "thorough" for Thoreau, instead of with the accent on the last syllable as Westerners are wont to pronounce it. Even flying at three thousand feet is a mental adjustment, for I *live* at six thousand!

The wing tilts, water catches sunlight, then flashes flat pewter. Traces of deeper green or a curving row of trees tell of other channels, and where the rivers ran before. I hear Edwin, sitting just in front of me, instruct our pilot: Would you turn a little more, please? Will you circle that swamp again? He's loved airplanes since he was a little boy and relates in *Dune Boy* how he tried to build one, and now the little boy grown up pilots us through the sky.

We have flown up and back over the Sudbury River; now it's time to do the same on the Assabet. We make a wide sweep around Egg Rock at the base of Nashawtuc Hill in Concord, and follow the "North River," as the Assabet was often called. According to local historians, Assabet is an Algonquin word meaning "the place where materials for making fishnets grow." If so, doubtless many settlers had problems with the euphonious but strange word and spelled it phonetically, according to their own ear. As early as 1650 it appears as Asibath, Isabeth, Elsabeth, Elzbeth, Elizabeth (a perfectly good English name which still appears on one of the tributaries), Assabeath, and Assabet. It was standardized in its present spelling in 1850.

How different is our overall view from that of the probable first white man to see the Assabet, William Wood. When he returned to England in 1632 he wrote a book called *New England's Prospects*, which, although full of cogent observations about plants and animals in this new country, was also promotional: to entice other Englishmen to America, he put the best face possible on the weather, the soil, the availability of food, stressing New England's virtues, minimizing its faults. Wood saw the confluence of the Assabet and Sudbury rivers at flood stage when he followed the Concord River south from its meeting with the Merrimack. He looked at Nashawtuc Hill from the east when the meadows around it were inundated and concluded that it was an island, and drew a map which showed the Assabet circling round the hill and making it so.

The Assabet, in its 31½ miles, is today a small, well-used river—often overused, as we can see from the air. It rises at an elevation of between 410 and 430 feet (depending upon your choice of source) near the Shrewsbury-Westborough town boundary and flows in a direction opposite to that of most New England rivers, generally north and northeast. It meets with the Sudbury in Concord at about 110 feet above sea level, for a fall of some 320 feet. It drains approximately 176 square miles, separated from adjacent drainage basins by the low divides characteristic of this gentle glaciated terrain.

Both the Assabet and the Sudbury are young rivers, established when glaciers melted ten thousand to fifteen thousand years ago, and as we fly over the landscape through which the Assabet wanders we see many drumlins, those rounded hills characteristic of glacial molding, and the raw scars of gravel pits, where glacier-deposited debris is mined. The "Great Ponds," kettle holes left by stagnating ice, glint like shiny coins as the plane constantly shifts our angles of reflection and refraction. (In the

middle of the seventeenth century, all lakes in the Commonwealth over ten acres were designated Great Ponds by the General
Court.)

Along the Assabet we see fewer of the meadowlands that
made the Sudbury so attractive to early settlers. The Assabet's valley is narrower, less hospitable. Its banks are high, approach more
difficult. Its waters can be swift and treacherous to cross. Farther
away from civilization in Colonial times, more exposed to Indian
raids, the land bordering the Assabet was slower to be taken up.
But its faster water made it suitable for mill development, which
brought new towns, economic betterment for some, and river pollution for the future.

Since there are few lowlands to absorb flood flows, a combination of melting snows and spring rain can send the Assabet on
a rampage. Major floods, associated also with hurricanes, have
been disastrous. When we reach the Westborough swamp where
the Assabet begins, the flood-retardation dam is a clear landmark,
barring the river within a mile of its beginnings, backing it up
into an area where once there were swamp and farmland.

Below the dam the river disappears as it curves under bow-
ers of trees, and there are mere glimpses of the small bridges that
span it; it becomes visible again under the Boston-Worcester turnpike, snaking across marshland, a stream stapled to the landscape
by bridges (the Assabet, in its thirty-one miles, has over forty
bridges; the Green River in the West, with which I am familiar,
has in its seven hundred miles but seven). A long squiggle of
white foam worms from the Westborough sewage treatment plant
down the Assabet's artificially straightened channel below. Then
the river resumes its natural quirking again, forming the north-
west-southeast boundary between Northborough and Westborough. Through a golf course, under more bridges, and the second
dam, in the center of Northborough, appears from the plane as a
narrow white line.

Out of Northborough the Assabet flows hidden, reappearing
as a long triangle behind the milldam at Woodside. Just before it
splashes over, it reflects the lovely gray stone of Wachusett Aqueduct. After Woodside the river works through sedge meadows,
threads of blue braiding around islands of green. Raw dirt, bull-
dozed ramps, fresh cement, mark the Tyler Dam Project, another
flood retardation dam.

The river slides around it and begins lazy loops through

open meadowlands, a short stretch of river above Hudson. Two major highways cross it in quick succession. We are flying low enough so that I can see the pale islets of duckweed on the river, white streaks of effluent, patches of sedge and pickerel weed, and even water lily pads! Two slivers of canoes ply the river, and I feel that old familiar tug, wishing to be *on* the river, not above it, with the seductive sound of water perking beneath the bow.

As we drone over farmlands and apple orchards laid like candlewicking on the hillsides, small valleys creasing the land between, the landscape looks like a huge crewel embroidery: close-packed French knots of green woolly trees, shiny satin-stitched river. The Assabet spills over a dam in the center of Hudson, flows out into the country after poking under railroad and highway bridges, then backs up behind the weir at the village of Gleasondale, with its long brick mill.

Past the Gleasondale mill the river turns, then slows once again, into the backwaters of the Ben Smith Dam above Maynard, which supplied power to the largest woolen mill in Massachusetts in the nineteenth century. An 1860 report notes that the Assabet's water level rose and fell according to the hours the mills were in operation, so heavy was the usage.

At the edge of Maynard, the river is obstructed by another milldam, the most troublesome one on the river at this writing. The structure is in bad repair and instead of the firm white waterline of the pour-over of a sturdy dam, the line here is jagged and broken. The impoundment is scum-covered and contains a lethal mass of sludge shot through with heavy metals from an overloaded sewage treatment plant that predates the current installation.

The last dam is at Damondale in West Concord and the river shoots through a breach on the right. When in working condition, the dam provided power for a cotton mill, and in later years, for the generation of electricity—the turbine, albeit inoperable, is still in place in the mill's basement. Below Damondale the river slithers between houses and under bridges, along the walls of the old Concord Reformatory buildings and under Route 2, its last bridge.

The Assabet's final miles, some of the loveliest reaches of the river, are hidden from view from the air. In secret, the river flows along the hook around Egg Rock and add its flow to that of the Sudbury and become the Concord.

Even from the air the contrast between the two rivers is patent. Where the Sudbury is reasonable and gracious, the Assabet is difficult and obscure. Where the Sudbury spreads out gently across its flood plain, the Assabet gallops and pounds down rock chutes and suffers no interference, largely following an old fault zone which dictates its course. The Sudbury gets ruffled once in a while, but only near its heading; it is more often a river of deep thoughts and beautiful flowerings. Where the Subury is pleasant and open, the Assabet is hard-working, carrying more, doing more, and perhaps suffering as a consequence.

The Assabet is a rock river, often rushing and noisy as it plows through obstacles, often a difficult river. The Sudbury is Emerson and Thoreau, afternoon tea, the Concord Social Circle and erudite conversation, canoeing on a summer evening. The Assabet is the industrial towns of Maynard and Hudson, Matthew Boone's bloody ambush, the roaring filth of an iron smelter, Brown's farmland covered by Damon's mill complex, plain names and undistinguished people and too many dams and too many wastewater treatment problems. But with, nevertheless, moments of brightness and beauty to gladden anyone who takes the time to find them.

As we bank and fly upriver, and watch the river stop at a dam and spread out into a reservoir time and again, I remind myself that the Assabet is a needed resource, and as such, is important to human existence, that there are balances to be decided upon, arguments to be adjudicated, life to be lived. I remind myself that utilization was inevitable in the scheme of things. Who on earth had time to notice its beauty and to boat this river when flour had to be ground, hay had to be cut, skins had to be tanned, flax retted, Indian raids survived, shoe soles pegged, cloth woven?

Not until the Concord romantics, living in a somewhat gentler era, was there time for wading the river and canoeing and taking "fluvial walks" and philosophizing and collecting plants. And even then, a river continued to be a place where you dumped your sewage, let off residue from the mills, and drowned unwanted kittens, just as it is still a place to toss beer bottles and old bedsprings and dead refrigerators and supermarket carts. The Assabet personifies the court ruling of 1871 in *Haskell* v. *New Bedford*: "One great natural office of the sea and all running waters is to carry off and dissipate, by their perpetual motion and currents

9

the impurities and offscourings of the land."

I remind myself again and again to be the pragmatist, not the romanticist—that is, until I swing my foot over the gunwale and dip a paddle into the water and watch the vortices spin counterclockwise behind the thin corkscrew ripple winding back from the bow.

2

EWJ The swamp—Cedar Swamp—spreads away over nearly fourteen hundred acres at the eastern edge of Massachusetts, fermenting with life in the late June sunshine. The pond—Cedar Swamp Pond—nestles at its center. It forms the hub of the wetland. Two hundred and seventy-four feet above sea level, nineteen acres in extent, it seems as remote and isolated as a mountain tarn or the Lake of the Dismal Swamp. Small brooks—Rutters, Denny, Jackstraw and Piccadilly—threading down from higher ground to the north, west and south join and empty into it. From its opposite side emerges the beginning Sudbury.

This we had seen outspread below us during our flight. On a later day in June, Ann and I launched our canoe beneath the high concrete bridge where, under two arches, one large, one small, the twin tracks of the Penn Central Railroad and the Sudbury River pass side by side, leaving the swamp behind. Stowing away an extra paddle, a knapsack of odds and ends, sandwiches and small cans of tomato and cranberry juice, we pushed away, met the surprisingly strong current head-on, and moved the first canoe length into the exploring of a river.

At first, sounds of civilization carried to us as we worked our way upstream: the roar and rattle of a freight train laboring along the right-of-way to our north; then a low rising and falling surf-like sound that swelled with our advance—the commingled swish and whine and blasting truck exhaust of superhighway traffic.

11

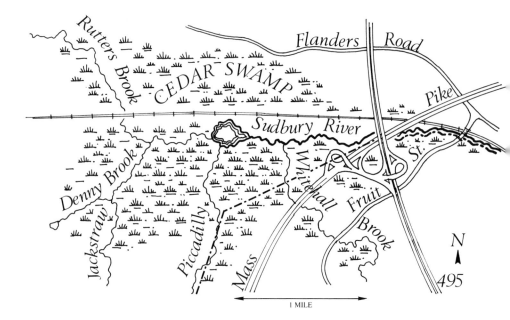

One of the paradoxes of Cedar Swamp is that hardly more than a mile from the solitude of the rarely visited pond at its heart, two of the main arteries of Massachusetts traffic intersect. Close to the eastern edge of the swamp, Route 495, running north and south, and the Massachusetts Turnpike, running east and west, meet and cross. In the course of a year, more than thirty million persons speed through this intersection. Few, if any, are aware of the swamp, or the pond, or the beginning Sudbury River.

As we paddled into the cavernous mouth of the single tunnel beneath the turnpike, the shadow shape of our canoe pushed across a wide band of brilliant lines of running light projected upward on the curve of the roof by sunlight glancing from moving ripples on the stream. Down either wall, higher than our heads, ran the straight line of the high water mark of spring. Once when my paddle struck the side of the metal canoe, hollow reverberations echoed along the tunnel, frightening a phoebe from her nest anchored to a rough place on the concrete and sending her flitting down the passageway toward the sunlight before us. We saw her tipping her tail on the branch of a streamside alder as we curved to the left and entered the double tunnel of the passage beneath Route 495.

When we emerged into the sunshine again, we pushed into a narrowing channel with steep mud banks winding across a corridor of smartweed. Slowly the surf sound of the highways receded, sank to a seashell murmur, then ceased completely as we wound deeper and deeper into the swamp.

At times we paddled with our outlook restricted by high walls of vegetation on either hand. At other times we came out into wide sedge meadows where the dried brown leaves of the previous year clustered around the clumps of sedges like the grass skirts of Hawaiian dancers. Once we navigated a series of six hairpin turns where the course of the river ran like folded ribbon candy and we found ourselves paddling back in the opposite direction close to the channel we had just left behind. For stretches of fifty yards at a time our way was narrowed by the masses of water smartweed pushing out from either bank. We skirted the edges of lowland woods, once where Canada mayflowers, or false lily of the valley, bloomed at the mossy bases of the trees, and a little farther on where the floor was carpeted with new sensitive

13

Wild lily of the valley (*Maianthemum canadense*)

ferns glowing yellow-green in the backlighting of sunshine.

The trees here were almost all red or swamp maples, with their shallow, widespread root systems. Only occasionally nowadays, and that most often close to the edges of the wetland, does an explorer of the area come upon the dense, gray-green spires of the white cedar, the tree that gave the swamp its name. In pioneer days it was reputed to form the most impenetrable thickets of any northern tree, and was in demand for boat building, for the interior finishing of houses, for cooperage, fence posts and railroad ties. Designated by Linnaeus *Chamaecyparis thyoides,* and known variously as the Atlantic white cedar and the Coast white cedar, its entire range is confined to the Atlantic coastal plain and the bordering land westward along the Gulf as far as Mississippi. Unlike the four-sided twigs of the familiar red cedar, its twigs are round or slightly compressed. Its wood is light and close-grained, durable and fragrant, brown tinged with red.

As we advanced we were unaware that the lay of the land was slanting slightly downward toward our rear, for there is no swiftness of current where there is not the gradient to produce it, and the flowing waters of the stream blended imperceptibly into the still waters of the swamp. Approximately twenty-nine inches of rainfall a year is the average for the United States. In the vicinity of Cedar Swamp it is more than forty inches. Here there is always rainfall, or melting snow. Here there is always water, high water or low in the cycle of the year, and the beginning stream can take its time, be tentative, probe this way and that, guided by gravity.

The apparently aimless staggering of the stream from side to side across the floor of the swamp traces the path of the lower ground. The deep slot cut by the channel—in places deeper than my paddle's length, probably over my head—indicates the permanence of the course of the infant river. "Thus in the course of ages," Thoreau noted in an entry in his *Journal* in 1855, "the rivers wriggle in their beds, till it feels comfortable under them."

All the standing water, all the flow beneath our canoe, had the same hue. This strong-tea color of the lifeblood of the lowland is derived from the tannin formed in the lush vegetation. The fleshy roots of the yellow water lilies, for instance, are so impregnated with tannin that in earlier times they were collected for use in tanning leather.

"... the flowing waters of the stream blended imperceptibly into the still waters of the swamp."

In the rising heat, the swamp air was rich with the primeval scent of mud and ooze and the dark, tannin-filled water. Everywhere around us, we sensed a world seething with life, silent life, often unseen life, life in earlier forms, multitudinous, newly awakening life, all the intermeshing life of the fecund swampland. Sometimes when we paddled over sunken branches, all their twigs festooned with long threads and waving streamers of green algae, we glimpsed underwater insects seeking shelter from the current. Once, paddling through mirrored clouds, we came upon a little bay swarming with water striders, and later, in another patch of still water, saw the surface cut by the gyrations of whirligig beetles. Inky black of wing and brilliant green of body, frail damselflies bobbed in uncertain flight over the stream before us. Every shoal of streaming waterweeds over which we pushed, even the small mats of pale vivid green duckweed that went drifting by, we knew harbored forms of life.

The voices of the spring birds, sometimes seen, more often hidden, were all around us. Off to our right, a marsh wren clattered its metallic little song and fell silent. Redwing blackbirds, riding on the bushtops, gave their harsh, chittering notes or their musical "Okalee." At one place where the stream made a wide stagger to the left and carried us along the edges of a lowland stretch of woods, the trees seemed full of warblers, their brilliant colors, darting bodies and incessant calling dominating the woodland, their voices intermingled—the "Wichity! Wichity!" of the yellow-throat, the drawling snore-like little song of the blue-winged warbler, the "Sweet! Sweet! I am so sweet!" of the yellow warbler.

Ducks, mostly mallards, shot up before us as we rounded sudden bends, and here and there a dark little duckling popped out of the overhanging vegetation, skittered across the water and shot out of sight again. In former years, Cedar Swamp was famed for its mallard, black duck, teal and wood duck, as well as for its furbearers—muskrat, mink and otter. All still inhabit the swamp, but in greatly reduced numbers. A few white-tailed deer remain; before the Europeans arrived, Indians hunted elk in Cedar Swamp.

Across this lowland are scattered several small areas of solid ground, believed to be the tops of low hills formed of glacial drift. On a few there are remnants of old stone walls where early set-

17

tlers carved out frontier homesteads in the swamp. There, also, are arrowheads, indicating the Indians used them as camping sites. The stone points that have been picked up date from the Early Woodland Period, from five to ten centuries ago.

Hardly two miles to the south of the beginning Sudbury up which we were paddling, the Old Connecticut Path, one of the most ancient and famous of the Indian trails, leading from the Connecticut River valley to the coast, skirts the swamp and, keeping to the south of the river, turns with it toward the north through what is now Framingham. It was along this path, at the beginning of the 1630s, that a small band of Wabbaquasset Indians trudged for nearly one hundred miles bearing heavy loads of corn from the fertile fields around Woodstock, Connecticut, to the hard-pressed colonists at Boston.

Three years later, three colonists, led by John Oldham, followed this trail on a return journey, seeking a suitable place to settle in Connecticut. In afteryears, the route became the main thoroughfare between the Bay Colony and the valley of the Connecticut River. Even today you come upon stretches of modern highway in the region that bear the designation "Old Connecticut Path."

The most famous of all the Indians associated with Cedar Swamp was Waunuckow, called Jackstraw by the settlers, one of the two red men taken to England from the Virginia Colony by Sir Walter Raleigh and presented to Queen Elizabeth. Later Waunuckow moved to the Bay Colony and settled on a hilltop overlooking Cedar Swamp in what is now Westborough. Because of his knowledge of English he was able to serve the colonists as an interpreter; he is said to have been the first Christian Indian to be granted land. Today, a bronze plaque on a fieldstone boulder at the corner of Bowman Street and Olde Coach Road in Westborough calls attention to his life here. And in and near Cedar Swamp, Jackstraw Hill, Jackstraw Brook and Jackstraw Meadow, through which the brook flows, commemorate the name the white men gave him.

Traditionally swamps have been disliked and avoided. In early days, they were considered only a source of mosquitoes and malaria. They were classed as worthless land providing neither fields for crops nor pastures for livestock. Their only use, except for supplying wildfowl in migration times, appeared to be as a place in which to dump old tires and worn-out baby carriages. Only in very recent years have swamps come to be valued for their own sakes. These two viewpoints, that the swamp is worthless and that the swamp has a special and important place in preserving the welfare of people, met head-on in the historic battle to save Cedar Swamp.

Westborough, in which almost all of Cedar Swamp lies, has had three boom periods in its history. The first began in 1810, when it became an important link in the busy Boston-Worcester stagecoach route; the second in 1835, when the Boston and Albany Railroad reached it; and the third in the 1960s, when the traffic of the two superhighways converged close to its eastern edge. The last brought a wave of expansionist fever to the community. Land values soared. The area was described as "an ideal distribution center located in the fastest growing area in a densely populated state." Billboards along the major highways proclaimed: "Westborough Welcomes Industry"; "Your Company Can't Get Any Closer to New England than Here"; "Transplant Your Plant." A flood of additional tax revenue was anticipated. In the past, because of the presence of large state institutions that paid no taxes, Westborough had felt tax-starved.

Industry responded. Leading companies, such as Digital, the computer-component manufacturer, Pittsburgh Plate Glass Company, Parke-Davis, the pharmaceutical manufacturer, and Cumberland Farms, sought property and began the construction of huge plants close to Westborough. They zeroed in on the edge of Cedar Swamp, on Flanders Road, because two decades before, when the idea that wetlands were worthless still prevailed, virtually all of the swamp had been zoned for industry. As each new industrial complex took form, it encroached on the wetland, subtracting from the size of the swamp. The climax came when Cumberland Farms bought ninety-two acres and erected a single building that covered sixteen acres to house its bakery, warehouse and national headquarters, serving its two hundred stores.

Westborough defended the "development" of the swamp by pointing out that the alternatives were farmland, which was shrinking, and woodland, which had increasing importance because of the growing demand for wood. "Worthless wetland" could most easily be sacrificed; it was the logical location for industry. But it did not seem logical to the people who lived down-

19

stream along the Sudbury. Through the ages, the lush vegetation of the lowland has built up layers of peaty material that in places have a depth of as much as thirty feet. Hence Cedar Swamp lies like a great sponge, able to absorb and retain vast quantities of water, which in flood times would otherwise be added to the torrent pouring down the river. Anything that reduces the swamp's size reduces its capacity to store up water. And as Sandra Dawson, director of legal services for the Conservation Law Foundation, in Boston, pointed out: "Westborough is upstream of the area and would reap the tax revenue without suffering the downstream effects."

This was the background of a struggle that extended over years and involved the State Department of Natural Resources, the U.S. Soil Conservation Service, the Massachusetts Audubon Society, the League of Women Voters, the Sierra Club, the chamber of commerce, developers, planners, industry, sportsmen and the selectmen and voters of Westborough.

The controversy reached its high point as the bicentennial of American Independence approached. On July 1, 1975, Cedar Swamp was named an Area of Environmental Concern—the first so designated in the Commonwealth. Unless preceded by a thorough environmental impact study, new intrusions into the wetland were blocked.

The ruling produced an uproar in Westborough. It was denounced as "another example of the state usurping home rule" and as a move that would have "a negative economic impact on the town." It was called "bureaucratic harassment and discrimination against the town." The selectmen demanded that the order be rescinded immediately. A spokesman for the chamber of commerce for the Worcester area maintained that Cedar Swamp did deserve protection, but as an "area of *economic* concern." It should be saved—for industry. In hearings and town meetings, speakers expressed such ideas as "We need to make our own rules for our own swamp" and "It is too late to save the swamp, so it should be developed."

At first the majority rejected all proposals that would have provided adequate protection of the swamp. Even a plan for floodplain zoning was voted down. Then a slow reaction set in. There was growing agreement that *"bona fide* wetlands," those that are wet 100 percent of the time, should be protected. The viewpoint of the people farther down the river valley received greater consideration. The swamp's value as a storage basin for floodwaters became better understood, the importance of the wetland more appreciated. In 1976 the plan for floodplain zoning—which had previously been rejected—was accepted by the voters of Westborough. One effect of this plan was to restrict building along the edges of the swamp.

On the June day when we paddled our canoe in the heart of the swamp around which controversy had so long swirled, the advance of the encroachments, the reduction in its size, seemed less of a threat. The defenders of Cedar Swamp were more alert and effective. The chances seemed good that never again would the designation "worthless" endanger its welfare. In the minds of more and more people it would continue as an "area of environmental concern."

To follow a river to its source is to make a journey backward in time—from the stream's maturity to its youth to its childhood to its infancy. As we pushed on, the character of our waterpath altered. The current eased off, the stream narrowed, the rank vegetation crowded out from either side, obstructions increased. Dark rows of painted turtles, running up the slopes of slanting logs, tumbled off into the water at our approach. Once I looked down and saw just below me, on the leaf of a pickerelweed lying on the surface of the water, a baby turtle no more than two inches long. Another time I bent close to watch a tiny black treehopper, its prothorax drawn up into a thorn-like horn or peak, that had alighted in the canoe. Footprints in the soft mud at the edge of the shallows showed where raccoons had been along the stream before us.

[More and more we are pushing ourselves across shallows. Buttonbush tangles. How stiff are their branches! I am hung up a dozen times. Once a branch gets stuck under the edge of the canoe and we extricate ourselves with difficulty. Now and then a small fish shoots across the shallows. Barring shallows, twists and turns, this is the story of our progress. Hairpin turns more difficult to navigate in this low water. Ann tries to use her paddle as a forward rudder. We pause to enter notes—I in a spiral-ring notebook, Ann on a yellow lined pad kept in a large yellow folding case. She prints everything—an improvement over my scrawl. I eat my tuna-fish salad sandwich little by little and consume the potato

"We pause to enter notes—I in a spiral-ring notebook . . ."

chips a bit at a time. It is, as everyone who has tried it has found, out of the question to eat potato chips in silence.

[Three times Ann has seen small water snakes. Being in front, she encounters things better than I do. Once she almost put her hand on one. Somewhere close by the pond must lie. For more than two hours, with only brief pauses for rest, we have been fighting the current. Now, in this ever harder going, our rests become frequent.]

We could see the trees ahead becoming farther apart, opening up where the pond lay extended. We were almost within sight of our goal. It could not be more than a few hundred yards away. But where the ditch-like channel made a right-angled turn to the right, and the outer bank was armored with the gnarled roots of swamp maples, a slanting log projected into the stream. It was wedged solidly in place, unlike previous logs that, slung lightly, had readily submerged as we pushed over them. For a long time we worked the canoe, inching around this obstruction. Almost immediately we came to another right-angled turn, this time to the left.

In the cycle of high and low water in the swamp, the high times come in the spring especially, and in fall; the low water in summer. Unavoidably, our trip was made a little late. Day by day the level of the water had been dropping. Would we be able to push our way through and reach the pond? The answer came suddenly. The water of the stream beneath us seemed to drain away. The canoe remained unmoving, glued in place by the mud. Moreover, just before us a green curtain of poison ivy, supported by tree branches and bushes, virtually blocked our way.

I could visualize the pond distinctly in all its colors and details—the outspread water, its surface a pale, delicate blue reflected from the luminous sky, the silvery, shining branches of the encircling swamp maples, their new "keys" clouding the treetops with a flush of red, the islands of floating water lily pads along the shore, the sense of a lovely, all-to-yourself lake that lies at the end of a struggle to attain it. For on a day earlier in spring, in a time of higher water, I had seen it open out before me when Roland Wells Robbins and I had reached this source pond of the Sudbury. Two pair of Canada geese, appearing immense, had circled low above the trees and had splashed down just offshore to swim about, giving their short calls of apprehension. Somewhere

"Two pair of Canada geese, appearing immense, had circled low above the trees and had splashed down just offshore to swim about, giving their short calls of apprehension."

close by, perhaps on a tussock of sedge, the female had her nest. The pond then had seemed lonely to Robbie and me, as remote as a tarn or forest pond in the great north woods. Today it basked in the June sunshine—so short a distance away, yet beyond reach.

Hemmed in by the narrow channel, we had no chance to turn around. Backpaddling, we navigated the first right-angled turn successfully, then came to the second, partially blocked by its slanting log. Here my end, the stern, wedged firmly among the swamp maple roots while the bow was snubbed from turning by the log. Ann saved the day. Climbing out, balancing herself on the log, she inched the lightened bow over the obstruction. Once we were headed downstream, the rest was easy.

We rode with the current. The channel widened and the current picked up speed. We slid easily over mud bars and water-weed tangles where we had pushed our way so laboriously before. We skidded around the hairpin turns and rode down straight sections with only an occasional paddle stroke to keep us on course. Going home we had more time to look around as the swamp moved by. All the way, now, we had the feeling: "We have been here before." We recognized little landmarks: a place where the amber flow of the stream slid over shallows of sand; a stretch of a hundred feet where long grasses trailed their slender leaftips in the current; a single high cattail stalk crowned by the fluff of its seedhead balanced like a billowing mass of light-tan foam at its top; Whitehall Brook drifting in from the south to form the first tributary of the Sudbury. Whitehall Brook, Piccadilly Brook—it is as though some homesick Londoner had contributed place names to the region of Cedar Swamp.

Occasionally, from the flooded lowlands, we heard the grating of frogs and once we drifted by a small water snake sunning itself—as the baby painted turtle had done—on a pickerelweed leaf lying flush with the water. For several hundred yards, a family of kingfishers went rattling back and forth across the stream ahead of us. Once more we paddled for a couple of hundred feet along a higher bank, at a woodland edge, where black birch saplings grew densely, the only place where I remember seeing them along the way.

The beginning Sudbury winds past innumerable such isolated plant communities. We found ourselves at one point suddenly surrounded by broad-leaved cattails; at another, by low willows that speckled the dark stream with little clots of floating catkin fluff. When we rested for a time by one swamp maple, Ann nibbled on watercress she found massed in the single patch we found that day.

A winding stream is a stream filled with surprises. And the more it winds, the greater the interest it holds. Beyond each bend lies a new vista. Each turning brings the possibility of something unusual. So it is that, in thinking back, I remember especially certain curves along this widely meandering early course of the Sudbury. There was the Curve of the Wild Roses, where all the outer bank of a sweeping turn lifted in a high wall of swamp rose bushes laden from end to end with the delicate pink of their innumerable blooms. There was the Curve of the Damselflies, where all around us the air was filled with the flutter of wings and the glitter of bodies as we passed through a concentration of fifty or more of the ethereal insects.

Then there was Mosquito Bend, where the smaller, less attractive insects swarmed about us and kept us slapping and dabbing on insect repellent until we left them behind. Elsewhere in the swamp in the sunshine of the day, we were virtually unbothered by mosquitoes. Strangest of all the surprises that greeted us was at the Bend of the Honeydew Rain. Here all the grassheads, all the slender descending leaves, were shining with sticky honeydew. Perhaps a host of tiny aphids were exuding the sweet fluid. In a syrup-like rain it descended on us. Our arms became sticky. My eyebrows became sticky. Ann's glasses became coated and had to be washed off. Only at this one place, at this single curve of the stream, did we encounter this phenomenon. When I bent down the long timothy-like heads of some of the high grasses, they shone and glittered, seemingly covered completely with a maze of tiny sparkling droplets.

[The rugged, exhilarating canoeing of going in; the "fun canoeing," speeding with the strong current, going back, past the long grasses dipping their slender leaves in the water. One paddle stroke going back equals four going upstream.] All too soon the faint sound of traffic strengthened. I remembered as we entered the turnpike tunnel the beautiful picture we had seen going upstream, the running ripples of light on the concrete.

This time we had a different illusion. We lost all sense of being on water, all ability to judge distances. The canoe seemed to be ascending a concrete roadway—the reflection of the concrete roof of the tunnel—and we seemed to be at the bottom of the water, many feet below the surface over which we moved. We had the feeling we could step out of the canoe and walk up the concrete roadway ascending before us. Only at the end of the passage did our senses adjust again to reality.

The phoebe was sitting on her nest again when we went under the turnpike. This time she was not frightened by our passage.

With paddles idle, we drifted the rest of the way toward the shelving ground of our landing place. Carried by the current of the stream, I wandered into thinking about all those other rivers, those streams of long ago that had flowed under the canoes of the Indians, the boats of the first colonists to push inland, under Thoreau's dory and the barges that had drifted downstream laden with bog-iron ore for the earliest smelters. Who could find them now?

For a river is not the river's course. It is not the river's bed. A dry bed is not a river. Then the river is absent. It is the flow of the water that makes the river and that is like the flowing of time. Time is a succession of seconds and minutes and hours and days. The river is a long sequence of other segments. It is made up of such fragments as the canoe length on which we rode, the moving water that passes a point of land and never flows there again. It moves on and is gone forever. It is something always disappearing downstream. Out of millions of such fragments are formed the rivers that flow through time. Where would our river, this small fragment on which we rode today, be tomorrow, or in another week, or when the year had ended? Who could find it then?

We grated on the gravel of our landing place and that small segment we had been accompanying moved away. For a moment I followed it with my eyes. Other fragments endlessly would pass this spot through future time. But never in all the course of history would this particular installment of ours, this particular union and combination of water, return again.

AH⅀ Edwin, the enthusiastic host, has written: "There are so many things to show you: exactly where Thoreau and his brother pushed their boat out into the current at the start of their Concord and Merrimack trip; where Thoreau took his 'fluvi-

27

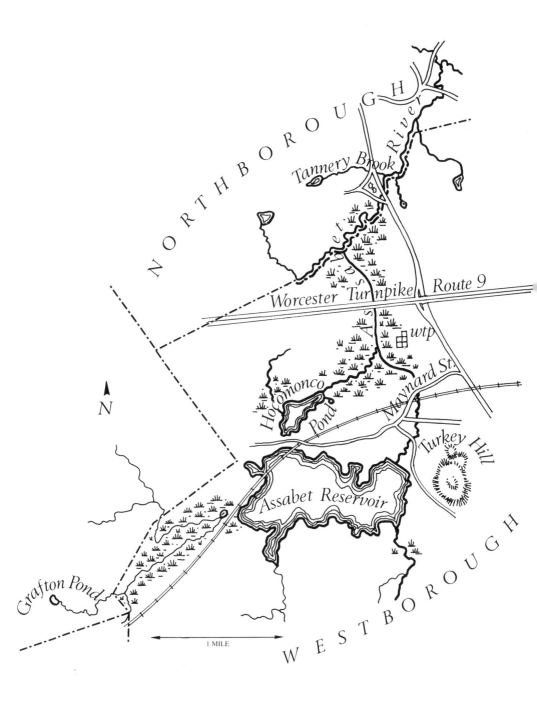

NORTHBOROUGH

Tannery Brook River

Worcester Turnpike Route 9

wtp

Maynard St.

Hocomonco Pond

Turkey Hill

N

Assabet Reservoir

Grafton Pond

1 MILE

WESTBOROUGH

al walks' near the Leaning Hemlocks, etc. etc. Just bring good weather and we will supply the rest! . . . There are some beautifully wild stretches on the upper Assabet before the dams begin that I can take you to in the late-winter halcyon days of mid-March . . ."

I certainly didn't bring good weather, and "halcyon" it isn't. I had forgotten there could be rain like this—insistent, pervasive, penetrating: Thoreau's "mizzling" weather.

Now Edwin, at home here, leads me, the stranger, across a vast open sedge meadow drifting with alternating mists and rain, into the hourglass-shaped swamp through which the beginning Assabet works. Every branch, every twig, my nose and my eyelashes drip. Even in the woods there is no protection. The leaves are not yet out and the rain plummets like lead shot through the empty branches, or else gathers on the underside of a limb and runs down into bigger drops which crash on the top of my hood. And because it's March, it's cold, hand-chilling, nose-reddening cold. The lowered skies, the rataplan of rain, make the swamp eerie and dark, just on the edge of sinister.

We slog through wet oak leaves and dead plant stalks. It seems as sodden underfoot as it is above. I leave a footprint-sized lake wherever I step. Edwin, being six feet tall, leaves deeper impressions, which fill in so quickly that they are obliterated in minutes. On one old tree trunk there is an opulent display of shelf fungus, greenish in the center, brown and ruffled on the edge, fresh filled with moisture. White wood chips litter the ground beneath a tree, perhaps, says Edwin, from a pileated woodpecker. A high bush cranberry thicket hangs full of last year's pale red berries. All the oak leaves, cinnamon brown, lie folded on the ground, all at a forty-five-degree angle, as if they've blown down and frozen that way. Although one expects to be able to see far into the swamp because branches begin high, the staggered verticals of tree after tree cut off any vistas.

Still, there is something intriguing here, perhaps the knowing that we walk where few others walk, where a river is gathering itself together. Edwin mentioned it in a follow-up letter: "I will never forget that little nameless stream wandering among the skunk cabbage spathes and under the first red of the swamp maples, descending with a series of tiny waterfalls into the source-swamp of the Assabet. The little cascades seemed to catch and hold all the brightness there was in the dull light on that still, rainy day and the sound of the falling water was the loudest sound among the trees. It was such a secluded, private spot, one of those special places with a kind of magic about it."

The red-purple spathes of skunk cabbage thrust up everywhere, the harbingers of spring, and as Thoreau did, in them I can see a summer ahead:

> If you are afflicted with melancholy at this season, go to the swamp and see the brave spears of skunk-cabbage buds already advanced toward a new year . . . Winter and death are ignored; the circle of life is complete . . . I say it is good for me to be here, slumping in the mud, a trap covered with withered leaves. See those green cabbage buds lifting the dry leaves in that watery and muddy place. There is no can't nor cant to them. They see over the brow of winter's hill. They see another summer ahead.

As we slosh along in the icy water, I try to imagine this swamp with the tongue of glacier that once filled it, that became detached and stagnated in place as the ice cover shrank; I think it couldn't have been much wetter and colder then than it is today. Behind the damming ice, glacial Lake Assabet formed. It lay mainly to the south of where the towns of Westborough and Northborough are now, with embayments reaching northward. Glacial Lake Sudbury, larger, lay to the east and north, and at one time the two were connected. At its highest level the surface of the lake lay at an elevation of 315 feet, almost precisely the level of the reservoir that today fills the lower half of this swamp.

Except possibly for ponds, swamps occupy the largest land area in the Assabet River valley, as they do in the Sudbury's. The red maple, American elm and white ash that are the dominant trees all require copious moisture, maintained by a high groundwater table and constant flooding; drainage eliminates the water-loving trees, especially red maple, which can be killed by a shift of as little as one foot in the water table. Water usually stands less than two feet below the surface; the swamps act as huge natural reservoirs, containing the high spring runoff, then slowly releasing it throughout the summer. Tree species and numbers in swamps tend to remain stable over the years; hence swamp forests are extremely valuable to wildlife, providing reliable food supplies and shelter, and because they are seldom entered by humans (by sensible ones, at any rate), undisturbed living.

A swamp seems hardly habitable, but the cover a swamp provides for wildlife was also cover for the few native Americans who remained in Colonial times, relics of the decimated Nipmucks, one of the seven subtribes of the Algonquin nation that for four thousand years called Canada to the Gulf of Mexico home. In the sixteenth century, Nipmucks had villages all along the Assabet, but by 1674, although they had an allotment of six thousand acres, only ten families, comprising a total of fifty people, remained to inhabit it. Those fifty were a remnant of a remnant. When the first English settlers arrived in 1631, the Indians had already been in spasmodic contact with Europeans for more than a century, and plague and smallpox had drastically reduced their numbers.

By the end of the eighteenth century, the few remaining lived an alien sedentary life. Hassanamicoes, who fought in the Revolutionary War, lived alone at the edge of this Assabet swamp, supporting himself by weaving baskets. He wandered through the town of Westborough, in and out of houses and barns without knocking, misquoting scriptures with marvelous originality; one memorable malapropism preserved: "If sinner entice thee, consent thou."

It is recorded that in the early 1800s an Indian named Simon Gigger lived on a small rise where the hourglass-shaped swamp narrows (later moving to the foot of Turkey Hill, which for many years was called Gigger Hill). At the turn of this century, there still existed stone remnants of his old shanty in the swamp, where he lived with his brother Daniel, his sister Sallie, and Bets Hendricks, a fiddler to whom he was miserably mean. In anger and rebellion she once flew at him with a scythe and slashed him so that his thumb "fell over into his hand." Also according to the story, it was readily healed by generous poultices of balm of Gilead, which grew around their cabin.

These Indians were the wretched shabby ghosts of the skilled and canny hunters who strode the hills, and their passing was unmourned. In 1724 the Reverend John Bulkley wrote a treatise with the presumptuous title "An Inquiry into the Right of the Aboriginal Natives to the Lands in America," which proposed that a man who toils on the land earns it as his right; the Indian who hunted and fished forfeited that right because "cultivating and subduing the earth, and having dominion, are joined together."

Charles Hudson, a local historian writing a century and a half later, likely summed up the prevalent attitude: "Viewed therefore, on a broad and liberal scale, in the light of a rational philosophy, or a pure and elevated religion, the disappearance of the native tribes should fill us with rejoicing rather than regret."

Like Cedar Swamp, the Assabet Swamp has not escaped alteration. Within two miles of its beginning, the George H. Nichols Multiple Purpose Dam was built in 1969 for flood control and fish and wildlife development, flooding the entire lower half of the swamp. A plaque set in a boulder reels off the reservoir's statistics: a water surface of 380 acres and total storage capacity of 2,856 acre-feet. It is a shallow reservoir with a maximum depth of fifteen feet and nearly five miles of shoreline.

After the disastrous effects of Hurricane Diane on both the Assabet and the Sudbury, federal funds administered by the Soil Conservation Service were used to devise and publish *A Watershed Work Plan for Watershed Protection and Flood Prevention* and to provide incentive for the establishment of the original Sudbury-Assabet-Concord Watershed Association, Inc., known as SuAsCo, an association of landowners formed to cooperate with state and federal governments in flood control. The work plan said that flood damage could be mitigated since a large part of it was caused by poor planning and land use management, inadequate handling of sewage and wastewater, lack of protection of the wetlands and marshes which served as reservoirs in times of high water, and inappropriate development along the rivers. The plan called for ten floodwater-retarding structures, eight of which, including the Nichols Dam, are on the upper Assabet watershed. (Subsequently, in 1963, a comprehensive study by the League of Women Voters advocated other flood-control measures, among them the acquisition of marsh and floodplain areas along the rivers for wildlife habitat. Their support was instrumental in establishing the Great Meadows Wildlife Refuge. The first watershed association went out of existence with the completion of the Work Plan. The present SuAsCo Watershed Association, a volunteer, nonprofit, tax-exempt organization, was established in 1975 which opposes the construction of dams for flood control but supports a natural flood control philosophy like that of the LWV: maintaining open floodplains and wildlife refuges.)

Alas, as the Division of Water Pollution Control of the Massachusetts Water Resources Commission put it in 1974,

> to date, the project [Assabet Reservoir] has not been a success. Trees and roots, not sufficiently cleared from the floor of the impoundment, supply large amounts of organic decay material (detritus), resulting in inferior quality water. Also, proper regulation of the amount of water released is absent. During the summer, extremely low water levels have left small pools of water scattered about the impoundment—filled with dead fish.

Ironically, however, the reservoir has added to migrant shorebird habitats, and the dead trees provide cavities for nesting birds and support for great blue heron rookeries. But it has so degraded water downstream that recommendations have been made to survey the impoundment with a view to possible reconstruction of the dam. The hard facts of the matter are that it *is* in place and it would be more productive now to come up with a sensible water-level management program that would protect water quality as well as wildlife habitat than to destroy it.

It is the end of July when Edwin and I explore the shore of the reservoir, but the day is cloudy and a brisk wind bears in from the southwest, a constant blowing that ruffles the water, frets the grasses and spits sand. Because I don't particularly care for what a fluctuating reservoir does to its shoreline, my humor matches the irritability of the day. The reservoir's large surface area means large loss of water through evaporation, and its shallows warm quickly, one of the factors encouraging the massive algal blooms which are offensive to both sight and smell.

I strike out along the shoreline toward Edwin, who is far ahead. Typically he paces slowly but purposefully. He stops and stands as I've become used to seeing him: cap bill pulled down, spiral notebook that fits into his shirt pocket in his left hand, taking notes in small neat script with a stub of a pencil.

I join him and we walk around the shore as far as the bay full of dead trees standing sentinel-like, trunks stark against a clotting sky. There is nothing pleasant about blackened broken-off trees. No rustling leaves, no metronomic branches. No grace, no charm, no pleasing patterns. A Carolina locust, dark wings banded with yellow, sails by, uncharacteristically quiet today; Edwin says they clack only when they can hover, and today there's too much wind.

Before we leave I climb up the ladder at the outlet works and look down twenty feet into the water gushing through the sluice gates, white and frothing and deafening. There is something about the incessant pulsating rush that is profoundly unsettling. The outlet works are fixed—that is, the conduit is of sufficient diameter to permit free flow of water under normal conditions so that the reservoir cannot rise, but to choke when the flow increases beyond a predetermined point. Water continues to flow out during flood, but at a lesser rate than it flows in. Because some of the storage capacity may be in use before peak flood stage, such automatically controlled reservoirs need a larger surface area behind than those whose flow is adjustable.

The drain-off produces a canal-sized river, an artificial channel edged with thick sedges, which disappears under a bridge just visible downstream. It is bound with tiny meadows on either side, and in their thick greenness I have an intimation of what the hayfields that so attracted the early settlers must have been like, sedges and grasses bowing in the wind, sunlight gleaming up and down their stems, the furtive sparkle of the Assabet.

The swampy meadows that now underlie the reservoir were part of a grant given to the heirs of Governor Theophilus Eaton of Connecticut, who founded the colony of New Haven in 1638. The General Court ordered the land surveyed on June 11, 1680, with instructions that "the irregular shape be reduced to a square or rhomboyds and do not prejudice any former grants," suggesting that early surveyors often fudged a bit. Two years later the heirs of Eaton sold it to John Brigham, at which time it was divided into thirds, one of which included some of the wet meadows. Then Jonathan Whipple lived just north of what is now the north end of the dam. He built and farmed the original homestead of some 250 acres on the river, growing corn and operating a grist mill. His son Francis was a representative to the General Court in the 1760s and his associates, John Hancock and John Adams, were frequent guests at the Whipple house, their horses' hooves clacking against stone as they galloped across the shallow Assabet.

In the early 1800s the Forbush brothers operated a dairy farm here, shipping milk to Boston. And in 1855, "three acres on the west side of the Afsabet River" were sprout land, acreage set aside for new tree growth for wood supply. The dam is named after the Nichols family, who most recently farmed here, and Fred

Nichols made a tape for the Westborough Public Library of his memories of raising sweet corn, repeating again and again, "good life, good life."

It is but a mile from the dismal reservoir to an enchanting—albeit man-made—pond, a tiny blue bean on the USGS Shrewsbury quadrangle, three millimeters by four. The source of the Assabet River is defined by the United States Board on Geographic Names as Latitude 42° 15' 15" N and Longitude 71° 40' 30", which lies at the confluence of the stream from this pond and another coming in from the east, unnamed (all the streams at the headwaters of the Sudbury are named: Whitehall, Rutters, Jackstraw, etc., which says something about early use and familiarity with the sources of the two rivers). That source is now covered by the reservoir. The Massachusetts Water Resources Commission puts the river's beginning at the outlet of the Nichols Dam. But Edwin has suggested the pond as the proper source, and I agree out of pure sentiment: here, in this charming place, is the proper beginning for a river.

I first saw the little pond in the full green warmth of June, on a day woven of birdsong and leaf rustlings and the chirr of crickets. As I walked up the slope toward it, I felt far away from city and town. Quite suddenly I found myself precisely at eye level to its surface. The perspective was startling. The surface of the water shone like burnished stainless steel. I felt as if my feet were even with its base, my height measured its depth, and the encompassing trees sheltered us both.

I continued walking and in no time looked down on a little idyll of a pond about an acre in size. It was an ice pond, the dam that created it built sometime around 1920; the gray granite blocks of the icehouse foundation remain at the far end of the dam. Spring fed, its water made the best ice, used locally or shipped to Boston. In the 1800s and early 1900s, before refrigeration, ice cutting was a profitable business; insulating ice cut in January and February with layers of sawdust enabled supplies to last through summer and also made good use of a by-product of the local sawmills.

I saw the little pond several times after—when leaves were off the trees, in the brisk chill of an early spring day, and in still another autumn. But now, sitting at my typewriter, envisioning it, out of all the remembered images, I choose the first time I saw it,

"I saw the little pond several times after—when leaves were off the trees, in the brisk chill of an early spring day, and in still another autumn."

in summer—its gleaming surface fringed by grassy banks sparkling with tiny yellow cinquefoils and strawberries, enclosed by
thick underbrush and trees, set in a thick flickering greenness,
perfumed with honeysuckle. Even though golden celandine and
dandelions spatter the grass, even though cherry blossoms float
white petals on the breeze, it is as if these are merely facets of
green, highlights and accents, and any butterfly that flies here,
any dragonfly, any cricket, any bird, has also to be green. There is
but a scrap of sky showing, and its blue is merely an aspect of the
encompassing verdure. The still corners of the pond stream with

Celandine (*Chelidonium majus*)

37

Honeysuckle (*Lonicera tatarica*)

algae like the green hair of a naiad, pearled with tiny bubbles. Tiny caddis flies and moths rise and float around me, and a hesitant crane fly takes wobbling flight. The air is soft, coming off those wonderful leafy life-giving infinite greens. And the silence, the shimmering verdant silence.

Edwin writes of going to Cedar Swamp Pond as going back to the river's childhood. Coming to this little pond at the Assabet's beginning is a trip into *my* childhood, for on that summer's day this pond brought back to me, in an unexpected rush a small enchanted dark pond in northern Michigan near where I spent childhood summers. I saw it but once, but I can close my eyes and see it still, so vivid was the impression it made. It was a secretive place, also close palisaded by somber trees, so that the water shone dark and scarcely quivered in the quiet, like some polished dark lens that held all its reflections within itself. There were delicate bell-like flowers and clusters of tiny mushrooms on long languid stems and soft pads of emerald green moss. The ground was thickly layered with pine needles and the leaves of many summers wreathed the pond edge. Although it was not damp, the air was gentle, and the odors of pine and moss and soil mingled together in a cool freshness that pleased even a child's senses. All the proportions, all the feelings, were right. Here was a place where I, a very timid child, felt immediately at home. I remember letting go of a safe hand and taking the path ahead alone, enticed and curious and oddly happy.

The green closeness of that pond and of this one is the opposite of the open expansive western world I now know, the adopted world of my adulthood, with its big blue skies and notched horizons and miles of rutted canyons bared to a shattering sun. This little pond, belonging to the Assabet's beginnings, holds many memories. It is a measure of where I've been and where I am.

3

EWJ It was called the Fiddleneck. It was referred to as Rocklawn. It was a place so unattractive and rocky that, according to H. P. DeForest's _The History of Westborough_, in early times,
although it was near the older settlements of Marlborough and
Framingham, no one occupied it. The town of Marlborough formally disclaimed ownership. Prominent citizens in Framingham certi-
fied that it did not belong to that township. Even the Indians made
no claim to it. This is the unpromising land through which the
young Sudbury River flows when it leaves Cedar Swamp behind.

Not far away, in the country east of Westborough, where
Fruit Street now swings south from Flanders Road, the legendary
John Belknap, in the early eighteenth century, carved out his pioneer farm. Old tales recall how he always worked in his fields
with a gun beside him and how, on winter nights, he sometimes
built a ring of fires around his stable buildings to keep the wolves
at bay. He was eighty years old when he finally married, choosing
Joanna Kimball, a twice-widowed neighbor, as his bride. A mile or
so from the Belknap farm, in the area where contention over industrial expansion into the swamp reached its height, one section
of Flanders Road bore the name of Contention Glade because of
the squabbling of the earliest residents.

Downstream only a rod or two from the river-and-railroad
Fruit Street Bridge, the character of the Sudbury changes abruptly.
All through the swamp it is largely a silent stream. But here the

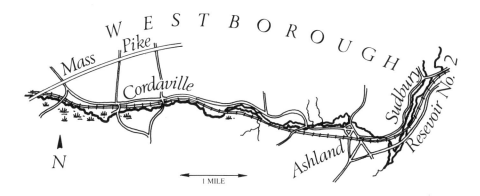

"But here the river breaks, its bed tilts downward, it foams along glacial rocks. Suddenly the silent river becomes the noisy river. It fills the air with a mingled rushing, thumping, gurgling, bubbling as its flow is ripped and shattered by the rocks."

river breaks, its bed tilts downward, it foams along glacial rocks. Suddenly the silent river becomes the noisy river. It fills the air with a mingled rushing, thumping, gurgling, bubbling, as its flow is ripped and shattered by the rocks. This is the start of the Sudbury's swift beginning, the rapid descent of its early miles.

When Ann and I first came to the tumbling water, we found a small boy, as silent and patient as a heron, fishing on the bank of a pool below the white water and the rocks. He told us that, off and on, he had been fishing there for days. But he had caught nothing yet. His hopes were buoyed up by the fact that sometime every spring, the Massachusetts Division of Fisheries and Wildlife releases young brook trout into the purer water of these upper reaches of the river.

I wandered across a little higher ground, across the remnants of an old stone wall, to reach the stream. A hairy woodpecker appeared to be riding waves as it crossed overhead. Among the fallen oak leaves I found the feathers of a blue-winged teal, the victim of an unknown predator. A chipmunk leapt in silence from root to root where a long, dead tree had been undercut by the river.

How vastly different the scene would have been if a project that was proposed a decade or so before had been carried out! This was the "channelization" of the young river: the removal of the obstruction formed by the boulders left by a glacial moraine just below the Fruit Street Bridge and the deepening of the channel by as much as eight feet for some distance upstream into the swamp. By lowering the water level of the wetland, it would have made it possible to build houses farther out into the swamp.

Eugene H. Walker, hydrologist with the U.S. Geological Survey, was assigned to evaluate the effects of the plan. He found that lowering the water level would affect wells near the swamp adversely, including two that provided almost 30 percent of Westborough's water. It would cause a lowering of the land surface, exposing the saturated peat and muck to drying, to fires and to oxidation of the organic material that would lead to a 50 percent loss. This subsidence of the swamp soil would permanently reduce the storage capacity of the swamp in flood times. The deepening of the channel, at the same time, would discharge into the river half again as much of the floodwater. There would be far-reaching changes in the type of vegetation in the swamp. Everything considered, the plan promised to be as disastrous, albeit on a smaller scale, as the ill-conceived draining of the Everglades. The scheme was abandoned.

As we gazed down at the quickening water foaming past us, hurrying away downstream, disappearing around the next bend, with other journeying water taking its place, we sensed in its suddenly increasing strength a pull, an urge, a tug to follow the moving water, to know its rapids and its quiet reaches, to see what lay beyond its many bends, to read the river's story as it was being written. Perhaps we were responding, in some vague way, to the attraction of the flowing stream as the stream responds to the pull of gravity on its water.

We had followed downstream the north bank of the descending Sudbury for perhaps five hundred feet when we came to a narrow ravine branching steeply off to the left. Choked with boulders, littered with fallen trees, it suggested some wild and picturesque gorge in the White Mountains, reproduced in miniature. In a long foaming cascade, water tumbled down its length. It twisted through narrow chutes between the mossy boulders, raced beneath the moldering trunks of the fallen trees, piled sodden leaves and shining foam in great masses against the upstream side of every rock and filled the woods with the clamor of its descent.

As we traced its course, stopping every few feet along the way, the realization dawned that the ravine must be man-made, was the flume of some ancient mill. Our surmise was verified on a later date by Robbie Robbins, who has combined a hobby and an occupation in a career in archaeology. From his experience in restoring the first ironworks in America at Saugus, pinpointing the exact site of Thoreau's cabin at Walden Pond and conducting excavations at Jefferson's birthplace in Virginia, he came to this ravine and its surroundings prepared by specialized knowledge to visualize what had been there when it all was new so long ago.

It was fun to follow him about as though accompanying a man with X-ray eyes probing beneath the surface of the ground. The old mill seemed to rise before my eyes as he reconstructed it from bits of evidence seen in mounded earth and scattered stone. Here fragments of foundation and a corner of rough masonry revealed where the mill had stood, jutting out over the flume. There was the wheel pit, the great blocks of stone that had suported the ponderous wheel still in place. The pit could have accommodated

44

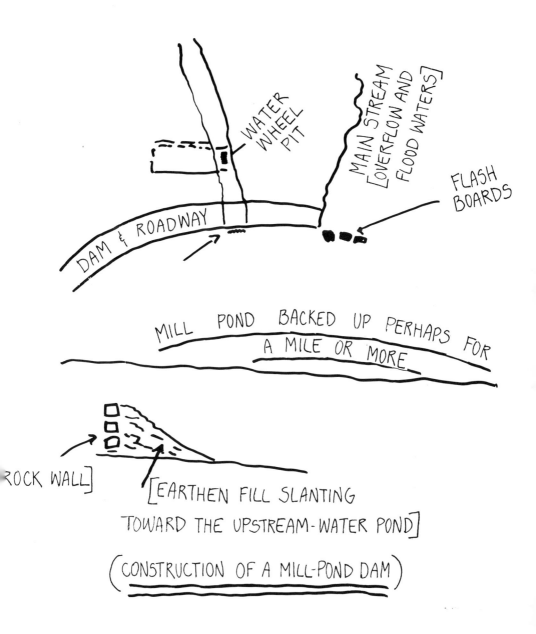

WATER WHEEL PIT

MAIN STREAM [OVERFLOW AND FLOOD WATERS]

FLASH BOARDS

DAM & ROADWAY

MILL POND BACKED UP PERHAPS FOR A MILE OR MORE

[ROCK WALL]

[EARTHEN FILL SLANTING TOWARD THE UPSTREAM-WATER POND]

(CONSTRUCTION OF A MILL-POND DAM)

EWT's diagram of the first mill, as Robbins reconstructed it.

a wheel ten or fifteen feet in diameter, even two wheels mounted side by side—overshot wheels, which supply the most power. There had been a drop of at least ten feet between the top of the dam and the wheel pit. The dam, which could be traced in a great crescent cut by the flume and the main river, had been sufficient to back up water in a shallow millpond extending upstream for perhaps a mile into the swamp. When it was in use, the main stream was the safety valve. In floods, the flashboards that normally kept the water in the pond, with the excess flowing over the boards, were lifted and all the floodwaters, diverted away from the mill, poured down the main river.

Robbie thought that while the ravine was man-made, little digging had been necessary. The builders just scratched a trench at the beginning; then water diverted from the river in floods cut deeper until the steep descent of the "flume" resulted.

Below the site of the mill itself the ravine plunged on. At one time it carried the torrent of the tailrace down to a pool it had scoured out at the bottom of the descent. Remnants of the pool are still there, we discovered, when we worked our way down the slope.

How old was the mill, and another whose ruins we discovered on the opposite side of the river, a little farther downstream? Robbie said that from the primitive dressing of the stone blocks—merely one side knocked off—they appeared to date back at least to the eighteenth century. And in the files of the Westborough Library there is a map dated 1830 which shows the two branching millraces and the two mill-sites. They were known as the Rocklawn Mills then. The first one we encountered is labeled "Grist Mill" and the second, the one slightly downstream, "Sawmill."

On another June morning, Ann and I launched our canoe close beside the old bridge that crosses the Sudbury at Southville and turned upstream, toward where the old mills and millraces had been. At first we slipped under huge weeping willows that lean out from backyards that run down to the water's edge. Then we were winding through lowland woods of shallow-rooted swamp maple, the flooring dense with water-loving plants—skunk cabbage, royal ferns, hellebore and sensitive ferns—and cushions of moss, all speckled with the red of fallen maple flowers.

More and more, as we advanced, the dark water was

"... the water was patterned with running lines and swirls and interlacing
designs of foam."

splotched with masses of floating foam. It collected in shining white clouds among the bushes and plant stems at the river's edge. The river widened before us. All across its expanse the water was patterned with running lines and swirls and interlacing designs of foam. Woven by the shifting currents below the rapids, they caught and held the sunlight, brilliant and glowing, against the dark background of the stream. Just beyond, extending from bank to bank, the tumbling white water of the rapids thundered down.

Back at the bridge, we stopped for a while before turning downstream toward Cordaville and the Cordaville Dam. Almost at this exact spot, more than a hundred years ago, Henry Parker Fellows and a companion had loaded camping gear and cooking utensils into a cumbersome rowboat that had been deposited at the Southville railroad station a few hours before. It was the beginning of their adventurous descent of the Sudbury River, the innumerable difficulties of which were chronicled by Fellows in his *Boating Trips on New England Rivers,* published in 1884.

Below the dam at Cordaville, the next community downstream, they found the river dry. Patiently they waited for the mill to commence operations and then floated away on the wastewater released below the turning mill wheel. In other places they dragged their heavy boat over rocks from pool to pool. The refrain that runs through the narrative is: here we found the stream "shallow and filled with many rocks." Unable to row, they often poled themselves along with their oars. Each time they came to a community of any size, they summoned the Adams Express Company to send a wagon to transport their boat to the other side of town.

Even at that early date, the river was heavily polluted by the waste products of the mills. At one point Fellows wrote: "The water was clogged with all sorts of impurities from the woollen mills and so muddy we could only guess at obstacles." And again: "The oars in poling sank through thick, yellow water deep into oozy beds of yielding, slippery slime, and the odor stirred up by the action was foul and miasmatic. Indeed, neither Styx nor Phlegethon, I suspect, is half so bad."

When Ann and I turned our light canoe downstream that morning, in the long-ago wake of Fellows's rowboat, we shot under the bridge, riding on a slender tongue or V of fast water. It

". . . we came to Cordaville and the torrent pouring over the high rock-and-earth wall of the dam. . . . All down the wooded hillside where we landed were old borrow pits from which rock and earth for the dam had been excavated long ago, overgrown now and green with moss and ferns."

"Ahead was a picturesque stone bridge supporting an abandoned road, and downstream, beyond it, lay the busy modern highway of the Cordaville Road. . . ."

was the last swift-flowing current we encountered until we came to Cordaville and the torrent pouring over the high rock-and-earth wall of the dam that backs up and slows the stream almost to the Southville Bridge, a distance of three-quarters of a mile.

Still tea brown from the swampland tannin, the river wound in and out among pleasant woods. Sometimes we paddled parallel to the railroad, the elevated right-of-way rising above us, just to our left. Once we caught the sustained, musical trilling of two American toads at the river's edge ahead of us. Our paddles motionless, we drifted. We were almost upon the singers before their far-carrying courtship song abruptly ceased.

When we came within sight of the brink of the dam at Cordaville we skirted warily along one edge of the impounded water. All down the wooded hillside where we landed were old borrow pits from which rock and earth for the dam had been excavated long ago, overgrown now and green with moss and ferns. In the ravine below the dam, timbers and tree trunks lay jumbled where they had been deposited by the high waters of some previous spring. Leaving the canoe, we threaded our way on foot down the ravine, past the flood wreckage, and little bays of quiet water imprinted with patterns of foam. The Sudbury was taking up its flow again. Ahead was a picturesque stone bridge supporting an abandoned road, and downstream, beyond it, beyond the busy modern highway of the Cordaville Road, we found a secluded launching place among skunk cabbage and the roots of red maples. It was buffered from the current, there beginning to race.

When we came back one summer morning a year later and launched the canoe from there, one paddle stroke drove it into midcurrent. We, like the Sudbury, were taking up our journey again.

Curiously, in our advance, the current of the stream seemed to speed up and slow down. The brown river hurried us along between walls of alder and osier. Then it would let us drift among cattails and tussocks of royal ferns. Where open wetland meadow stretched away, lush with springtime grass, redwing blackbirds alighted, scarlet epaulets flaring. Noticeably the volume of water increased. The river, moving downstream, attracted other water as it flowed. We had thought to reach Ashland, but beyond a wide, sloping meadow, the stream narrowed. Huge rocks reared above the water, obstructing the way. We pulled the canoe up and

51

walked to the first bridge downstream. The view in both directions revealed barriers to our passage, fast water rushing in a shallow flood down a rocky bed to where the Sudbury swung to the left and passed under the railroad into the town.

Ashland, originally called Unionville, long known as "Clocktown," is the home of the pioneer Warren Telechron Company. A sign on the road entering from the west reads: "Welcome to Ashland. Home of the Electric Clock." The Sudbury River runs the whole length of the town and was its creator, supplying power for the mills that attracted workers. Here at Ashland, on the western edge of Framingham, the river begins the great bend that shifts the direction of its flow from east to north. Here the rushing stream is transformed, impounded in the reservoirs of Framingham.

AHZ   In their upper reaches the Assabet and Sudbury are more alike than different—delightful larking streams that had enough fall to power small mills. The Assabet's first drop, from the pond at its beginning to the Nichols Reservoir less than half a mile away, is some one hundred feet. Confined for a mile in the reservoir, the river begins to pick up speed as it flows under its first bridge, less than a quarter mile below the Nichols Dam, at Mill Street in Westborough (as is true of most of the bridges on the Assabet, the kindest thing one can say about this one is that it is unpretentious).

One summer's day, Edwin and I lean on the bridge railing, tree branches arching above us, woven together like tiercerons, leaves flickering as the water flickers below. Basketball-sized boulders piled up in the stream for riprap create tiny waterfalls, and we stand hypnotized, watching the water froth and pour in the shadowed reach or out in midstream, where it pillows up and falls lacy with bubbles, constantly changing, constantly moving, constantly spellbinding. It is obvious why this was the site of an early mill. Water velocity is good, the steep banks high enough for safe building. The earliest corn mill was built here by Oliver Ward in the winter of 1724.

In the new country, generous inducements frequently were offered to millers: free land, guaranteed water rights, and sometimes free labor for construction. Mills were in essence controlled monopolies, with the number limited and charges strictly regulated. Early millers had to be skilled in many areas, for building and running a mill involved engineering expertise, mechanics, hydraulics, architecture, and local politics. Consequently the miller frequently became a respected and influential member of the community—Joel Parker, who later owned the mill here on Mill Street, was referred to as the "Honest Miller." On the other hand, many millers had scant reputation for honesty and some of the most stringent fines of early times were levied on millers who charged not wisely but too well. Perhaps they were tempted to seek extra recompense for what could be a dangerous job; not a few graves are marked with a millstone, and "through the mill" still means surviving really hard times.

With our overview from the bridge, Edwin and I speculate on precisely where the wheel might have been set. By Colonial times the wheels were set vertically in a millrace through which the water flow could be controlled, and connected by a shaft to the millstone. Ordinarily millstones were granite, quarried in full-sized chunks from local deposits, and did well for the coarser grinding of corn meal, buckwheat, and rye flour. For finer grinding, limestone wheels were imported from France. Some weighed more than a ton and must have required ingenuity as well as strength to set in place. If a millstone marked a grave, in spite of the expense and difficulty of obtaining a new one, it was because it was considered bad luck to continue using a stone that had caused a death.

Setting the two millstones was crucial—close enough to grind finely, far enough apart not to touch and spark. But despite care, mill fires were frequent. Just downstream on the Assabet, Fisher's mill burned in 1880, causing $1,000 damage, and the one at the Nourse place on an upstream tributary burned in 1877, the loss of $1,600 a considerable investment in those days.

In 1735 Oliver Ward sold his mill to Jonathan Whipple, who in turn sold to Eleazer Rider, who built another mill, the last to be constructed on the premises, in 1780. The celebration at the raising of Rider's mill was attended by the Reverend Ebenezer Parkman, the faithful diary-keeper from Westborough:

> Tho Things are Dark as to outer Circumstances, yet God is my Refuge. I would beg Grace to hope and trust in Him! Squire Baker came and invites me to the Raising of a Grist Mill and a Saw Mill. I went. The Company was double, but all supped together at Mr. Rider's.

The Reverend's reference to dark circumstances describes the loss of income, once paid by both settlements of Northborough and Westborough. When the former broke away to form its own town, it refused to contribute any longer to his salary. Since Westborough was also remiss at the time, Parkman was in true and serious danger of starving.

The mill complex was eventually sold to Joel Parker in 1800. Parker had a lively pair of daughters who delighted in arranging festive parties, at which Simon Gigger would play his fiddle for dancing that lasted until sunup. Although a few glasses of hard cider put him to sleep, according to a Westborough historian, his fiddle somehow kept on squeaking.

Water pepper (*Polygonum hydropiperoides*)

"All the little crisscrossing parallel lines that fret the water surface constantly thread back and forth, weaving and raveling, plaiting and fraying . . . and
eelgrass streams in the swift current."

Broad-leaved arrowhead (*Sagittaria latifolia*)

The banks where the mill stood rise steeply and one must go just a little farther downstream to be able to walk beside the river. On a summer's day it flows demurely working along with that gentle conversational murmuring that I love, sliding silkily over the stones, shallowing out, slowing and spinning, speeding up, spreading lines of ripples from every obstruction. Flowers are knee high: water pepper, yellow evening primrose looped with bindweed, a stand of bouncing bets and fleabanes. At the water's edge tiny mints and blue veronica tangle together; compass plant and hawk's-beard blooms share the same lemon yellow. Sedges rustle pleasantly against my legs. A little storybook stream, lush and green, fresh and singing.

Below the next small bridge the tea-colored water is golden brown in the riffles, sharp little corrugations across the whole ten-foot width of the stream. All the little crisscrossing parallel lines that fret the water surface constantly thread back and forth, weaving and raveling, plaiting and fraying. Clumps of jewelweed and black alder line the banks, and eelgrass streams in the swift current. Arrowhead and pondweed sway with the water's pulse. Lush sedges bear heads as large as willow catkins. One can almost forget the world above—the lapping gabbling water is nearly loud enough to mask all other sounds except the conversation of a red-wing blackbird. When I close my eyes the river fragrances are as gentle as its sounds, and without the distractions of the visual world, the lyrics of the river flow through my head.

Its charm must have captivated Edwin too, for he wrote: "I keep remembering the upper reaches of the Assabet. That beautiful, beautiful river! I had never heard about it before. Nobody seems to know about it. It was like exploring a new stream."

Bubbling downstream, the river doubles in width, riffling along, full of tattings of foam where it gathers over rocks, scalloped where it bounces over a ledge. Maynard Street, where another bridge spans it, was named for Amasa Maynard, a prominent and well-to-do man who lived nearby, and apparently was not above a practical joke.

Dr. Stephen Ball, Northborough's doctor and apothecary—a contemporary writer remarked "that any one passing Dr. Ball in the dark could recognize him by the odor of drugs exhaled from his old gig"—also had a gristmill and sawmill on Hop Brook, a tributary to the Assabet. Evidently Dr. Ball made frequent visits to

Maynard. Such is the humor of the river that one almost hears the conversation that transpired one evening toward the end of dinner. Perhaps the good doctor had turned up once too often at mealtime, or perhaps Maynard had been treated once too often by the doctor's favorite method—first bleed, then dose with a severe emetic, on top of which administer a doze of calomel, a purgative, and then jalap, a Mexican herb used as a cathartic. Or perhaps Maynard was just a dedicated practical joker. At any rate, on the evening in question, Mr. Maynard informed Dr. Ball that what he was eating with so much relish was Maynard's old mare. Not until the discomfiting meal was over did Maynard admit to remembering that he had, ever so providentially, swapped the old mare for a side of beef.

Just downstream the river curves and there is a deep pool that was once a place to swim, surrounded by overhanging birches that made sparkling shadows. Rachel Dearing, a child after the turn of the century in Westborough, now an elegant New England lady, remembers that she and a friend wedged a board seat just large enough for the two of them between two birches. Here the two little girls, sometimes with a purloined piece of sponge cake in hand, came to share dreams beside a river that was clear and pretty.

The Assabet chatters on for less than a mile more before it spreads out into marsh; less than a mile beyond that, the Boston-Worcester turnpike crosses it. And somewhere between Maynard Street and the turnpike it becomes canoeable. Or uncanoeable, as the case may be, the judgment depending upon water level and one's willingness to bat through overhanging thickets, rafts of water-soaked logs, and the assorted debris of civilization's offcasts.

It is with regret that I have had to replan the late-May canoe trip on the upper Assabet to which both Edwin and I had so looked forward. Edwin has been under the weather and has urged me to go ahead while I have a chance, Colorado being a rather far commute. Actually, knowing Edwin's enjoyment of open sedge meadows and wide gracious waterways, I am rather thankful he's not here, for once we get under way, we get swatted in the face, stuck on logs, and beset by odors from the Westborough wastewater treatment plant.

If it can't be Edwin, I can think of no more delightful companions than Anne and Lael (Mike) Meixsell, expert canoers who have traveled many northeastern rivers. Their interest in the Assabet is proprietary. As former president and one of the founders of the present SuAsCo Watershed Association, and now executive director, Mike is concerned with the health of the three rivers within his purview. This confined and difficult reach of water must be for them an exercise in background education.

Mike plops the canoe in the water beneath the Boston-Worcester turnpike bridge, and we head upstream. From the start the woods are thick. I glance up through layers and layers of leaves to see a fly dangling in a spiderweb and leaves dotted with galls. Tent caterpillars are all over, their silhouettes moving restlessly inside their tents. Dry stalks of sensitive fern, spore-spiraled, cluster on the narrow bank. The leaves of the bloodroot wrap the flowering stems as if to protect the flowers. Solomon's seal nods deeper in the woods.

Old boards, cushioned with green moss, are wedged in the stream. The river flows around them, crinkling and pleating. Red maples have dropped their samaras and the canoe bow parts flotillas of them. Water boatmen dart out from the shore as the boat disturbs the water.

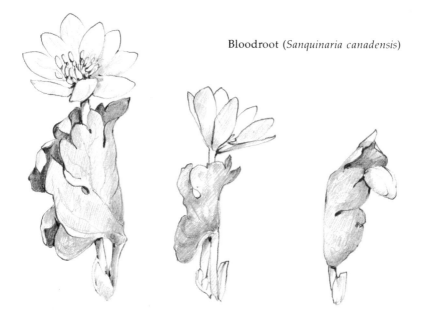

Bloodroot (*Sanguinaria canadensis*)

We enter a clearing. Spiraling upward, a broadwing hawk scribes helices in the sky; the black line on the leading edge of the wing and bronze tail show clearly and I think: If Edwin were only here to see *that!* One of the things I have treasured most on our canoeing days is the way in which Edwin, without a moment's hesitation, can identify birds from a mere snippet of sound or the briefest glimpse of flight pattern and habitat.

It takes the three of us about an hour to go upstream as far as we can go—we can't even get as far as the Maynard Street bridge. Bushes hang lower and lower over the stream; branches

Solomon's seal (*Polygonatum pubescens*)

and logs sit higher and higher in the water, and everyone's enthusiasm quickly dims when it is more work to paddle than to walk. We maneuver a turn and start back downstream. The river's appearance becomes progressively worse as we near the inflow streams from the Westborough and Shrewsbury wastewater treatment plants, and the turnpike bridge. The water is scummy, the surface lifeless. Occasional miasmic odors envelop the canoe.

I have a sense of canoeing on a dead stream, overloaded and overenriched, supporting only sewage and red bloodworms, suckers and carp. The river has no animation. It is a lifeless, listless, river Styx. A gray line of scum along the bank marks the last high water of sewage-laden effluent. Pods of scum float beside the canoe, dirty gray-white with unsavory excrescences in the center. Edwin has just sent me a quote from William Wood's *New Englands Prospect* that has a ring of irony when I read it after canoeing here: "For the Countrey it is as well watered as any land under the Sunne . . . it is thought there can be no better water in the world . . ."

Along with visual pollution and foul odors, for the canoer who likes quiet there is noise pollution on this stretch of the Assabet. Such sounds may be music to other ears—I can remember campers who could not bear the utter stillness of the woods. To me they are anathema, the droning of traffic, the annoying mosquito hum of tires that filter upstream from the Boston-Worcester turnpike.

Traffic has proceeded over this marshy reach of the Assabet that the turnpike now crosses since time immemorial, and settlers were crossing by 1638. Governor Winthrop first noted the need for a true road in 1649, but it was not formally laid out, by Major John Pynchon, until 1683, preceding the better-known Boston Post Road by a decade. The General Court order for its construction read:

> Whereas the way to Kornecticut, now used being very hazardous to travellers by reason of one deepe river that is passed fower or five times over, which may be avoided, it is referred to Major Pynchon to order ye said way to be laid out and well-marked. He having hired two injins to guide him in the way for fifty shillings, it is ordered that the Treasurer pay them the same in country pay towards effecting this worke.

When Pynchon looked the country over he could find no better route, it is said, than the path trod by local cattle.

Within the century General Henry Knox force-marched fifty-five cannon over this segment of road from Fort Ticonderoga to General Washington in Boston, where they were mounted on the hillsides of Dorchester and used against General Howe in the spring of 1776. The cannon weighed from one thousand to five thousand pounds each, and were pulled by oxen "borrowed" from Northborough farmers because teams had to be changed every ten miles. After the war, one thousand of Burgoyne's British soldiers passed this way, prisoners of war on their way to Boston.

In 1798 Washington crossed the Assabet here during his tour of New England—"Bay horses with two negro boys as riders, the horses attached to a travelling-carriage, in which sat General Washington," remembered a spectator. His confrère Marie Joseph Paul Yves Roch Gilbert du Motier, Marquis de Lafayette, traveled this route in 1825 to the laying of the cornerstone of the Bunker Hill Monument—"a very large man, slightly lame, and carrying a silver-headed cane."

By 1805 travelers needed a more direct route from Worcester to Boston than the original boustrophedon path which had wandered northward from here to Marlborough, and thence eastward. A petition was presented by Aaron Davis and 145 others, and in March 1806, the General Court empowered Davis and four associates to establish the turnpike route as it now exists, "to make, lay out and keep in repair a turnpike road from Roxbury to Worcester, commencing at or near Roxbury Street ... " and to erect toll gates, collect tolls, sue or be sued.

Private toll roads operated under a charter, and were "improved roads," which probably meant minimum boulder removal and some bedding over soggy places. Gates were usually placed every ten miles, and each turnpike had its own name and individual charges. The General Court had set the official tolls in 1805; no tolls could be collected from persons going to and from church or the gristmill, or on military duty. It is to be expected that tollgate-keepers developed a healthy cynicism about some travelers' final destinations and piety, and a tollgate-keeper was in turn generally disliked by travelers.

Aaron Davis's turnpike was four rods, or about twenty-two feet, wide, and laid out as the crow flies; it tried to ignore obstacles, such as the Assabet marsh that puddled out on either side of the river. William Howe, a subcontractor from Worcester, was bankrupt by the causeway across this particular part of the marsh. He had to build it three times because it showed an alarming tendency to sink out of sight when no one was looking. The third time he must have felt was the proverbial charm, for he brought the road inspectors out for final approval. When they arrived there was no road to inspect. The Assabet muck had simply imbibed it.

It was finally completed, however, and tollgates erected at either end. By 1831 the number of travelers averaged 22,000 a year. Four stages ran daily between Roxbury and Worcester, and the fare was two dollars per person for the dozen people wedged inside and the five or six clinging on top.

Then in July 1835, the railroad come to Westborough, a little English engine pulling twelve cars full of dignitaries. Guests were invited "to partake of a collation at Brigham's railroad house," and the ladies got a free ride half a mile down the track and back. Embarrassingly, the train was so overloaded that it could not make it back up the grade to town and its complement of town boys had to disembark and walk.

Nevertheless the railroad was a success. Perhaps seeing that the life he had known would be irrevocably disrupted by the mechanical monstrosity, an innkeeper who maintained an inn and stables just up the turnpike overlooking the Assabet sold out and then hanged himself from his own oak tree. Upkeep for the turnpike became too expensive—lessened road travel meant insufficient tolls—and by 1841 ownership had been transferred to the various towns through which it passed. Most of them also found it too expensive to maintain, and narrowed it. Rachel Dearing remembers sledding on the "old sandy dirt road" around 1910, down the long hill onto the "Assabet Meadows"; in the wintertime the ice was notable for air holes "where the river breathed," which could trip an unwary skater. Not until the advent of the automobile did the turnpike come into its own once more. Today it is a major four-lane highway, the Worcester Turnpike—Route 9.

For about half a mile below the turnpike bridge, the Assabet plods along an abnormally straight path. It was channeled here at the turn of the century as part of an early flood-control project.

Dredging removes the pool-and-riffle sequence normal to rivers and renders the channel bottom uniform, decreasing the variety of plant and animal species that characterize a healthy natural environment; it frequently lowers the water table as well as greatly increases bank cutting, still in evidence today. But none of these considerations carries much weight if it's your meadow that's being flooded. Then, as now, land users in the floodplain blamed the river when things went awry. In January 1901, Northborough farmers claimed that their hay meadows were being inundated and ruined because Westborough had recently installed filter basins upstream. The *Worcester Daily Telegram* reported:

> Mr. Appleton's [town surveyor of Westborough] survey of the river, showing its extraordinary natural condition was a complete surprise to the farmers. They have claimed that the whole cause of the sluggish condition of the stream was from the Westboro filter beds. It now appears that the Assabet river is not and never was a flowing stream, and could never be with such an irregular bottom. At one place there is a mound of sand that rises very nearly perpendicular to the surface of the river, holding back a large area of water and retarding the flow of the stream.

The fall of the stream here was less than two feet per mile, the minimum necessary for a good flowing stream. The surveyor recommended that the obstructions be dredged out and the channel straightened, reducing the river mileage and increasing the fall. One victim of the channelizing was the bar in the river large enough to be named Hasting's Island; it was believed to have been an Indian camping ground.

Canoeing this reach has all the charm of cross-country skiing on mud flats. The artificially straight banks are treeless more than eighty years after they were carved out; muck at the sides is bared by low water and has an odor best left undescribed. Large skeins of *Oscillatoria*, a multicellular filamentous blue-green alga which is one of the more unattractive growths of polluted waters, float around the canoe. Not only is it mucilaginous when fresh; it breaks free from anchorage and forms large slimy mats which reek when they die. Its name comes from the active movement that the trichomes, by which the algae reproduce, exhibit—they glide, slide, and oscillate. *Oscillatoria* also reproduces by cell division and fragmentation, which means that there is rapid and extremely efficient reproduction at all levels with any encouragement, as from the phosphorus-enriched effluent of a wastewater treatment plant, or the nitrogen-enriched runoff from heavily fertilized farmlands. I try to fish a skein of it up onto my paddle with some thought of putting it in a bottle until I can get it home and under a microscope. It slithers away, the bubbles held in its slippery matrix looking like glass beads as it slides back into the water.

At the moment of my preoccupation the river is suddenly invaded by two dogs that romp out of the woods and, seeing us, come bounding toward us. They splash furiously, spraying black water, and plunge in to swim alongside; every time one of them gets close, he tries to climb into the canoe. When we are forced toward shore because of logs in the stream, the dogs gleefully run along beside us, shaking as they go, ignoring our shouted warnings. One is chestnut, the other fawn and cream—now both dark brown.

They are oh-so-eager and oh-so-friendly, and stick to us for more than a mile, never giving up trying to jump into our laps. We must make a strange procession: three adults brandishing paddles and hollering, two dogs trying to distribute their affections equally, and one spattered canoe. It is with great relief that we hear a distant whistle; the dogs stop in their tracks, and then take off for home.

Along shore, mud flats exposed by low water have dried and cracked into plates. Heron tracks, eight inches across at least, measured by my hand span, are deeply impressed. Inside the tracks ants and flies explore, and tiny beetles pick their way among new green sprigs.

There are other tracks, with a line between them from a dragging tail, that lead to a large depression in the slime. In it wallows a huge snapping turtle, the shell at least twenty inches long, plus head, plus tail. Snugged in the mud, it is burrowed so deeply that its back lies about an inch below the surface, its knobby black eyes and dog-like head just visible.

It is a chelonian that I'd hate to meet on land. Although a snapping turtle moves ponderously, it can react with deceptive quickness, catching fish, frogs, and insects with ease. It eats almost anything else available—snails, crayfish, mice, small birds—and has an unpleasant reputation for catching a duckling's leg and pulling it under water.

The comparatively small plastron of a snapper allows free

articulation of the legs and long neck but modest protection: its head, larger than that of most turtles of comparable size, can't be completely pulled in between shell and plastron. The snapper's strong beaked jaw and irascible disposition are protection enough against almost any potential predator, and its tail, longer than its carapace and crested like that of an alligator, adds to its fearsome aspect.

When Mike pokes this one with his paddle, Anne and I involuntarily stiffen, I suppose both of us with visions of it launching itself like a behemoth toward the canoe, taking a crunch out of the hull and then finishing off the occupants. But it only burrows deeper, heaving the muck around it, powerful legs pushing, finding traction difficult in a medium that does not push back. Slowly it works deeper. Staggering odors arise. I would like to add to the general biology of snapping turtles that they have *no* sense of smell.

As we continue, the woods thicken. My map shows that ahead of us is a bridge which marks the boundary between Westborough and Northborough in this patchwork quilt of contiguous New England towns. The Reverend Joseph Allen described the original bounds of Northborough in 1826:

> Beginning at the southwest corner, at a heap of stones on Shrewsbury line, it thence runs east, nineteen degrees north, four hundred and eighty nine rods, to a stake by the river Assabeth; thence, in a northeasterly direction, as the river runs, one hundred and seventy six rods, to the County road, near the dwelling house of Phineas Davis, Esq.; thence, by said river, one hundred and ninety four rods, to a stake and stones; thence east, twenty degrees north, eight hundred and sixty four rods, to a stake and stones on Southborough line.

The complex of Davis houses still stands on a gentle rise above the river. The original house and 79 acres of land along the Assabet came into the family when Isaac Davis bought them in 1781, for 1,800 ounces of "plated silver" (coin plate of mint standard, not silver plate as we understand it); currency was still so unstable a decade after the Revolutionary War that weights of silver were in use instead.

Just before we reach the houses the river widens for a moment into a little, still pool. The dark passageway through which we've been paddling, shuttered with willow and ash, opens into

Glossy buckthorn (*Rhamnus frangula*)

the light. Entering the bright cloud-mottled pond, we instinctively lift our paddles across the gunwales for a moment, not wishing to disturb the sudden stillness. I have the odd sensation of being inside a New England primitive painting: Phineas Davis's rectilinear house a little out of scale, stylized trees with carefully delineated stylized leaves, the traditional weeping willow in the foreground, the grass a little too smooth and too green, a world frozen on a wooden panel, well-varnished against fading.

As the river narrows again, we go under the bridge that marks the boundary between Westborough and Northborough. Just beyond, Tannery Brook, unlabeled on modern maps, empties into the Assabet. Once it carried the wastes from Davis's tannery, established in 1778.

Tanning converts hides and skins into leather by impregnating them with tannin, which came, in the eighteenth and nineteenth centuries, from the bark of hemlock, fir, sumac and several species of oak, and chestnut and its wood, and, according to Edwin, even the roots of the yellow water lily. Although black oak was preferred, easily available hemlock was in prevalent use in the northeast.

67

The process was so slow and laborious, and leather needed so badly for so many uses, that most farmers were willing to pay to have their hides tanned professionally, or for the finished leather. First the hide was split and trimmed, then soaked to soften it. A limewater soaking loosened hair, but some tanners simply stacked the wet hides until they began to rot, when the rank skins could be scraped clean. Vats, usually six feet long, four deep, and four to six wide, were filled with layers of ground bark and hides and then flooded. For as long as a year the hides were turned frequently, allowing the tannin to penetrate. When ready they were fished out, washed in the nearby stream, dried on a rock, and softened by pounding and working.

The smell of a tanning yard was vigorously offensive and living downwind from one must have been very unpleasant. Furthermore, great amounts of water were needed for the tanning process and the products thereof were flushed away downstream. The oxygen taken out of the water in tanning one hide was the equivalent of the oxygen demand of eighteen people. Clearly the production of many hides put a heavy drain on both Tannery Brook and the Assabet; just as clearly, that drain was acceptable in the context of society's need for leather. Until local bark supplies declined, the Davis tannery business prospered for almost a hundred years, producing as much as twenty thousand dollars a year—a handsome income for the eighteenth century.

Downstream from Tannery Brook, we dawdle in the general pleasure of being on the river, and I ask myself: Why are a few hours on even this river—this dirty, woefully polluted river— pleasant? Part of the answer is that I've learned that unsavory passages do not last long, that there are moments of remoteness when the trees close in. Although the river runs through towns and under bridges and bears the noise of traffic which leaves welts in my ears, it somehow always sidles away and becomes itself in a matter of rods, filtering everything through its screen of trees, blocking other horizons with its own high banks, rippling and glinting. If, in getting to know a river such as the Assabet, we cannot shirk the less pleasant passages, we can at least explore those passages with anticipation of something better.

And so as I see trees bending over the river ahead, I anticipate its return to its usual animated self, changing as the landscape changes, slowing and quickening, tying together past and present and tomorrow, bright in the sunlight and glowing in the shadows, answering back and knowing that no matter what is done to it, it somehow persists in shining through, and that if I am just patient, just around the bend, there downstream, where the willow waves and the alder arches, is what I am looking for.

When I settle into the bow seat and dip my paddle into the water, I feel as Emerson felt when he lived at the Old Manse and went boating on the Concord:

> My house stands in low land, with limited outlook, and on the skirt of the village. But I go with my friend to the shore of our little river, and with one stroke of the paddle I leave the village politics and personalities, yes, and the world of villages and personalities, behind, and pass into a delicate realm of sunset and moonlight. . . ."

4

TWO In 1843, when its growing population had reached eighty thousand, Boston engaged Loammi Baldwin to find a new and abundant source of water. At the time, Baldwin was one of the few trained civil engineers in the country. He had supervised the building of the first inland waterway dug in America, the Middlesex Canal. He also was the man who introduced the Baldwin apple, a fruit he discovered growing on a wild tree near Woburn when he was surveying the route of the canal. Tart and juicy, with fine keeping qualities, it became the most popular winter apple of New England.

Concentrating on upland water to the west of the metropolis, Baldwin investigated fourteen possible sources within twenty-five miles of the state capital. In the end his selection, which became known as the Cochituate System, centered in Lake Cochituate and the upper Sudbury River basin in the Framingham region. The Indian word Cochituate, pronounced "Cochit'uit," means "Place of Falling Water" and refers to the lake's nearness to the Saxonville Falls—the "Rocky Falls" or the "Falls of the Sudbury," around which, in the days of waterpower, the industrial center of Framingham developed, and which is now replaced by a flood-control dam of concrete.

Old maps record the meandering course of the river advancing from south to north through Framingham. Modern maps show this serpentine interrupted, the stream lost to view for

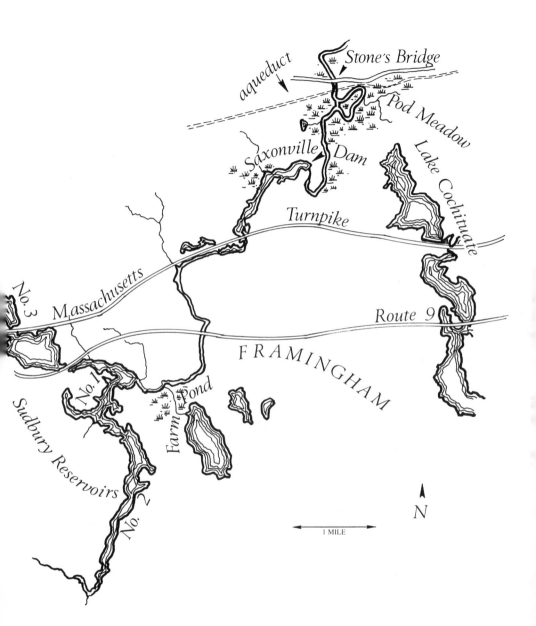

aqueduct

Stone's Bridge

Pod Meadow

Lake Cochituate

Saxonville Dam

Turnpike

Massachusetts

Route 9

No. 3

FRAMINGHAM

No. 1

Farm Pond

Sudbury Reservoirs

No. 2

N

1 MILE

miles, a drowned river buried beneath the water of several long, linked lakes that trace the course of the invisible stream. The far-reaching effect on the river of Loammi Baldwin's decision is still apparent more than a century and a quarter later.

To the citizens of Boston, Framingham seemed far away at the time of Baldwin's choice. But dams were built and reservoirs impounded and aqueducts constructed. Work began in the summer of 1846; in October 1848, the first of the upland water reached the metropolis. It was greeted by the historic Water Celebration on Boston Common, and for half a century afterward the upper Sudbury basin adequately supplied the needs of the growing city.

The Framingham reservoirs have not been used to supply water to Boston since 1931. As pollution decreased the quality of the river water, new sources had to be found and the search was extended farther west, first to the Wachusett Reservoir, north of Worcester, and then to the vast Quabban Reservoir, sixty-five miles inland from Boston. The Sudbury Reservoirs are retained on a standby basis only, as a possible source of water, if heavily chlorinated, for use in an emergency.

It was along the old Cordaville Road, the highway that once carried the stagecoaches east from Worcester, that Ann and I approached this land of reservoirs. Even the river that passed under the highway in Ashland was not the rushing, headlong stream we had known, and as we advanced, we could see the slowing, the sudden check, the transformation of the Sudbury, its water spreading out and growing still behind impounding dams. At times we looked across expanses of water a fifth of a mile wide. The river that we had seen foaming around rocks, swirling among tree roots, here lay quiescent, a blue mirror reflecting the urban scene that walled its banks.

On streets that seemed continually carrying us nearer the water then veering away again, we tried to follow the banks of two elongated bodies of water—Reservoir Number 2 and Reservoir Number 1—toward the center of Framingham. It was an odyssey of frustration, a wandering through a maze in which no two streets ran parallel. The side streets were marked with signs, but money is saved in Framingham by not marking the main streets: if you are on one of them, you ought to know its name, after all. It is possible to go for miles without seeing the name of the interminable street you are following. When we came to the first reservoir, a huge factory with a high brick chimney lay ahead. Were we on Myrtle Street or Cherry Street? We stopped for aid at a filling station, asked the attendant to point north. He didn't know north from south. A real city man. I decided that next time I went to look for someplace in a city, I would take a compass.

Not far beyond where the extensive Reservoir Number 3 is linked with Number 1, just before the river is shunted to the east around Bare Hill, below Dam Number 1, the Sudbury becomes a flowing stream once more. Its rate of flow is 1.5 million gallons a day. The figure can be given exactly because, by law dating back to the time of the Middlesex Canal, that amount of water must be pumped from the reservoirs into the bed of the river. The canal operators complained that, as a result of the draining away of water for Boston's use, the Sudbury downstream from Framingham had become a water-starved stream and the lowered level of the water was interfering with the operation of their enterprise. The legislation that was passed on their behalf is still in effect.

For about four miles we kept company with a river again, though a river confined, with buildings crowding close, a canal-like urban stream that began to widen into another impounded pond as it neared the Saxonville Dam. Here, where once the Falls of the Sudbury roared unchecked and unharnessed, at the ancient meeting place of the Nipmucks and the salmon, we had reached the final dam on the Sudbury, the last of the impounded water. Below it, feeling liberated, we took up the course of our river research once more. And gradually we left behind the discarded baby carriages, bicycle frames and old tires that had been dumped down the bank into the river's edge through the outskirts of Framingham. We were in a green world again, in contact with, part of, the flowing stream.

Each river has a life of its own, almost as completely its own as the life of a person. What happens to it, where it flows, are recorded so surely, its individual characteristics are so clearly established by the nature of its bed and banks, the vegetation that grows along its course, the soil it carries in its waters, that the chemistry, content and flavors of its water produce a combination as distinctive as a fingerprint. It is thus that the salmon, returning from the sea, recognize the river of their beginning from all other rivers.

The Sudbury is remarkable for the steepness of its initial

gradient. All the dams built along its course are concentrated in this descent. In its first twelve miles—from Cedar Swamp to the Great Falls of the Sudbury at Saxonville—it descends 160 feet. Below the falls, the river levels off, its swifter current left behind. It meanders. It becomes a placid stream, its descent ebbing to less than a foot in a mile. Its youth has been tumultuous; its maturity is tranquil. Except in time of flood, it is almost a river becalmed.

Fine-leaved and many-branched, masses of hornwort, or coontail, rose in dense submerged shoals or whalebacks streamlined by the current that swept the interlacing stems into constant movement. We slid among them, now and then catching the momentary glint of some small fish darting from the sheltering plants into the open water of the channel, to twist and shoot out of sight again. Unseen, a host of tiny forms of life find safety in the dark-green hornwort. For certain fishes it provides food as well as shelter, and in autumn, waterfowl—black ducks, pintail, mallard, wood ducks and blue- and green-winged teal—feed upon both the plants and the seeds during pauses in their southward migration.

Pondweeds and bur reeds, the lush fountains of the huge arrow-leaved water arum, occasional clusters of the little water shamrock, *Marsilea quadrifolia*, resembling four-leaved clovers, appeared beside us and slipped away to the rear as we advanced. Duckweed, *Lemna minor*, dangling the thin threads of their unattached roots beneath their little leaves, drifted by, clustered into floating islands, or lay caught, matted among the stems of plants by the stream's edge.

We glided above shallows alive with motion, sinuous with the writhing strands of slender ribbon leaves—the wild celery, or freshwater eelgrass. Like the hornwort, it attracts migrant waterfowl in fall. Along other shallows, where white water lilies bloomed, we paused, anchored among the lily pads, surrounded by the waxen cups of the flowers. The air was filled with their intensely sweet perfume.

In places we seemed riding down one of the most beautiful streams in the world—overarched by swamp oaks clad in the dark green of their large leaves, walled in along quiet reaches by *Pontedaria*, the pickerelweed, with the still water reflecting, in inverted images, the intense blue of its flower spikes.

It was not always so. Ever since Colonial times, the Sudbury has been befouled in various ways. Once, on another trip down this section of the river, we stopped to talk to an elderly man who had lived most of his life on the bank of the stream not far from the ruins of Stone's Bridge. He recalled how, in former days, he used to see the river here running bright red one time, vivid green another, brilliant blue another. It depended on the color of the dye emptied into the water by the large carpet factory at the Saxonville Falls.

It was in connection with water emptying into the Sudbury River that the first law in America aimed at controlling pollution in streams was enacted. In 1663, within ten years of the founding of Marlborough, its citizens voted in favor of the following resolution:

> It is ordered that no person shall lay or put any fflax or hemp into any pond or brooke within this town, where cattle use to drink, on penalty of paying to the town's use twenty shillings for every offence; and whosoever hath now any fflax or hemp in pond or brooke aforesaid, shall cause the same to be taken out within four and twenty hours after the date hereof, on penalty of paying the said sum.

[Duckweed increases in the slower stretches of the stream, clinging to the bank and its vegetation. As we go I photograph the reflections of the pickerelweed, and the reaches of the stream. White-eyed vireo in the hot still woods of noontime. Everywhere the long moving skeins of the waterweeds. White wild morning glories in bloom. Massed high grass, reed grass at one bend in the river, in the sun. The stream reminds me of the lower Assabet. So beautiful a river. Rocks are clothed in brownish pelts of algae or algae-like waterweed. One landmark is a maple tree leaning far out. Two large rocks loom up ahead. Crows cawing away to the east. The rank smell of mud. Two wood ducks fly up and alight on the limb of a tree high above the water ahead of us. Take off again. Jays begin to scream. We have been seen. A silent robin in the deepening shade beneath the streamside trees. Frogs "talking" in a little side stream or inlet. Interlaced among the high grass are the vines of the morning glories. Nightshade in purple and yellow bloom. A green heron flaps up to alight on a dead limb high over the water.]

Although occasionally we caught the sound of motor traffic

75

"The stream reminds me of the lower Assabet. So beautiful a river. . . . One landmark is a maple tree leaning far out."

along some nearby highway and although we knew that houses must be close at hand, we saw almost no signs of human contact with the river. We seemed to be winding along some remote and solitary stream, riding with the current down the narrow groove of its shaded valley, far from civilization. The impression remained with us all the way downstream until we came to the upper arm of the famous Framingham Ox-Bow, that most striking landmark of the river.

Long ago at this point, the stream had encountered an unbreachable barrier of heavy glacial gravel, and its water had been swung to the east into a wide loop, circling back to resume its former course about a hundred yards downstream. For uncounted centuries, the traveler on the Sudbury had his choice of paddling or rowing an extra mile, or of dragging his craft across the hundred yards of the Ox-Bow's neck.

Such was Henry Thoreau's choice when he reached this point in ascending the river on the final day of July in 1859. He and his friend Ellery Channing had started upstream that day rowing Thoreau's homemade dory, and intending to go all the way to Saxonville. It was one of the sultry dog days of summer and along the way they refreshed themselves as best they could by dipping up the warm and muddy-tasting river water in a clamshell they carried in the boat. Buttonbushes had reached the height of their blooming and swarmed with honeybees. They noticed that they could hear the humming of the insects as much as six or seven rods away.

When they came to the Ox-Bow, Thoreau paced off the distance across the solid neck. He found it was almost exactly a hundred yards. He and Channing gazed up the river from the other side. Then they turned back. This point, sixteen miles upstream from Egg Rock, was the farthest Thoreau ever ascended either the Sudbury or the Assabet.

Ninety-eight years after that day—and two years after the disastrous deluge that accompanied Hurricane Diane—the neck of the Ox-Bow was finally cut. The level of the stream above the cut was lowered approximately two feet by the straightening of the river.

Just above the shallow rapids of the cut, we turned into the upper arm of the Ox-Bow. Here we found the ultimate in the slowing of the river, a permanent ending of its normal flow. The former channel was a long-stagnant pond. Movement, the life of every river, was gone. The dead water was dense with algae and waterweeds, the scum on the surface fretted by the zigzagging trails of turtles and ducklings. A high wall of gravel loomed up before us, blocking the way. We were in a cul-de-sac. The story of that wall of gravel forms an important part of the story of the cut that was made through the neck of the Ox-Bow.

Around us, across hundreds of acres, stretched the excavations of extensive gravel pits. Indeed, all the country of the Sudbury and Assabet rivers is a land of gravel pits. In this part of the East it is not gold or diamonds that represent mineral wealth, but gravel and sand, legacies of the melting glaciers.

The land lying within the loop of the Ox-Bow is owned by the New England Sand and Gravel Company. The difficulty with cutting the neck of the bow had been that it would cut off the owners from access to their land. In the end an agreement between the state and the gravel company stipulated that in return for an easement permitting the cut to be made, the company would be guaranteed the right to construct a causeway across the loop of the Ox-bow to reach the enclosed land. The obscuring wall, on top of which is a roadway of gravel, fulfills the state's pledge and cuts the former course of the river into two separate sections. The lower end of the Ox-Bow, which lay behind it, was to be perforce the revelation of another day.

It was July when we entered it, having paddled upstream from Stone's Bridge. The stagnant water, green with algae and warmed by the summer sun, stretched away, curving to the right. Again, there was no current. Except for a breeze, it was as easy to paddle in one direction as the other.

Over most of the way we traced the boundary line between the towns of Framingham and Wayland, which ran down the center of the water path that led us on. When we paddled near the right bank we were in Framingham; when we paddled along the left we were in Wayland.

The pathway of dead water led us into the wide, lush lowland known as Pod Meadow, a country wild and beautiful and unexploited, a land of songbirds and wildflowers. Maples and willows lined the banks. In places we saw wild grapevines clambering over the bushes, dropping in green festoons from the higher branches, curtaining the trees. Yellow and blue iris shone in brilliant clusters along the edges of the waterway, and in the treetops, Baltimore orioles.

I think I will always remember our unhurried advance most of all as the time of the orioles. We caught the rich notes of their songs overhead. We saw the brilliant flashes of color as the males darted across the stream. Once when we were trying to see an oriole singing almost directly above us, we came to a sudden halt. The canoe was aground on a submerged rock. Backpaddling, we extricated ourselves amicably. Thoreau's account of a similar situation, as related in *A Week on the Concord and Merrimack Rivers*, ends: "So, each casting some blame upon the other, we withdrew quickly to safer waters."

But along the severed stream there were birds of other kinds as well that we remember: a great crested flycatcher, with rusty tail and lemon-yellow underparts, high in a maple tree reiterating its hoarse and carrying call; a silent robin, flitting from perch to perch among the bushes; a lone black-billed cuckoo, sleek and streamlined, appearing among the trees of the Wayland bank, crossing over the water, and disappearing among the trees of Framingham. We had drawn close to what used to be called the Farm Bridge, the span that carries the road from Wayland to Pelham Island across the river, when we saw ahead of us an osprey on half-furled wings hanging in the breeze. Probably its home was on the shore of Heard Pond, where a few of these birds, so reduced in numbers by pesticides once sprayed on the lowlands of the Sudbury's floodplain to control mosquitoes, nest and raise their young.

As we went on, the water became more stagnant, more dark and opaque, more dense with algae and waterweeds, its surface sown with thousands of tiny floating bubbles. Our canoe slid among them, cut across long thin streaks like strands of spider silk that stretched along the surface. We slid among lily pads and through patches where the paddle-shaped leaves of the pondweed covered the water. We drifted past banks dense with feathery horsetails, and others where sensitive and royal ferns were massed. Painted turtles splashed off slanting logs at our approach. All across the Pod Meadow lowlands we could hear the redwings calling.

At the top of the loop, we caught sight of a high rectangular shaft of gray granite, half buried in bushes on the left-hand bank.

Like some marker in the wilderness, it stood in isolation. We swung close to inspect it, but the riddle of its purpose remained until later a Geological Survey contour map of the Framingham quadrangle provided a solution. It is at this precise point that the Framingham-Wayland boundary leaves the river to angle away across Pod Meadow toward Lake Cochituate.

Ten or fifteen minutes later, we landed at the foot of the causeway of gravel. On this side a path leads to the top. As far as we could see were excavations, and dusty roads, followed by huge trucks, winding east and south between high gravel banks. To the east the silvery pylons of a high-tension electric line trooped in single-file across the landscape. We turned away and began the return journey, following the looping line of water where once had run the Sudbury, back to the living river. As we entered it we ceased paddling for a moment to watch two horses, smooth-coated and in perfect condition, feeding in a small fenced-in pasture, an acre or so in extent, that descended to the water. And swinging downstream, riding with the current once more, we paused again to enjoy one of those temporary little landmarks of a few days that impressed themselves on our minds: more than seventy-five yellow iris massed together in one immense golden cluster on the marshy edging of the stream.

It was just beyond the yellow iris that we came to the last reminder of Boston's water and of the impact of its procurement on the history of the Sudbury. Ahead of us an immense cylinder of steel arched up and over the river. Eleven and a half feet in diameter, supported by massive abutments of stone at either end, it emerges from the ground on one side of the stream and disappears into the ground on the other. When we paddled beneath its arc, a river flowed under our canoe and another river, a greater river, flowed above our heads. For the cylinder is a short visible link in the Weston Aqueduct, which carries water under high pressure from the Wachusett Reservoir to the mains of Boston. Through the steel channel fifty million gallons a day rush from west to east above the Sudbury River.

Around us as we passed beneath the arch, huge drops of water plopped down on the smooth surface of the stream. One struck me squarely on the head. At first we thought the aqueduct was leaking. Then we noticed the moisture collecting on the outside of the cylinder. The colder water of the flood charging

"Ahead of us an immense cylinder of steel arched up and over the river. When we paddled under its arc, a river flowed beneath our canoe and another river, a greater river, flowed above our heads."

through the aqueduct was condensing the moisture in the warm air of this humid July day.

AHZ The first trip in Edwin's new canoe! A perfect May day on an entrancing stretch of the Assabet, the mile or so just upstream from the town of Northborough, which contains so much of what a river meant in the lives of those who settled beside it.

When Edwin wrote that he was going to buy a canoe and didn't want to go fifty-fifty, as we had agreed to do on expenses, I demurred. He insisted. He marshaled a dozen arguments—a prize debater warming to his task—concluding with one I could not possibly resist: "It seems to mean so much to me to have a canoe of my own at last." And after *much* correspondence a postcard arrived, dated March 29, 1978, with the jubilant sentence: "I HAVE BOUGHT A CANOE!"

From reading Edwin's notes, it is obvious that he carried out the pursuit and capture of his canoe with typical thoroughness and devotion to detail:

> The main goal of this first trip of the year to Concord is to make arrangements for a canoe. Waiting for the boathouse to open is too uncertain. We want to be able to be out at dawn or stay out later in the evening and not be dependent on hiring a canoe. I thought of making arrangements with the Rohans at the South Bridge Boat House to keep a boat for the season. Or finding a secondhand Grumman canoe for sale. I want a 15-foot canoe, a little shorter, a little lighter, than the 17-foot canoes Ann and I have used. I want to be able to get it on and off the car-carrying rack by myself. And on these winding and relatively placid streams we will not need a larger canoe.
>
> I had thought of getting a canoe and then finding someone—some friend of a friend of ours—who lives on the rivers to let me store it on his property. But everybody is against the idea. Canoes are being stolen at every chance. I thought of chaining mine to a tree. Mary Fenn says they file the chain and go off with the canoe. Mrs. Rohan says in one case they chopped down the tree and slipped the chain off the stump! Everyone says the best thing is to keep the canoe on my car, take it home and bring it back when I want to use it.
>
> No Grummans are for sale secondhand. This is the time of year everybody wants one. Sold secondhand mainly in the

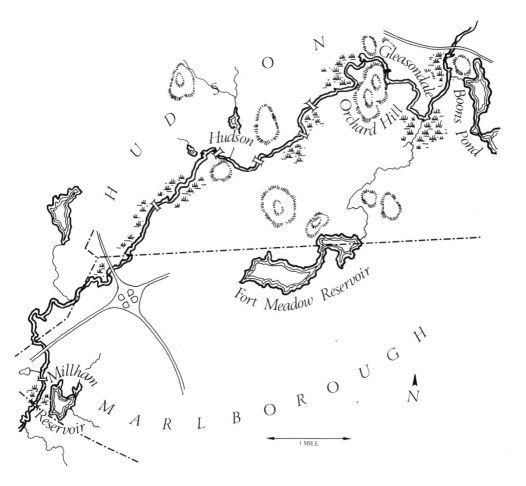

HUDSON

Hudson

Gleasondale

Orchard Hill

Boons Pond

Fort Meadow Reservoir

Millham
Reservoir

MARLBOROUGH

N

1 MILE

fall. If "canoe for sale" is put up on a bulletin board, the canoe is usually snapped up in a couple of days.

The Rohans are the dealers for Grumman canoes in Concord. Have canoes in stock. Have two 15-foot models. I left a deposit on a new canoe. Total—including 2 paddles, 2 cushions and $16.75 sales tax—is $363.75. I will leave it [in Concord] and take possession sometime in April. They put on a sticker reserving it for me. So now I am—almost—the proud possessor of a canoe of my own. I have always wanted to own a canoe.

I couldn't have been very old when my parents presented me with a canoe on Walloon Lake in northern Michigan, where we spent our summers. The circumstances of its arrival are lost in the haze of time—perhaps it just struck my mother as a good thing with which to occupy a restless child. Or perhaps, because she had loved spending time on the water as a young woman, she wanted to be sure her daughter knew the same. It was an Olde Towne canvas canoe, a broad-beamed stable boat with air locks in the sides, virtually untippable, painted a homely dark green.

After a few rudimentary instructions, I went out alone in my life jacket, my mother standing on the dock, watching. She had diminished alarmingly in size when caution caught up with me. Ahead was a frightening expanse of choppy water. Behind was the dock and safety. The canoe wouldn't turn around. My mother's instructions were lost on the wind. Tears pricked my eyes.

And then I did something right and the canoe responded and I suppose, although I didn't know it then, I learned something about the stimulus of fear and, in the first flush of confidence, the rewards of independence.

It was in that canoe that my mother took the stern and I the bow, and we paddled westward until the sun shattered on the serrated pines and the sky flushed deep and marvelous colors, and then we turned, no shadow running before us, just darkening water, the damp smell gathering on the surface, the trees along shore fusing into one somber silhouette, to reach the boathouse just before its white facade dimmed beyond recognition and it was night.

Edwin had brought his new canoe in April, but we had not been able to go out; in his notes he recorded:

The flag is flapping wildly when we go to breakfast. A cold and violent wind. I feel *I cannot stand it!* Not once to use the

84

new canoe. But I become stoical and we head for the Concord Library. On a windy, cold, unseasonable day, the research room in the basement is a sanctuary.

On this sunny day, launching the canoe is easy. Edwin has devised an ingenious wooden stand which holds it steady as he raises or lowers it from the top of the car. Characteristically, he has named it—he calls it his "Steady Eddie."

As we christen the shiny hull with mud on the keel instead of champagne on the bow, a black duck and her ducklings slide into the water so close together I think they're a muskrat until they separate into ducks, heads constantly pivoting. The hen remains all but immobile, watching; the ducklings rotate about her. Then all proceed upstream in a line as if moored to the same string.

The Assabet upstream from Northborough curves tightly, small, smooth, grassy-banked, golf-course manicured on each side, a placid little English stream. Whirligig beetles endlessly pucker the surface film by darting back and forth through it in swift quadrilles, propelled by strong middle and hind legs. I snatch one up from the water and hold it under my hand lens. Its double eyes are just visible: compound eyes on the upper part of the head through which surface movement is perceived, and another set beneath the waterline for underwater vision.

The openness does not last long; shortly woods bind the river, and every twig has its complement of insects and arachnids. When I brush against an overhanging branch, harvestmen shower onto my notebook; they rest there with four of their eight hairlike legs forward, four back, their tiny oval bodies suspended in the middle like some spidery lunar vehicle. An ambush bug still clutching a twig drops in their midst, a lethal-looking little baggage: blunted snout, front legs as muscular as those of a weight lifter held up in menace, orange-pink eyes. Spittlebugs have bubbled bright white clots all over a dogwood. Bumblebees hang from bitter nightshade blossoms, small purple bells with turned-back petals and a cluster of protruding yellow stamens. Dark blue-gray damselflies dart among the brighter blue blossoms of pickerelweed. Tiny white caddis flies flutter helplessly, caught on the surface of the water. Above them, a row of barn swallows, backs metallic navy blue, are perfectly arranged on an empty branch as if brushed there by a Chinese calligrapher.

85

Bitter nightshade (*Solanum dulcamara*)

Suddenly I am aware of a larger object, unmoving, unblinking—*very* much the largest frog I've ever seen, like some dark cloudy jade Buddha with a yellow throat, enigmatic, all-knowing. There he sits, big muscular legs folded under his squat tailless body, surrounded by this ideal habitat of overgrown stream thick with pickerelweed and arrowhead to hide in, and snails and dragonfly and damselfly nymphs to feed on.

These males begin calling before the females emerge from muddy hibernation. Even after breeding season they often continue to call, defining their territory. Air is forced into sacs from the lungs through an opening at each side of the tongue or at the mouth corners; when calling, the bullfrog takes a gulp of air, shuts his nostrils and mouth, and then shuttles the air back and forth over elastic vocal cords, perhaps the first creature on earth to make sound by using vocal cords.

Judging from the number of bullfrogs in, on, and around the stream, this is a bumper year for frogs; all along the way they jump, plop, flip, spring, slide into the river. Behind us, like water gurgling out of a jug, or an off-key twang on a bull fiddle, one

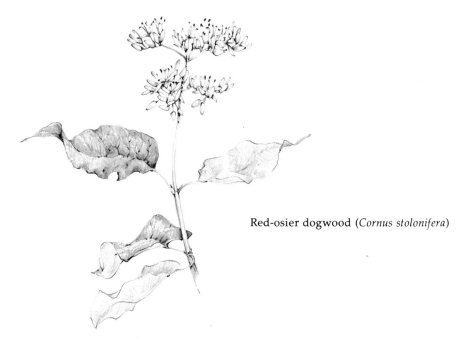

Red-osier dogwood (*Cornus stolonifera*)

sounds off, then another, the most ponderous love song on the river.

A white-tailed dragonfly takes off from a pickerelweed. It has a good three-inch wingspan and makes a soft clatter, moving just fast enough so that I can't tell if it's male or female. The female has three black spots on each wing, while on males white spots are interspersed, which flash as they fly in their swift erratic fashion. Their common name comes from the distinct whitish bloom on the abdomen.

I remark to Edwin that I wish I had my net with me so I could capture one to examine at leisure; I have just had a college course in entomology and a whole new world has opened up to me. My rhapsodizing is met with an uncharacteristic and rather ominous silence from the stern of the canoe.

Then Edwin's voice: He never found it necessary to kill an insect; he just put it in a jar and took it down to the next meeting of the New York Entomological Association, of which he was a member, where someone identified it. Then he took it home and released it where he had found it.

I assuage my conscience with the economics of long-distance nomenclature, but the honest fact of the matter is that some of us are collectors and some of us are not. Still, ever after, I feel like a pillager and plunderer of the countryside and every time I stick a pin through an unprotesting thorax, I think of Edwin's Schweitzer-like respect for the insect community.

A letter is there when I get home: "The dragonfly with the chalky-white abdomen that alighted around us as we ate lunch . . . is *Plathemis lydia,* the White Tail. It is the older males that have the powdered chalk appearance. One alights in sunny places ahead of me when I go down the lane for the mail these days. When at rest it always holds its wings slanting forward and down."

The river, closeted by vegetation, runs quietly here. Along the bank, tiny white trailing chickweeds and starflowers shine like constellations in a grassy sky. Duckweed clusters on the tips of hornwort where it rises to touch the river surface; on one a damselfly, abdomen tucked under, lays her eggs.

To animals with a three-to-four-week life span, the warming weather gives an intense push to procreation. All up and down the river the damselflies dart in pairs, in the horizontal P configu-

Starflower (*Trientalis borealis*)

ration of mating—male the staff of the P, female held between head and thorax by claspers on the male's tail, curving her abdomen around and up to remove a packet of sperm on the underside of the male's abdomen.

The female damselfly is guided to the proper egg-laying site by both visual and chemical clues, often inserting her eggs directly into plant tissue. The male sometimes hovers above to prevent other males from mating with her; sometimes he holds her, as in mating, as she descends beneath the waterline to deposit her eggs in plant stalks, providing the necessary pull to help her break back up through the elastic boundary. I watch one such pair slowly backing down a pickerelweed stem; for a second the male remains holding the female as she oviposits, then unexpectedly releases her and darts away, leaving her there. As we pass, I lunge for the stem to save her, nearly upsetting the canoe—and miss, and we are past. There she must remain, unable to push through the water/air interface, until she drowns.

We approach a handsome stone railroad bridge. As water swirls around the cement base it dimples, the indentations showing darker against dark, rotating quietly downstream. If it weren't for these and the duckweeds that spin slowly by, singly, doubly, triply, but seldom more, there would seem to be no current, only the smooth reflections that scarcely waver with the breeze.

As we enter the arch of the bridge a disembodied voice says, "You'll never make it!" Three boys sit on the parapet on the other side of the abutment, six legs dangling over, three heads watching our progress. He's right. We stop rather suddenly. I get out, safely shod in Nellie's waders, to pull the canoe over a little bar of gravel.

Originally these rails carried the cars of the "Agricultural Branch" of the Boston & Worcester Railroad, which arrived in Northborough in 1856. The branch ran from Northborough to South Framingham, where it connected with the Boston & Worcester, and Northborough was the end of the line until after the Civil War. In 1866 the branch was extended to Fitchburg and became the Boston, Clinton & Fitchburg Railroad. Railroads in New England more frequently than not have exceedingly complicated histories, changing hands and names, maintaining interlocking directorates and breeding new companies with the rapidity of guppies. Eventually this one became the Northern division of the

90

New York, New Haven & Hartford; the bridge was built when this segment was owned by the Pennsylvania Railroad.

The water deepens and canoeing again becomes easy. Edwin scoops up a young painted turtle, the size of a silver dollar, and passes it to me on his paddle. Its neck is the brown of the river, its plastron a lovely salmon. The shell is marked with vermilion, the head with Naples yellow stripes. As I hold it upside down to examine it, it tucks its head in and pulls its tail round to one side, fitting both perfectly between shell and plastron. I place it on my notebook, wrongside up, a neat little package.

It brings back memories of my childhood, for painted turtles are the most abundant turtles of the Midwest and East, where lakes and streams have muddy bottoms and plentiful vegetation. They feed under water, consuming algae, grass, moss, insects and tiny mollusks, and scavenging as well. Supposedly they have some difficulty swallowing when out of water. In winter they hibernate in mucky stream and pond bottoms and edges. Eggs are laid mid to late June in the late afternoon or evening. The female digs a nest in soil near the water, dropping in four to eight pinkish eggs, which she tamps down into the dirt and covers carefully.

The turtle remains rocking on its back, so I turn it over. Its head protrudes enough for me to see the yellow streaks behind the eyes. It samples the air, then withdraws. A minute green aphid disturbs a hair on the back of my hand; in my concentration the aphid feels as if it had spiked boots on. The turtle continues motionless. I reach to pick it up and just as I do a flipper extends, then another. My hand moving across the page makes it draw in its head but only for a second; almost immediately the head and tail pop out again, the head up, ready to travel.

Tentatively it pulls up onto the folded USGS map tucked into my notebook pocket. Slowly, doing a kind of terrestrial breaststroke across inked road and swamp, brook and house, it makes its way home. Edwin quotes Thoreau's *Journal* entry of May 1853: "A turtle walking is as if a man were to try to walk by sticking his legs and arms merely out the windows."

It bows its head, raises it once more, and then, to my delight, scuttles right across the map precisely where it is in actuality and drops into the water so quickly that I miss the splash and see only the tiny disk rotating slowly down into the dark river.

The river slows still more in the backwater from the Main

Street Dam at Northborough. The original dam, built in 1739, provided waterpower for Samuel Wood's fulling mill. There was another dam about where we are now, in the impoundment of which total-immersion baptism took place, something which could scarcely occur today, for the water here is very high in nutrients and suffers bacterial blooms. The present dam downstream, completed in 1855, has a hydraulic height of fifteen feet, concrete and stone completely hidden by the thick sheet of water which sends a formidable reverberation upstream.

Just beyond the dam is the stone bridge carrying Northborough's main street, built in 1849. As did Stone's Bridge on the Sudbury, it replaced a timber bridge which had borne historic footsteps. One April noontime, Peter Whitney, Northborough's patriotic minister, was giving a rousing oration to Northborough militiamen when word came of a skirmish at Concord. The men dispersed to get their equipment, boots thudding back and forth across the bridge. Before they left the same day, they assembled at Samuel Wood's house, by the bridge, for Whitney's last exhortations and benediction.

Main Street—and thus the bridge—is part of the old Boston Post Road. Known as the Old Connecticut Road, it was the first designated post road in America. Early in 1673, mail was scheduled for delivery between New York and Boston, and thereafter, on the first Monday of each month, riders set out from New York. The Assabet crossing must have been one of their distance markers. It was not until 1753, when the ingenious Benjamin Franklin, odometer in hand, measured distances along New England roads and caused stone mile markers to be installed, that such landmarks became less important and coach and postal rates, based upon distance traveled, could be standardized.

The first stagecoach contract to carry mail was awarded in 1785 to one Levi Pease, who maintained fast extra-fare coaches and reduced the normal mail run from six days to a day and a half between Boston and New York. All ablebodied men in the area between sixteen and sixty were required to contribute time toward post road upkeep, with high penalties for noncompliance. By 1826, four stages a day ran, both east and west, Sundays of course excepted. In the mid-1830s, before the railroad, more than two thousand mail and passenger coaches clattered over the Assabet each year.

Samuel Wood's fulling mill, hard by the bridge, was one of the earliest mills on the Assabet. It was established on the east side of the river in 1751; his deed read, in part, "to stake by the Assabett River—thence Northwardly by said river as the river runs—eighty nine rods" to his neighbor's boundary. Wood served the town throughout his life, and was a militia captain in the Revolutionary War. His mill finished some seven thousand yards of dressed cloth per year.

The production of linen and woolen cloth was a home industry in the Northeast from the earliest days of the Colonies, and one of the earliest commercial industries to supplement it was fulling. It was necessary because wool came off the loom dirty and loosely and unevenly woven. It needed to be cleaned, felted and shrunk.

Fulling comes from the Old French *fuler,* meaning "to walk or tread upon." Before fulling mills were established, there used to be fulling parties, where the soap-saturated hand-woven woolen cloth was put in a tub and everyone stomped on it, to both clean and compact it. The result was lots of clean feet but inadequate cloth, and an early Colonial priority was the establishment of fulling mills. However, since it was a fairly expensive process, many colonists wore homespuns, with minimal finishing, at least for everyday.

When hand-woven cloth was brought to the mill, it was first washed well in hot soapy water to remove the surface dirt and some of the lanolin. Then it was put into a trough with "fuller's earth," an absorbent clay which takes up grease in the wool, and later washes out, and thumped for hours by vertical pestles, harnessed to waterpower. The clean wet cloth was stretched on frames to block it. When dry, it was laid over poles and "curried" with the dried seed pod of teasel, a daisy family species, *Dipsacus laciniatus,* still seen growing along the roadsides in this country. Teasel pods are covered with hooked spines unequaled for raising the nap on wool. However, since they do so unevenly, the fuller then wrapped the cloth around a cylinder to make the nap stand up and skillfully trimmed it, hefting long-bladed shears that weighed up to sixty pounds.

In the immediate vicinity of the Main Street Bridge in Northborough, which is now small business and residential, there was a succession of businesses typical of many small streams such

93

as the upper Assabet. Water privileges provided nearly free energy, and production continued as long as there was a demand for the product. Machinery was relatively small and simple and easily adapted to different products, allowing great variety and diversity, and hence considerable economic resiliency. By contrast, on bigger rivers, which supported larger industry, usually textile manufacture, a town's economy often became so closely keyed to one product that its fortunes rose and fell with those of the mill, as happened at Maynard, downstream on the Assabet.

Wood's fulling mill was first at the Main Street site. In 1782 there was an iron factory. By the early 1800s the Hunt brothers had a shoe factory; they pegged and nailed the soles to the uppers by hand, a method outmoded by the invention of the sewing machine. Wesson rifles were manufactured here between 1838 and 1850 by Daniel Baird Wesson and his brother, Edwin. And in 1861 Edward H. Smith had a bone mill in which oyster shell was ground up for cattle and chicken feed.

One of the more ingenious users of Assabet waterpower in Northborough was Thomas Blair, who lived in Samuel Wood's old house. In 1894 the Camera Company and in 1907 the Blair Lite Company were in operation. Blair invented a cash register, the combination wrench, attachments for sewing machines, and quite possibly film—at any rate, Eastman (which became Eastman Kodak) bought out Blair's patents.

Blair's cash register, a sample of which remains in the Northborough Historical Society, is a captivating device. A divided tray alongside the register holds metal tabs of different colors and denominations. To ring up a sale, you insert the appropriate tab in a slot in the register, which pops open the cash drawer and then drops inside with a satisfying plunk. At the end of the day a total of the tabs told the day's receipts more quickly and easily than counting money.

In the late 1800s the old Wood mills were occupied by Milo Hildreth, who manufactured tortoiseshell jewelry and buttons (a rage for ornaments of this sort caused the near extinction of Atlantic tortoises). There was evidently some dispute between the town of Northborough and Hildreth. To settle it, a committee was appointed, and all agreed that Hildreth ought to build a culvert and

> if the said Hildreth should change the location of the present Culvert and continue it over his canal to the Assabet River, he

is to hold the Town harmless forever from any damage in consequence of passing over said canal; and the said Hildreth for himself, his heirs and assigns, does hereby promise and agree to hold said Town harmless from any and all damages in consequence of said culvert passing over said canal forever.

For this the committee agreed to pay Hildreth two hundred dollars.

Also in Wood's buildings, by the first part of the nineteenth century, was Samuel Fisher. Unlike most of the small shop and factory owners, of whom we have record only through deeds and account books and impersonal town documents, Samuel Fisher kept a diary full of observations of everyday life in the 1830s: on this same day, over a century ago, May 23, 1837, he planted "beans cucumbers mushmellown Squashers & etc."

Fisher was a cabinetmaker, wheelwright, and carpenter, and must have been most dexterous, for he made cheese presses, bedposts, brick walls, window frames and sashes. He made bobbins for the Davis cotton factory downstream on the Assabet, and one to three-quarters of his day frequently was devoted to this as well as repair work on the factory's looms. He was, in short, the kind of skillful practical man so needed to keep the various businesses of Northborough going.

He kept meticulous records of deaths and funerals, the age of the deceased, what was preached on the occasion. In his day, waves of illness took many children; early records show that in 1746 some thirty children died of dysentery, and in 1749–50 "throat distemper" took some sixty more, the first to be buried in the new church graveyard. In 1839 Fisher wrote:

May 3 about 4 oclock found Elen a live without much apparent alteration   She had continued through the night in great distress   She finally Died about 10 minutes before 6 oclock this morning 3d May 1839   Aged 2 years 18 days   Doct Davis Examened her sore on her neck and found it had ulcerated to a considerable extent it had eaten the interior juglerer vein about half off which caused the bleeding there were also sores in the head as matter Discharged at the ear and proverbly there was canker in the head   She probernly Died from Loss of blood but would have died from Disease had she not blad
about the house & at the shop
4 about home and attended the funeral of Ellen Frances Fisher

"I measure one of its extravagant leaves by my hand span and find it twenty inches long and a foot wide."

"Reflections of treetops waver in the water, dark peaked patterns, positive and negative shapes interfingering in the ripples from a paddle stroke. Sunlight dancing off the white pine needles sparkles within the water. The forest floor itself shimmers in watery waves. . . ."

this after noon at 4 oclock May 4th 1839 who died May 3d 1839   Aged 2 years 18 dayes

The daily entries continue—the following Sunday morning he found his hog dead and went to a meeting—a close-mouthed, contained litany of planting and mending and repairing and making, the lack of elaboration telling in the most piercing way what it was like to lose the child you had held in your arms.

We turn back upstream. This morning, a century and a half later, the charm of the river blossoms and burgeons all about us. Arrow arum carries big white blooms that look like calla lilies. I measure one of its extravagant leaves by my hand span and find it twenty inches long and a foot wide.

Reflections of treetops waver in the river, dark peaked patterns, positive and negative shapes interfingering in the ripples from a paddle stroke. Sunlight dancing off the white pine needles sparkles within the water. The forest floor itself shimmers in watery waves, the wreath of monkey flowers and ferns on its edge doubled quivering in the river. A tiger swallowtail butterfly drifts by in a dreamlike silence. Deep in the woods, angelica marches in green palisades, its flowering heads spheres of green lifted high

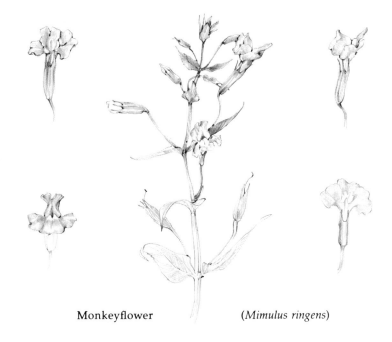

Monkeyflower   (*Mimulus ringens*)

above the other herbs. Wild grapevines languish over the grasses and shrubs, festooning every available support, echoing the iconography of an early Christian sarcophagus where the arabesques of marble vines interweave through eternity, world without end—an appropriate symbol of immortality.

All the luscious variety of greens and all the river musings, birdsong festooning the trees, the soft aroma of elderberry flowers, surround us as we slide on the silken silvery skin between two worlds. Water drops tick off the paddle blade to dot the water film and spread interlocking circles outward, the quiet breathing of the river, boundaries at once lucid and dissolving: quintessential riverness.

We take out at the small bridge on Brigham Street, where the openness of the Brigham farmland still remains in the golf course that replaces it. A "rabbit-ear" fence follows the road, gray boulders laid to form a fence with spaced slabs set vertically, notched to carry wooden crosspieces. The glacial erratics studding New England's meadows provided a seemingly unending supply of boulders for New England's lovely old walls. A rabbit-ear fence required a minimum of stone hauling and provided a maximum

Sensitive fern (*Onoclea sensibilis*)

of protection. This one is made even handsomer by the drifts of wildflowers that find shelter beside it—vetch, buttercups, ground ivy, violets, and strawberries.

By the early 1800s, when this fence was built, farming was beginning to prove of so little profit here that there began a general exodus westward; by the 1860s many of these hard-won fields had been abandoned to the woods. Natural events hastened the demise of farming: crop-damaging frosts occurred in the unusually cold summer of 1816. Hay that normally sold for $30 a ton went for $180. The aberrant weather was caused by dust circling the earth from the explosion of Mount Tambora in Indonesia in 1815, an eruption considerably larger than that of the better-known Krakatoa.

As I stow Edwin's "Steady Eddie" back into the car after he has loaded the canoe on top, a few word fragments penciled on the wood pique my curiosity. At my question, Edwin replies that when he and Nellie were in England working on *Springtime in Britain*, they heard about a gravestone in a small Cumberland churchyard cemetery, from which these penciled words were taken. For Edwin the epitaph summed up the essence of the theme

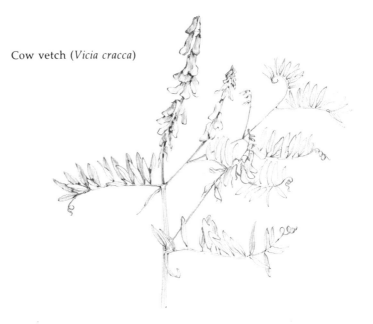

Cow vetch (*Vicia cracca*)

Ground ivy (*Glechoma hederacea*)

that ran through the books of those nature writers he most admired—their "letters to the world." The full inscription read:

> The wonder of the world, the beauty and the power, the shape of things, their colors, lights and shades: these I saw. Look ye also while life lasts.

That evening the sunset is spectacular. The dust from the first large eruption of Mount Saint Helens has sifted into New England.

5

EWJ   Where the river, just below our halting place, rushes
          down a wide and shallow bed, where the water wind of
the shifting currents fills the stream from bank to bank with the
sinuous undulations of thousands of ribbon leaves of the freshwater eelgrass, we rode toward the most picturesque of all the landmarks along the Sudbury. Once seen, the impression it makes is
indelible.

We came upon it first one October day when we had turned
off the Old Connecticut Path, now Route 126, south of Wayland.
A side road carried us west toward the river. Beside the stream an
immense weeping willow screened the view. As we passed it, the
aspect downstream was revealed with dramatic suddenness, as if
there had been a swift parting of a curtain. Like some ancient
Roman aqueduct set down in the New World, the remains of an
old stone bridge stood stark and lonely in its river setting. With its
weathered blocks of stone, its four remaining arches, its western
end fallen away, it seemed surrounded by a venerable air, envel-
oped in an atmosphere of great antiquity.

The official name of the stone bridge is Stone's Bridge, derived from the name of one of the earliest colonists to buy land
from the Indians and settle in this area, where Framingham and
Wayland join. At one time the family's holdings, extending to the
Saxonville Falls, were known as Stone's End. Until the nineteenth
century, this bridge was known as the "New Bridge" to differenti-

Sherman Bridge

S U D B U R Y

W A Y L A N D

Great
Meadows
National
Wildlife

Causeway Bridge

Refuge

Wayland

Wash Brook

Heard Pond

Pelham Island

Stone's Bridge

N

1 MILE

"Like some ancient Roman aqueduct set down in the New World, the remains of an old stone bridge stood stark and lonely in its river setting."

ate it from the "Old Bridge," built in 1646, farther downstream. It was not called Stone's Bridge until around 1820. At this point, as along part of the dead stream of the Ox-Bow, the Framingham-Wayland boundary runs down the center of the river. The old stone bridge is bisected by it, its eastern half in Wayland, its western half in Framingham.

A bronze plaque at the eastern end of the ruined bridge records that here the historic Knox Trail crossed the Sudbury. It was one of the most dramatic achievements of the early days of the American Revolution, that dragging of nearly sixty of the cannon of Fort Ticonderoga three hundred miles on sledges pulled by oxen and horses over nearly impassable roads in midwinter to aid General George Washington in the siege of Boston. General Henry Knox, commanding, was twenty-five years old at the time, a young Boston bookseller turned soldier. Most authorities agree that the "noble train" of Ticonderoga cannon proved the decisive factor in forcing the British from the city in 1776.

For a long time it was believed that the four arches of the old stone bridge had supported the train of Revolutionary cannon across this vital link in their route to Boston. The assumption was—and the first impression of great antiquity seemed to bear it out—that the now-ruined bridge was of Colonial origin. Several historical publications have placed the date of its building at about 1722. But recently, careful investigations of old records by Helen F. Emery, of the Wayland Historical Commission, in connection with the bicentennial celebration of 1976, have revealed new information.

The trail she followed through the town records of Wayland, Sudbury and Framingham, through those of the Middlesex County Commissioners and the Commonwealth of Massachusetts, were complicated by gaps and vagueness in the archives. In one instance a town treasurer had maintained that the records he had kept belonged to him and took them with him when he left office. But as evidence accumulated, the history of the various bridges that had been constructed at the spot became clear.

As early as 1674, a wooden cart bridge was built at this location by Samuel How. The place selected, with its relatively shallow water and firm bed, had long been used as a fording place by the Indians. Framingham records of April 7, 1674, state:

In answer to the petition of Samuel How, referring to some allowance to be made him for his expenses about the bridge he had lately erected upon Sudbury river above the towne, he is allowed of all travellers, for a horse and man, $3^{d.}$ and for a cart $6^{d.}$, until there be an orderly settlement of the country high-way and some disbursement.

In 1773 bills were paid for timbers such as are used in build-ing wooden bridges, for construction of a new and stronger bridge at the site. If General Knox crossed the Sudbury here, it was over this strengthened bridge, which was made of wood, not stone.

When was the wooden bridge replaced by the bridge of stone? Mrs. Emery found in town records entries of payment for building material used only in the repair of a wooden bridge—planks and joists and spikes—as late as the mid-1850s: in the spring of 1855 the town of Wayland paid $2.98 for 166 feet of plank to repair the bridge. About this time, references to plans to replace the wooden bridge with a new bridge of stone begin to appear in the records, but the evidence trails off. Nowhere could Mrs. Emery find a definitive record of the actual building, and so it seemed for a time that her search had reached a dead end.

It was an entry in the twelfth volume of Thoreau's *Journal* that supplied the missing link. Recording details of the trip he and Channing made up the Sudbury as far as the neck of the Fram-ingham Ox-Bow, on July 31, 1859, Thoreau tells of his conversa-tion with a man he encountered near the end of his upstream advance. In the high water of spring, he was told, the river had risen five feet from its present level at the bridge on the edge of Framingham. The man pointed out the high water mark on the stone construction. To this Thoreau adds: "It is an arched stone bridge, built some two years ago." That, apparently, pins down the date of the building of the present structure to the year 1857.

[Mrs. Emery proves to be a dignified graduate of Vassar with an additional degree from Harvard, a former teacher at Smith. When I show her the Thoreau *Journal* quotation ... she shakes hands with me and almost jumps up and down. It is, she says, such a precious day! Her idea is that the state must have paid for the bridge, so no costs appear in the Wayland town meeting minutes.]

Thus, in spite of its venerable appearance and the legends

that surround it, the history of the four-arched stone structure known as Stone's Bridge extends back only to a few years before the Civil War. The end of its life as a carrier of traffic came almost exactly a century after it was built. As the river rose above the arches during the flood that accompanied Hurricane Diane, the stone structure acted as a dam stretching from one side of the river to the other. The stones had been laid without being cemented together, and the pressure of the water flowing through the cracks washed away the gravel which had been put on the bridge to form a solid support for the asphalt hardtop. With the gravel removed from under it, the road collapsed.

It could have been repaired. The four arches of the bridge were intact. But money was available for flood relief and it was decided to build a new bridge—the Potter Street Bridge, just upstream—and to straighten and widen the road. The western arch of Stone's Bridge was then removed, to reduce its effect as a substantial barrier in times of high water.

[There is a waterweed growing near the bridge, unknown to me. I go down to the river's edge on the upstream side of the bridge with a pail and a long-handled rake. Rake out strands of the waterweed. Take a pailful with me to have the weed identified by Dr. C. Barre Hellquist of the Biology Department of Boston State College, who lives nearby and is an authority on waterweeds. I present my pail of waterweed apologetically—botanists want specimens pressed and on herbarium sheets and not in pails. But he identifies it as soon as he looks into the pail. It is *Potamogeton epihydrus;* this is the commonest kind in the region. Alkalinity of water determines what species of *Potamogeton* grows in a stream. Limestone makes for alkaline water; granitic rock for acid.

[From the bridge, I look downstream. Waving freshwater eelgrass, or wild celery, grows all across the shallow bed of the river. Its leaves ruffle the surface of the water. I tell Ann this is the "white water" of the Sudbury. What a contrast to the raging water of the rapids she has been running in the West!

[Freshwater eelgrass or wild celery (*Vallisneria spiralis*) is listed as one of the most valuable foods for wild ducks in the Northeast. In fact, canvasbacks are so fond of it that their scientific name is *Aytha valisineria,* the specific name a variation or a misspelling of *Vallisneria.* Ann Haven Morgan, in *Fieldbook of Ponds and*

108

Streams, describes the interesting method of reproduction employed by the plant:

> The small greenish female flowers are borne singly on the ends of long spiral stems so supple and springy that they are not pulled underwater when wind ripples its surface. The short-stemmed male flowers develop near the base of the plant, several hundreds of them in each cluster, the separate flowers becoming detached as they mature. A bubble of air in each one buoys it to the top and there it opens and floats along the surface till it meets the female flower. The male flowers congregate in great numbers about the larger female ones to which their sticky pollen finally adheres. After pollination the spiral stem of the female flower contracts and pulls the maturing fruit down into the water.]

By chance Ann and I set out on our long-awaited all-day trip down the Sudbury from Stone's Bridge, on October 15, my Freedom Day, my Independence Day, my Freedom Bell Day—the day I escaped from *Popular Science* into the free-lance life. How fine a way to celebrate it, this thirty-fifth anniversary of my own personal Fourth of July!

In college I developed interests that have remained with me ever since—but I did not prepare myself for making a living! My grades were good, I was elected class president and president of several organizations, I won the extemporaneous speaking contest, went to three state oratorical contests and was on the state championship debating team. I made many friendships that have lasted through life.

But I had no idea what I wanted to do. At one time I thought of becoming a lawyer—heaven help me! By graduation day I had decided I was going to become a writer. But what does that mean? It never occurred to me I could make a living and support a family writing about nature. I took none of the studies I should have taken: biology, zoology, botany, etc. (I am not sure that I am sorry. Self-education in a field that becomes intensely interesting has its advantages.)

Several years after I was out of college I went to New York and got a job with *Popular Science.* On my own time, as an aid in illustrating magazine stories, I had taken up photography and as a sideline hobby had been taking action and sequence pictures of insects. They sold well to Sunday supplements and magazines. I had assembled quite a collection when Dodd, Mead & Co. wrote asking to buy a set of pictures I had taken of Rube Cross, a man who tied dry flies. They wanted them to illustrate a book Cross had written. (Years afterward, Edward H. Dodd, Jr., recalled that on the day Rube Cross had originally brought in his manuscript, there had been an elevator strike in the building where Dodd, Mead had its offices. Cross might have decided to go to another publisher. Instead he climbed the stairs *eleven floors* to the Dodd, Mead office. If he had decided otherwise, the stroke of luck that meant so much in my life would never have occurred.)

When I delivered the pictures, I took along one hundred or more of my insect pictures to demonstrate the kind of work I was doing in case Dodd, Mead ever needed insect photographs to illustrate some future book. Mr. Dodd suggested that I write a book and illustrate it with my own photographs.

Grassroot Jungles resulted. It attracted an unusual amount of attention and was given the front-page review by *The New York Times Book Review*. From then on, I was on my way. But four years went by, and I was past forty-two, before I could see my way to give up my job and become a free lance, devoting myself day after day to books, instead of working on them nights and weekends. All the wonderful things that have happened since commenced on the day I made that decision and walked away from *Popular Science*—my personal Independence Day, October 15, 1941.

On this October 15, we awoke to a day windy and cold, largely overcast, but as we unlashed the canoe and slid it down the steep rocks to the water's edge, the sky began opening up, and the sun came out soon after we started. Riding on the sweep of the current curving around the open end of Stone's Bridge, carried over shallows alive with the waving of the living ribbons of the waterweeds, we headed downstream.

The sun shone. The wind blew. We were off on an adventure! Most of the time the wind was behind us. It recalled the old Irish blessing: "May you have the sun in your face and the wind at your back." As we paddled with leisurely strokes, I felt as alive and alert to all around me as some wild animal, some fox that hears a mouse in the grass. Ann was wearing hiking boots; I was wearing moccasins that could be easily slipped off if we upset. An optimist and a pessimist in the same canoe!

For perhaps a quarter of a mile, our course was straight, slightly west of north, walled in by almost vertical banks of mud and interlacing roots of grass and sedge. We followed the ancient trough of a natural canal: cutting across this portion of the river runs a line of weakness in the earth's crust called by geologists the Weston Fault.

Then, in an almost right-angled swing to the east, the river carried us for another three-quarters of a mile on a new course. The current moderated, the banks sank lower, became less like the walls of a canal. Our view of the wetlands extending away around us expanded.

We were drifting nearer to a second point of dramatic change in the life of the river. Here, about a mile downstream from Stone's Bridge, just before the meander of the five bends below Heard Pond on Pelham Island—a wriggling of the stream that appears as a blue-tinted squiggle on contour maps of the area—the Sudbury River undergoes a transformation as abrupt as that which occurs at the Great Falls. In the space of only a few hundred yards it becomes a river of yet another kind.

We felt the current slacken. We saw the dense wetland vegetation of the banks move by more slowly. The clear water that had run between the canal-like walls we had just left behind grew more murky. All the features of the streambed, all the little pits that had snared the dark, decaying leaves of the previous autumn, all the things that we had viewed as through a window of clear glass, began to fade away, curtained by the increasing silt of the slower river.

The gradient of the stream had suddenly flattened out. And all things followed. From here on, as it wanders down the bed of the ancient glacial Lake Sudbury, it descends only about an inch to the mile. It becomes placid, drifting, vagrant, the unchanging river. All the rest of its course, all the way to Egg Rock and its confluence with the Assabet, its character remains virtually unchanged. In a wide and lazy flow, its brown water pursues its deliberate way down the green width of its valley. Its time of sudden alteration is reflected in many things, in subtle changes in the dominant waterweeds it supports and in the kind of fish that inhabit its more murky waters.

In a world of patchy, straggly, tentative beginnings and inconclusive endings, there is about a river an artistic unity, a begin-

111

ning and a middle and an end. But among all the rivers that I have known, the Sudbury is unique in the way in which its middle is telescoped into a relatively small proportion of its length. It had reached maturity and attained the characteristics of old age in a space that we traversed with only a hundred or two paddle strokes.

In the now wandering course of the river, it swings to the east to circle around Pelham Island, a low drumlin deposited by the glaciers, before continuing its flow into the north, and borders the wild stretch of sedge and bur reed and cotton grass known as Beaver Hole Meadow. Thoreau noted that the meadow was the home of rails and marsh wrens and "green bitterns," and there he measured great bur reeds that rose to a height of five or six feet.

Herbert Pelham, who had come from the fen country in England, acted for the government of the Bay Colony in clearing obstructions from the river, and was awarded five hundred acres in lieu of cash payment for his services. The Heard family later bought the land. Hence Heard Pond (Pelham Pond in Thoreau's day) on Pelham Island.

[Heard Pond in Indian days was the annual scene of a great summer encampment, with as many as five thousand Nipmucks living along its shore. Indian villages probably made up of "beehive huts." Poles bent to center point and tied with rawhide, then covered with skins. Along the river are found myriads of tiny points that are sometimes called bird points because they were probably used to kill birds and very small animals.]

For some time as we rounded Pelham Island, well before we reached Heard Pond, we had been glimpsing white rectangles beside the stream, signs bearing the stylized picture of a flying goose and the words: "Area Closed to Pursuing, Hunting, Taking, Capturing or Killing." They indicated that the adjoining lowland was a protected sanctuary administered by the Fish and Wildlife Service. Almost all the land bordering the Sudbury River from Heard Pond to Lee's Bridge, just above Fairhaven Bay, is now part of the Great Meadows National Wildlife Refuge.

Nevertheless, along the Sudbury there is hunting. A tangle of state and federal laws and local ordinances is involved. And the Corps of Engineers plays a part: Although a dam on the Concord at Billerica has prevented commercial traffic on both the Concord and the Sudbury for a century, the corps, which has control over navigable waterways, still maintains that both the rivers are navigable. Massachusetts state laws require that hunting be permitted on all navigable rivers. Here states' rights come into the picture: state laws take precedence over federal laws in such matters. Hence hunting has to be permitted on the Sudbury even where refuge land is posted on either side: hunters can legally shoot waterfowl from boats. But what if they shoot a duck and it falls on land posted and protected as a refuge? Here the Fish and Wildlife Service has decided that the dead duck is better recovered and eaten than left to go to waste. If the hunter leaves his gun in the boat, he is permitted to break the law and trespass on the sanctuary to recover the duck. This is considered better "resource use."

There seems to be additional bending of the law in the hunter's favor. Hunting is legal on certain private tracts along the upper part of the river, over which the Fish and Wildlife Service has no control. But there are other tracts of land that are really part of the wildlife refuge but which, because of lack of funds, have not yet been posted. Since wardens know that if they take hunters caught hunting on these tracts to court the case will be dismissed because there are no signs on the land, they wink at hunting in such places for the present.

[In earlier days, when the marshes along this winding river teemed with waterfowl in fall and spring, hunters made two "harvests": they killed the breeding birds returning to their nesting grounds as well as the migrants going south in autumn. Now the spring flight is safe, and modern hunting groups, such as Ducks, Unlimited, buy up marshland in Canada to preserve it as breeding areas for wildfowl. They do a distinct service, for destruction of habitat can cause more widespread harm than hunting. J. N. Darling, when head of the Fish and Wildlife Service, had a slogan: "Ducks can't lay eggs on picket fences." They have to have the right conditions for nesting. Where vast lowland areas have been drained and turned into farms—as in the Kankakee Marsh in Indiana—the damage to waterfowl has been great. The cutting of forests, as well as the slaughter, contributed to the extinction of passenger pigeons.

[But there is another consideration. When, in a time of expansion, lowland is being drained and the waterfowl production reduced, then, especially, the birds need relief from hunting pressure. Even if hunting represents a small proportion of the harm being done, it may be the final straw, the added strain that makes the difference.

[Hunters say hunting is necessary to control wildlife populations. And there is a point to this argument too. But hunters are not a substitute for natural predators. The lions take the weak and sick, the poorest stock, while the hunters pick the best, the largest and strongest, the superior animals. One aids evolution by strengthening the breed, the other weakens it. Bring back the lions!

[Can hunting be classed as a sport? Can anything in which one side does not have a sporting chance be called a sport? Where is the "sporting chance" for the birds in modern game bird shooting? The hunter has a dog to smell out the birds and tell him where they are hidden because he does not have an adequate sense of smell himself, and then when the bird, which is only trying to hide, is forced from its cover, he shoots it with a scatter gun that fills the air with lead pellets because he can't shoot straight enough to hit it with a single bullet. This doesn't seem much more sporting than drowning out a gopher by pouring water in one end of its hole to drive it out the other, at which you have placed a coiled rattlesnake. Until the birds and the rabbits have guns and can shoot back, where are the equal chances?

[Some hunters are superb naturalists, accurate and with a wide range of information about the ways of wild creatures. And some naturalists have been hunters. J. J. Audubon, of course, never did get over his insatiable desire to kill more and more birds—for sport and not just for painting. In his day, probably the most terrifying sight a bird could see was John James Audubon approaching! John Burroughs used to carry a cane gun, but later in life he said he found he could not enjoy the woods fully unless he left the gun at home. Of course, we must judge these men in the context of the time in which they lived. The study of birds, before modern field guides and field glasses were available, was based on having the dead bird in the hand. (I wonder how many birds Roger Tory Peterson has saved through his books with their quick aids to identification?) Nevertheless, John Muir never seems to have carried a gun or been a hunter. Thoreau sold his gun when he was in his twenties.

[In "Higher Laws" in *Walden*, Thoreau speaks in favor of hunting and calls it an important part of his early education. But he says: "I . . . sold my gun before I went to the woods." And: "As for fowling, during the last years that I carried a gun my excuse was that I was studying ornithology, and sought only new or rare birds. But I confess that I am now inclined to think that there is a finer way of studying ornithology than this. It requires so much closer attention to the habits of the birds, that, if for that reason only, I have been willing to omit the gun."

["In Boston yesterday," he wrote in his *Journal* on May 10, 1854, "an ornithologist said significantly, 'If you held the bird in your hand—'; but I would rather hold it in my affections."

[Canoeing Heard Pond once with Mary and Fuzzy Fenn, I heard the curious "chippering" call of the ospreys and we saw among the *Pontederia*, rusted and dead in the fall, curious pink-red objects, bobbing in the water. They proved to be numerous shotgun shells, open ends up, the brass bases holding them in a vertical position. Once we saw a place that seemed trampled down by a herd of elephants. The duck hunters had left their boats and waded to an island where trees provided a hiding place. There were hundreds of shells bobbing in the water among the weeds. Halfway home, we turned back to look at a beautiful bird, a trim little blue-winged teal, floating on the surface, bobbing up and down, its bill upthrust, its feet held tightly to its body—a victim uncollected by the hunters.]

AHZ   It is spring when Edwin and I launch the canoe just below Northborough. In the woods alongside the Assabet, dozens of pink lady's slippers bloom in the shadows and wild lily of the valley carpets the ground, just eye level as we skim by in the canoe.

Soon the river opens out into islands of sedges which we work through blindly, letting whatever current there might be direct us, canoeing a tranquil pond as the Assabet slows and widens in the backwaters of the next dam at Woodside, less than a mile below the Main Street Dam in Northborough. Alongside us now runs Hudson Street, named for Ebenezer Hudson, a fife player at the Battle of Bunker Hill.

Like some well-preserved relic from Avignon, the Wachusett Aqueduct arches across the Assabet ahead of us, its graceful proportions doubled in the river. The aqueduct is made of cut gray granite blocks, the curves of its large arches repeated in smaller

Wild lily of the valley
(*Maianthemum canadense*)

"Like some well-preserved relic from Avignon, the Wachusett Aqueduct arches across the Assabet ahead of us, its graceful proportions doubled in the river."

ones on the cornice. Built in 1898, it was one of the first constructions authorized by the Metropolitan Water District, which had been created but three years earlier to bring still more water to Boston. Once it carried 65 billion gallons of water a day, connecting Wachusett Reservoir watershed to Boston, thirty-two miles away. Now it is no longer in use, and water is transferred via a deep rock tunnel, the Wachusett-Marlborough Tunnel, completed in 1965, which empties into the Sudbury Reservoirs to the east and underlies the Assabet about a mile downstream.

We beach the canoe and walk up the road, which gives access to the top of the aqueduct. The view is resplendent. Upstream, reflections and ripples glitter, the fluttering waves catching blue sky and sunshine, a breeze bowing the sedges, the whole visible reach of the river scintillating.

Downstream, almost beneath our feet, the river pounds over the milldam. Eleazer Howe had the first gristmill at the site in the 1720s. He sold to Ephraim Allen, also a miller, who built a bridge across the Assabet here in 1780; rebuilt in 1812, it is still known as Allen's Bridge and is still in use.

In 1814 Isaac Davis, from above Northborough, with eight partners bought six acres on both sides of the river, including the water privileges, for $3,000. In 1816 he complained about his property assessment and achieved a reduction of $182.70, surely as considerable an accomplishment then as it would be now.

Davis reorganized the company in 1831, named it the Northborough Cotton Manufacturing Company, and with an additional investment of $15,000, bought out his partners. He ran it for twenty-six years, selling out in 1851 to David Wood—hence the present name Woodside. The unlucky Wood saw the mill burn to the ground soon after purchase, rebuilt it, and watched it burn again at the end of 1866, notwithstanding the fact that the first firehouse in Northborough had been established in 1847 close by the mill and volunteers no longer had to depend upon a bucket brigade sloshing water up from the Assabet.

In 1867 Wood, who was as persistent as he was unlucky, began rebuilding once more, and eventually operated two woolen mills on this site, which made "shoddy" and "satinet." The former, from which our derisive adjective comes, was woven from "shoddy yarn," a yarn made of wool wastes that worked up into a very inferior product. Satinet, with a cotton warp and woolen filling, was inexpensive to make but presentable, serviceable and long-wearing.

The present building was built by Wood in 1888; long and narrow, of brick pierced with many windows and enlivened by nice detail work, it nestles into the riverside. Inside, I find it pleasant and airy. But I do not think I would have found it so, stuffed with constantly roaring machinery under these low ceilings. After Wood's death in 1900 the mill stood idle, and the structure has had a varied history since, coming into its present use as a store in the 1960s. It also has a place in local literature: sometime after 1900 an anonymous poet, sitting at the mill's window, wrote fourteen improbable stanzas, beginning:

> Rushing and roaring, hear the thunder
> Of a powerful streamful of water—
> The "Elspeth"—is now in spring freshet
> In full flood it flows without ceasing.

Outside, the waterwheel is still in place, but the millrace now is interrupted and no longer carries water into the wheel; the powerful bore of water instead pours back into the river. Its volume and velocity intimate that there was plenty of power once, when it was needed.

We take to the water again below the dam, through the rocky run at Woodside, past the model house built in 1855 of Assabet clay bricks manufactured in Albert Goodridge's brickyards; bricks made of glacially deposited clays sold for half a cent each in 1850 (it was not a profitable business). Almost as soon as we depart the narrow channel, the land levels out, the water slows, and once again we weave between sedge tussocks.

Everything seems to be going on at once, but softly—a grasshopper sparrow calls, a bullfrog pontificates, two fluttering sandpipers riffle the air with their wings, a blue jay yatters, five mallards swish ahead of the canoe, a ring-necked pheasant's squawk grates across the water, the ubiquitous blackbirds chirr.

Ahead of us is the last of the flood-control dams to be built on the Assabet, so new that it looks like cement teeth ready to eat the river, which, now confined in an artificial channel, still perks around the side. The dam is straight lines, hieratic, like those cruel Assyrian reliefs of the eighth century B.C., in which all sinews and muscles are delineated in a vocabulary of brutal overriding power.

119

Somewhere, back upstream, lost in the midst of the thick greenery, is the entrance to Stirrup Brook. On a knoll by the brook, just a quarter mile from where it enters the Assabet, stood the garrison house of Samuel Goodenow, one of four men to receive tracts of land in Marlborough in 1672.

Without fortification, nearly defenseless against Indian raids incited by the French, who supplied the Indians with arms and alcohol (supposedly the French also instituted the custom of taking scalps, as a tally of the number of settlers killed), constantly on edge because of news of scalpings and massacres, early colonists declared certain houses in a community to be "garrison houses," make-do where there was neither money nor labor to erect stoneworks or other defenses. These were no more than ordinary farmhouses with a good well (which not every house had—often the "well" was merely a depression in the ground with a low wall to keep livestock out), a supply of arms and ammunition laid in, and a modest surrounding palisade. To each house four to six families might be assigned. When rumors of Indian restlessness were abroad, families gathered at their assigned house, sometimes unable to go out even to till their own land until danger was over.

It was a fearsome time, when the dread of attack must have been almost as devastating as the attack itself; death lurked in the woods and terror just up the hillside, and not even the open fields were safe. Since women were left to do all the farm chores and heavy work while their husbands and sons were away on required militia duty, it was they who watched a child kidnapped, a sister scalped, a house destroyed, an orchard girdled. When Indians were brought, under protection, to Marlborough, it is told that the white women rioted in an attempt to reach and kill the Indian women.

In August 1707, the families of Gersham Fay, Jonathan Forbush, Nathaniel Oaks, as well as Goodenow's own, gathered in Samuel Goodenow's garrison house in response to rumors of marauding Indians. One blooming afternoon, when they must have felt secure, Mary Fay, expecting her third child, and Mary Goodenow went out from her father's house to gather herbs in the shoulder-high meadows along Stirrup Brook. How glorious the sunshine, how reassuring, how lovely, this world full of life and summer.

Collecting herbs was not an idle afternoon's pastime. The

120

natural larder of Stirrup Brook provided plants for household uses, food, and medicines. An early 1660s account by Alexander Young an English minister, praised the bounty available in the new country simply for the picking: "strawberry leaves innumerable, sorrel, yarrow, carval, brooklime, liverwort, water cresses, great store of leak and onions and an excellent kind of flax or hemp."

Rushes, readily available at the river's edge, tough-stemmed and sturdy, laid on the floors and periodically changed kept dirt floors cleaner, or could be woven into seats and baskets. Bedstraw was a step up from hay in a mattress, maintaining its loft better because of the infinitesimal hooks on stems and seeds, and was sweet-smelling in the bargain. Angelica grew tall in wet places, and was an excellent medicinal herb as well as being good candied. Wild garlic and onions, chicory, mint and all the numerous "sweet herbs" were there for the picking. From ginger and sassafras, elderberry, apple and fox grape, housewives prepared all kinds of cordials and brandies, beers and shrubs.

Herbs were also needed for medicinal uses. Even into the nineteenth century, Dr. Ball of Northborough had a recipe for "Unguentum Polychre," one of his favorite cures, which read like an inventory of the meadows alongside Stirrup Brook:

> Green Tobacco, Henbane, chamomile. Cheese Mallows, Bitter sweet Root, Melilot, Yellow Pond Lily Root, Night Shade, Heartsease, Dock leaves, Plantin Leaves, Saint John's Wort Mouse Ear Garlicke Comfrey Leaves Buds of Walnut Old David's Weed Garden Scurvey Grass Burdock; Elder Heat all Catnip. Carpenter Weed Marsh Mallows both sorts, Chelindine Fenney wort yarrow low balm Gout Root Leaves.

In late summer Stirrup Brook runs two feet wide, tightly bound by small spindly trees interwoven like a mesh. Beyond them spreads a meadow of close-packed green. Near the stream the grasses rise taller than my head; in the meadow they are well above my knees, with shoulder-high milkweed, Queen Anne's lace, waist-high goldenrod. So lush. So beautifully lush. And yet so deceptive, for that lush growth entangles your ankles; the wet ground beneath is hummocky and treacherous to walk across.

And what did the herb gatherers chatter about? Did Mary Fay speculate on whether the child she carried would be a boy or a girl? She already had one of each, and they were home this halcyon day, and it must have been a treat of sorts not to be carrying one and having the other clinging to her skirts. Mary Goodenow was lame and doubtless walked slower, but perhaps she was the more thorough gatherer, seeing more, finding more.

And did the rustling of the summer leaves and the susurration of the grasses, and perhaps the sound of their own voices, obliterate the horror spreading out of the woods? What direction were they facing when the sky blackened?

Mary Fay ran, clumsy body, clumsy shoes, clumsy meadow grasses catching at her ankles. Reaching the garrison house, she shoved the gate closed. Was it then she looked back to see that Mary Goodenow was not following?

Only one man was at the garrison, the rest in the fields. He and Mary Fay fired and reloaded and fired again until the Indians retreated across Stirrup Brook and faded back into the woods. Mary Fay's child, a daughter, was born three months later and "was subject to a constant trembling, caused, it is supposed, by the mother's fright received at this time."

The next day twenty militiamen, alerted by Daniel How,

Ground pine (*Lycopodium obscutum*)

marched out of Marlborough, found the Indians, killed nine of the reported twenty-four who had attacked, watched the others flee like bad omens, still there to haunt and harass. In the pack of one of the dead was found a horrid talisman, blood-dried and stiff, the scalp of Mary Goodenow. And so they searched along the trail and when they finally found her, the hours of August heat had softened the mutilated body and they simply buried the remnants of a woman where she lay.

I walked to the site on a March day when the wind shunted through the pines, sharp and chill. Runners of ground pine snagged my feet. Clouds continually shuttered the sun. The wind resonated like a nightmare river rushing down. Even without leaves on the trees I could see but twenty feet or so, the view blocked by high brush that formed endless shifting palings. Branches abraded the sky. In the distance a rifle discharged, a sound with a double echo, sullen and ominous.

A small sign marks her grave. Death is not out of place here. The sounds of the rifle, the bitterness of the wind. It was not so that August day when the sun was warm and the meadow was silky green and two young women, one the age of one of my daughters, stooped and picked, walked on, gathered more, filling their baskets.

The trees that were here then are gone, but the same rocks were here that day, miserable mean rocks, absorbing the terror and giving it back to me almost three centuries later. And no sun, no sun at all.

6

𝓔𝓦𝓙 The wealth of the Assabet has lain in its water power, turning the wheels of early factories. The wealth of the Sudbury has lain in its river meadows, supplying fodder for the livestock of the pioneers. It drew farmers and gave rise to agricultural communities like Wayland and Sudbury.

At the time the colonists arrived in America, New England was mainly a land of forests. Natural open spaces were few; grasslands were rare. Where Indians cleared and cultivated tracts, keeping them open by annual burnings, the land reverted to forest as soon as it was abandoned. One of the most pressing problems of the colonists, therefore, was to find pasture, and winter fodder, for their cattle. The only early source of hay in the Bay Colony was the tidal marshes along the coast; experiments in feeding cows and oxen on acorns failed. The value of livestock quickly quadrupled. It was even suggested that wild moose be domesticated and harnessed to the plow instead of oxen.

And so it was that when, sometime before 1633, William Wood, author of *New Englands Prospect*, returned in an Indian canoe from his journey up the Merrimack and Concord, the most exciting news he brought back was his discovery of extensive wild hayfields. "These marshes be rich ground, and bring plenty of Hay," he wrote,

> of which the Cattle feed and like, as if they were fed with the best up-land Hay in New England. . . . in divers places neare

the plantations great broad Medowes, wherein grow neither shrub nor Tree, lying low, in which Plaines growes as much grasse, as may be throwne out with a Sithe, thicke and long, as high as a mans middle; some as high as the shoulders, so that a good mower may cut three loads in a day.

It was Wood's report of ample fodder for their livestock that led to the first inland movement away from the tide and the founding of the first Bay Colony settlement in the interior, Concord, in 1635—near the Great Meadows of the Concord River, and close by, as well, the "grass-ground" of the Wayland-Sudbury region, which gave the stream its Indian name: Musketaquid, the "Grass-Ground River."

When Ann and I pushed out from the gravel slope of the fan-shaped launching place beside the Route 20 Bridge, we turned downstream into this region where the Sudbury winds between wide margins, where once the Grass-Ground River flowed. The acres of high, dense grasses are gone now. Instead of wild hay-fields, jungles of entangled buttonbushes, with flood wrack caught among their lower branches, walled us in on either hand. Beyond these impenetrable barriers we could glimpse distant houses on higher ground, and on the wide stretch of the river flowing north, off to our right, we caught sight of bright-colored moving figures—golfers at the Sandy Burr Country Club. In the distance ahead of us, the white tower of Wayland's First Parish Church—a square tower with a clock on each of its four sides.

An original Paul Revere bell hangs in that tower. Beneath it the congregation heard the first singing of the famous Christmas carol "It Came Upon a Midnight Clear," written by the Reverend Edmund H. Sears, pastor of the First Parish Church. And only a little way to the north is the first free public library in the Commonwealth of Massachusetts, established in 1848.

[In Wayland call on a former caretaker of the church on the green, whose steeple we saw from the river. He says the four clocks are run by the same clockwork through two drive shafts with gears. One shaft turns clocks on east and west sides; the other clocks on the north and south sides. This keeps all the clocks in time . . . all show the same time. The old wooden-works clocks of earlier day have been replaced.

[On to Wayland Library to see if I can get the date when Lydia Maria Child's famous children's poem—and song—about

125

Buttonbush (*Cephalanthus occidentalis*)

Thanksgiving was published. Local story it was at the Causeway Bridge over the Sudbury. Mrs. Benjamin introduces me to reference librarian, who brings out all of Lydia Child's books, and two biographies of her. Find what I want in *Flowers for Children*, the volume, published in 1850, in which "Over the River . . . " poem first appeared. It was called "The Boy's Thanksgiving Song" according to one biography, *The Heart Is like Heaven, The Life of Lydia Maria Childs*, by Helene G. Baer (U. of Pennsylvania Press). The original text in *Flowers for Children* gives the title: "The New-England Boy's Song about Thanksgiving Day." And the first lines were:

> Over the river and through the wood,
> To grandfather's house we'll go,
>   The horse knows the way,
>   To carry the sleigh,
> Through the white and drifted snow.

(Not grandmother's, but *grandfather's*.)

[If the poem was printed in 1850, two years before Lydia Child came to live in Wayland, it could not have been written about the Sudbury. Thought to have been written about Medford, where she lived as a child, and the Mystic River and her grandfather's house in Medford Hill. (It is also attributed to the Charles River!)

[This is definite proof that the story of the Causeway Bridge and the two maps showing the house where they started and the house where "grandmother" lived are not true. Unloved is the exploder of popular local beliefs! But have that pinned down for certain.

[So I come back to the motel with two scalps on my belt. A good afternoon's work.]

The way to see the most, by land or water, is to travel slowly. This we did during that particular canoe day on the river. We dipped our paddles into the barely moving water only occasionally. We drifted with the lazy current. We turned aside to investigate little nooks among the buttonbushes. On the still water of one, a small feather floated, evidence of the feeding of a hawk in a dwarf willow close by.

Like a second barrier beside us, the inverted images of the mangrove-like tangle paraded slowly by. Looking back, we saw the images lengthen and contract in the rippled wake of our canoe. Once we saw two black ducks make a skittering landing on the river behind us.

Creeping in this manner downstream, disturbing nothing as we advanced, we watched the life of the muddy shallows, paved with muck, where the heads of painted turtles popped up from beneath the surface and where, occasionally, fish broke the water and then arrowed away, trailing an elongated V behind them. Under a wide sky we drifted with the turnings of a lowland stream, meandering through a landscape such as the Flemish artists loved to put on canvas.

The clearest picture of what the broad river meadows bordering this portion of the stream were like in the early days is found in the voluminous report of hearings held by the Joint Special Committee of the State Legislature in 1860. Published under the title *The Flowage of Meadows on Concord and Sudbury Rivers,* it runs to between four hundred and five hundred 9 x 5¼-inch pages, including the twenty-six pages of fine print at the end of the book that list the committee's expenses. The most eloquent testimony came from the farmers living in the Wayland-Sudbury region.

Flowage, in the legal sense, means flooding, as by a dam. And it was the dam at Billerica, on the Concord, first erected to provide waterpower and later heightened to increase the flow into the Middlesex Canal, that destroyed the meadows, for the level of both the Concord and the Sudbury rivers rose behind it, flooding the grasslands as far upstream as Farm Bridge at Pelham Island. The resulting legal action, after half a century of complaints, produced one of the historic confrontations of the time. It pitted the power of industrial expansion against the embattled farmers. Some of the most distinguished jurists of the East appeared in the case, and Henry Thoreau, as the leading surveyor in Concord, was employed by the River Meadow Association to collect facts about the depth of the rivers and their rise and fall, for use by the lawyers representing the farmers.

Thoreau's *Journal* during the summer of 1859 is filled with entries relating to the rivers at various points all the way from Wayland to Billerica. In a letter to Elizabeth Hoar, who was in Europe at the time, Ralph Waldo Emerson reported: "Henry T. occupies himself with the history of the river, measures it, weighs it, and strains it through a colander to all eternity."

The factual material that Thoreau amassed was of value to the case of the farmers, 117 of whom signed the petition—among them many whose surnames appear on the maps of the region in such place names as Heard Pond and Sherman's Bridge.

> Sixty-five years ago [the petition of the farmers pointed out], the Meadows were perfectly accessible to the heaviest teams, up and down the river, to its brink, and immense loads for three and four cattle were hauled from them, without the slightest difficulty from slumping. Such teams were habitually driven across the stream, at certain points, when not loaded, and occasionally when they were. But from about the year 1804, when the Canal Proprietors had made two additions to the height of their dam. . . . the Meadows became so soft as to be impossible for teams, except in times of extreme dryness. . . . Since the last addition to the dam, thirty years ago, these lands have been, with slight exceptions, inaccessible not only to teams but to grazing cattle.

(For a time hay was "poled" out, high mounds being carried by two laborers with the supporting poles on their shoulders. But this proved too expensive and soon only an echo of the practice remained, in such names as Pole Brook near Fairhaven Bay.)

In the days when the meadows were in their original condition, the yield was from one to two tons an acre, and the demand was always beyond the supply. Farmers in the Wayland and Sudbury areas were able to make considerable additional income by "boarding" the cattle of the less fortunate during the winter months. As the petition put it: "Fatting oxen, working oxen, and milch cows throve well upon it."

The calamity of the Billerica dam not only prevented access to the meadows; slowly it destroyed the valuable hay itself. For when the water level is raised, sedges, which require, or tolerate, more water than the meadow grasses, replace them. Drowned out as well were the great wild cranberry beds and the source of meadow muck used to fertilize fields of sandy loam. John Sherman testified that on eight acres of river meadow he used to harvest 150 bushels of cranberries each year. Other farmers recalled how they had seen waving fields of high, thick hay replaced by "lily ponds" and inundated areas filled with pickerelweed, how they had been used to fish at the edge of the river in a place where the water now stood above their heads. The sale of real estate was paralyzed. Meadowland once worth $100 to $150 an acre had dropped in value to $10 an acre.

The defense of the dam proprietors, as nearly as one threading one's way through the maze of testimony at this late date can deduce, was that while damage had been done to the meadows of the farmers, this was more than offset by the benefits bestowed on navigation on the rivers by raising the water level. That navigation at the time was virtually nonexistent seems to have been lost sight of. But in fact, the dam owners did not need to present even a logical defense to avoid paying indemnity to the injured farmers. Because of a series of laws, some of which jurists have thought were of doubtful constitutionality, they were immune from prosecution. Chief among them was legislation providing that they were liable for damages only when the claims for such damages were presented within one year. As a matter of practical application, it was only after several years that the damages became fully apparent. By then all recourse to law was prohibited.

In its conclusions, the legislative committee sympathized with the meadow owners. It seemed to agree with the statement in the petition: "We believe that the meshes of the Middlesex Canal Act were woven by the subtle fingers of lobby legislation." But little could be done. The river meadows were destroyed and the river meadows remain destroyed.

In the remembrances of the farmers recalling former times in connection with the river meadows, the names of many of the grasses—redtop, *Agrostis alba*, also known as White-top, water twitch, fine john and summer dew grass; herd's-grass, or timothy, *Phleum pratense*; bluejoint, or reed grass, *Calamagrostis canadensis*; fowl meadow grass or false redtop, *Poa trifolia*; and the tall reed canary grass, *Phalaris arundinacea*—appeared in the testimony at the legislative hearings. But the type of fodder that was valued most of all was known variously as pipes, pipe grass, shave grass or joint grass.

Discovering this led Ann and me into a mystery that we were not able to solve completely. At first, even the name, "pipes," seemed a minor mystery within a major mystery. Then in the *Journal* kept by Thoreau we found the plant that was referred to in the district by that name. It is the silica-filled scouring rush, the horsetail, *Equisetum hyemale*. Apparently the term was applied indiscriminately to various other species of horsetails as well.

Thoreau speaks of seeing "pipes" rising to a height of two and a half feet in wet parts of the riverside meadows, and one entry in his *Journal* talks about "a noble sea of pipes... a broad stream of this valuable grass growing densely...." William Stone, of Sudbury, recalled during the hearings that he used to harvest a ton and a half of pipes on an acre of his meadow. Edward Rice, of Wayland, remembered six acres dense with pipe grass. He declared it was the best kind of hay that he knew of for livestock, better than English hay. His tract of pipe meadow, he thought, was the most valuable part of his land. Both cattle and horses ate the dried horsetails voraciously. Other testimony brought out that this meadow crop was so nutritious and attractive that creatures would suspend their chewing even on the finest English hay upon hearing the particular rustle of the pipes upon the scaffold and wait to be served with them.

Yet these plants are so filled with silica they were used to scour out pots and pans in pioneer times. If one is placed in acid that eats away the vegetable matter, the silica framework of the horsetail will be left. And the tremendous appeal of this fodder becomes even more of a mystery when one realizes that every book on the poisonous plants of North America includes the horsetails. They are listed among the dangerous plants of the western ranges. At first their injurious effect on livestock was attributed to the mechanical action of the silica in the digestive tract. When poison was detected, it was early attributed to a fungus growing on the horsetails. It is now known that the plants themselves contain deadly aconitic acid, an alkaloidal nerve poison named equisetin.

Horses that have fed extensively on this food lose weight. No longer able to control their muscles, they sway and stagger. In the end they lose the power to stand, and go down, struggling violently but futilely to get up. The pulse becomes slow, the extremities cold. Finally, worn out by their struggles, they die of exhaustion. Yet horses are said to seek out horsetails and to eat them voraciously.

So the riddles connected with these ancient, primitive plants, which have descended through nearly 300 million years from their treelike ancestors of the Carboniferous period, continue to accumulate. Why should grazing animals be so attracted to something so deadly? What impels them to seek it out? Do horse-tails have a salty taste? Why does not instinct warn the animals of their danger? I have seen muskrats gathering large mouthfuls of the scouring rush and swimming with them back to their feeding places at the edge of a pond. Do the various species of *Equisetum* contain different amounts of poison at different stages of their growth? Specifically, is the concentration greater when the plants are young than when they are full-grown and at the stage when they were harvested on the river meadows? Compounding the mystery, which none of the innumerable authorities I consulted had been able to dispel, is the fact that the plants in their early stages, sprinkled with flour and fried, formed one of the favorite vegetable dishes of the Romans!

In following the Sudbury all the way from Cedar Swamp to Egg Rock, Ann and I found only a single place where one could experience what the colonists had experienced when they first stood amid the close-packed stems of the high, waving grasses of the river meadows. This is a corridor of original wild hay, a sur-viving remnant in the form of a strip about 150 feet wide and perhaps a quarter of a mile long. Bordered by white pines and red maples, with Hazel Brook winding through it, it leads down to the river not far from Sherman's Bridge. Bobby Robinson, one of the most knowledgeable among all the many knowledgeable people who helped us with the history and ecology of this particular seg-ment of the river, had shown us how to reach it.

We came to it first on an autumn day. [Running blackberry vines set traps for my feet near the edge of the woods. A nest woven of black rootlets has fallen from one of the pines. Now all along the edge of the hayfield the brilliant, rich reds of the high bush blueberries, mingled with the low alders. High in a slender maple, the bulky mass of leaves that forms a gray squirrel's home.]

Growing season, seed-producing season, had been left be-hind. The juices of spring, greenness of summer, were gone. We pushed our way into a gray-yellow sea, rising and falling around us. Everything was in motion. We stood in the midst of a moving world, the air filled with the sibilant rustling of the dry leaves. The tops of the moving plants rose, in places as high as my shoul-ders and almost to the top of Ann's head. In the exposed portions of the corridor, all the slender stems slanted toward the east, away from the river, tilted by the prevailing winds. As near as we could tell, the grass in the last of the hayfields of the river consisted mainly of reed grass and reed canary grass.

Perhaps this corridor of grass had hardly altered since the days when the red men initially inhabited the banks of the river—within recent years, excavations made close by have brought to light Indian artifacts that date back eight thousand years. Now, as part of the Great Meadows National Wildlife Refuge, this remnant of the past will have permanent protection.

Later, in other seasons of the year, I saw it under many conditions. Once, on a midsummer day, I measured off a square foot where the grass grew densely and counted the number of stems it contained. The result showed that in that particular place, the slender stems were so closely packed together that they numbered nearly five hundred to a square yard. Without trees or bushes, the unbroken stand of native grasses stretched away in the sunshine. Nothing but grass, dense and high and lush, rose from the wet soil. The seeds of larger growths could find no room to start.

Standing there, surrounded by walls of close-packed stems, I imagined myself one of those early colonists, hungry for pasturage, walking in the midst of such a promised land. I visualized them swinging their scythes in long sweeps, watching the grass falling in swaths across the meadowland. Thoreau, in his *Journal*, has given a vivid picture of the mowing along the Sudbury in August:

> I hear their scythes cronching the coarse weeds by the river's brink as I row near. . . . I see a platoon of three or four mowers, one behind the other, diagonally advancing with regular sweeps across the broad meadow and ever and anon standing to whet their scythes. Or else, having made several bouts, they are resting in the shade on the edge of the firm land. In one place I see one sturdy mower stretched on the ground amid his oxen in the shade of an oak, trying to sleep; or I see one wending far inland with a jug to some well-known spring.

On the last day of July, on the third of a series of ninety-degree days, the imagined became real for me. With Tom Goettel, assistant manager at the refuge, I brought an old scythe, well-sharpened, to the corridor of grass. I had not swung a scythe since I was a boy, but in the midst of the wild meadow, it all came back,

"I had not swung a scythe since I was a boy, but in the midst of the wild meadow, it all came back, and for a time I saw the ranks of the high grasses falling beneath my regular sweeps."

and for a time I saw the ranks of the high grasses falling beneath my regular sweeps. As I stood leaning on my scythe, looking at the fallen grass, looking at the dragonflies that hovered and darted and alighted around me, looking at the drifting clouds overhead, my eyes seeing what in this very place perhaps other eyes had seen in another age, it was as though three centuries had not passed.

But now all the treasure beside the river, growing so rank three centuries ago, had dwindled to this single slender strip. Never again would the riverbank miles be dense with primeval hay. Even so, with the treasure of earlier days gone, the former meadowlands still have a special value in this modern world. They are the safety valves of flood times, the broad expanses where the river can spread out into extensive reservoirs that store up significant quantities of the excess water, reducing flood damage downstream.

In still another way they aid in times of high water. In a flowing stream, the current generally moves fastest near the surface at the center of the channel. Along the sides and bottom of the stream, friction slows down the water. The velocity is greatest where friction is least. Thus when the stream spreads out it increases the width of its base where friction is at a maximum. Even though the velocity in the submerged river channel is great, in these pond-like expanses the water is hardly moving. This retards the transportation of the water and provides a further delaying action in the flood. It was the wide expanse of the former meadows of the Sudbury that reduced the damage in the great flood of 1955, while the narrower Assabet was harder hit.

In its serpentines, a river is a river of expectation. What lies around the next turn? In its placid reaches it is a river of reflection. For Thoreau the Assabet was "the river of ripples," the Sudbury "the river of reflections." For Ann and me, as we neared the end of our unhurried exploration, that day in October, of what once were meadows—now a river without rocks, without rapids, a relaxed stream where long ago wild meadows extended for as much as a mile across the floodplain—the Sudbury became a river of reflections of a different kind.

We found ourselves comparing memories of the individual paths by which we had reached the same relationship with the out-of-doors, how our fascination with nature had developed and how writing about nature had become such an important part of our lives.

For me, life has constantly grown better. The worst was the first part. Joliet, when I was growing up, was predominantly a steel town, a railroad town, and the site of the state penitentiary. The air was always filled with coal smoke. The tracks of three railroads ran near our house. In our neighborhood there was a mixture of nationalities—Irish, Swedish, German, English. And it seemed swarming with boys who wanted to fight. I was rather sensitive and peacefully inclined—a soft-boiled egg in a nest of hard-boiled eggs. I toughened up later on, but at first I seemed to have no way of coping. One thing I developed that has stood me in good stead: a capacity to assimilate a tremendous amount of punishment without giving in. I was no hero, but if I couldn't conquer, I wasn't completely conquered either.

This was the great pressure on the outside. But there was another kind of pressure on the inside. My mother had been a teacher and our home became a schoolroom and I was the only pupil. Relatives were always telling me that as an only child, I was bound to be spoiled. The only effect I could see of being an only child was that I was the only one around and everybody could devote all time and energy to correcting me. I was the twig being bent in the direction in which I should grow. Most of the time I felt like the most bent twig history has ever known.

So my early years were spent between two great pressures. I was in the jaws of a nutcracker and something had to give. It gave in the direction of the out-of-doors. At Lone Oak, my grandparents' farm in the dune country of northern Indiana, I took wing; I was free; I could fly away from all my troubles.

It was important for me then to be alone with nature. In the spring, my mother used to take me to see the wildflowers in Davidson's Woods, in Joliet. She was also interested in nature and she appreciated the beauty of things, but such expeditions were filled with lessons. There were morals to be observed everywhere. That was not the way I went to nature when I was alone. I enjoyed it wholly for its own sake, feeling a closeness to everything around me that I could not explain. There were times when I was little when I felt I had been delivered, by mistake, to the wrong planet. But not when I was alone with nature in the freedom of Lone Oak.

136

At first, I suppose I thought of the out-of-doors as a place where I "felt good," where there were trees to climb, ditches to explore, rabbits to watch. During all my childhood summers on my grandfather's farm I plunged wholeheartedly into a world of rabbits and katydids and orioles, running barefoot, endlessly entranced with what I saw around me. I was trying to write a book about nature on my grandfather's farm when I was nine years old.

As time went on, a new relationship with nature developed, a dawning sense of the wonder and the beauty of it. I was still pretty young when the first instance of this kind occurred. Among the vines covering a circular grape arbor at Lone Oak I found two pale-green, ethereal luna moths that had emerged from their cocoons and were clinging to the grape leaves. I had never seen anything so beautiful before. They appeared as a kind of revelation and I kept returning to gaze at them over and over. So far as I can recall, that was the first time I had a deep appreciation of beauty for its own sake.

I was older, perhaps ten or eleven, when a second event occurred that is as vivid in my mind now as events of an hour ago. I was helping Gramp bring in wood for the night on the last evening before I had to return to Joliet at the end of a Christmas vacation. Everything was still. In the sunset, all the fields of snow to the west lay tinted with delicate pastel hues. Something about the moment, the stillness, the beauty of the tinted snow, the feeling of the minutes ticking away with my return to home so imminent, the somber mood of the time, produced a profound impression on my mind. At that moment, and in afteryears, I seemed standing at one of the great turning points in my life. Whenever, in all the years that have followed, I have seen the snow tinted by the sunset, it has all come back to me.

It was when I was at Lone Oak, when I was still young, that I began a habit that has had great importance in my writing. This was the development of a memory for specific details. So often I would think, in my happiness: *This* is something I want to remember always. *This* is something I never want to forget. And I would look around, memorizing the sights, the sounds, the scents, the mood of the moment, so later on I could project it on my mind and relive that happy time. This has become a lifelong habit. I still practice it without thinking, as I have done during these halcyon days on the rivers of Concord.

For Ann, the great turning point came some twenty years ago with the purchase of Constant Friendship, with its aspen grove, its high ponderosa pines and, at its heart, the pond of spring-fed water. It was about Constant Friendship that she wrote her first book, *Beyond the Aspen Grove,* and all her other books that have followed have been based on her personal experience, personal contact, personal observation in nature. Writing them has also entailed a certain element of risk. Yet sitting in the bow of the canoe on this peaceful eastern river, only five feet tall and weighing only 105 pounds, she looked almost frail—the last person one would expect to have run the rapids and threaded through the canyons of the classic wild river of the West, the Green.

In both Ann's books and mine, it seems to me, the same pattern has been followed. We have found something that is very precious to us, our special relationship to nature. We feel a desire to catch and hold and preserve the moments that mean so much to us, to be able to return to them and relive them again. So we begin putting down a record of those times we would gladly live again—and the books follow in time. Others, if we have been successful, sense what we have sensed, feel what we have felt, learn what we have learned. And they, too, may catch fire as we have done. Such an approach embodies an elemental sincerity, and a *joie de vivre,* that cannot be counterfeited.

There is something else that happens, if fortune favors us. A kind of magic light fills the pages. How it is achieved, I do not know. Probably in writing of nature we unconsciously portray what we are writing about as seen through tinted rather than clear glass. The elements around us are as they are described, the facts are accurate, but we see it all in a special light, a vision of our own.

As Ann once wrote, in response to a review I had just sent her of her latest book: "After the pleasure of reading it, I reflected that all it means is that I can keep on writing and drawing. It's the work, always the work—the research, the fieldwork, the learning, the trying, the pushing back old boundaries—that is what it's all about. It's lovely to have someone like what you do, but what really counts is that you get to do it. A good review is simply a ticket to tomorrow."

In reply I quoted from Robert Welker's biography of William Beebe: "If a book sells widely or an article is well received, the author is bound to be pleased, but a dedicated naturalist is moved by more compelling reasons. There is news to tell of what has been sought and found; and there is also challenge and joy, beauty and wonder and devotion to be imparted in words that capture and hold them best, and perhaps endure the longest."

Still, there is the other side of the coin—the pressures. Ann's are different from mine—she says her work time is defined by interruption. One pressure, for me, was having to make a living. Particularly in the beginning, my writing was a life-and-death matter. I was the breadwinner, the whole support. My books had to sell sufficiently to bring in enough to keep us going. Otherwise the whole wonderful prospect of being able to support a family by doing what I wanted to do most would disappear. I had to hold the level of interest high or all was lost. But I had to do it legitimately, without faking, without distortion.

The other pressure is the loneliness of authorship, and this is so for Ann and me—and for our families. It is a sacrifice we all make. I once asked Nellie—I suppose hoping to be patted on the head—"What is it like to be married to an author?" Ask Nellie an honest question and you get an honest answer. She said, "It's a little lonely."

There is a sense of withdrawal. I am only in the next room; I am accessible; I am there if there is any emergency. But I am withdrawn. I am living in another time and place; I am to a certain extent disconnected from the present; I am concentrating intensely on a project that goes on and on. But the loneliness of authorship is a shared experience. There are the self-centered, get-out-of-my-way authors who ride roughshod over such considerations. They couldn't care less about the effect their actions have on others. But Ann and I are not of that kind. And so we make what compromises are possible, work toward our writing goals, aware of the double responsibility we carry. As it must be for everyone, our close involvement with nature has been only part of our lives. But for each, it has become a part of expanding importance. As Thoreau wrote:

> I love Nature partly *because* she is not man, but a retreat from him. None of his institutions control or pervade her. There a different kind of right prevails. In her midst I can be glad with an entire gladness. If this world were all man, I could not stretch myself, I should lose all hope. He is constraint, she is

139

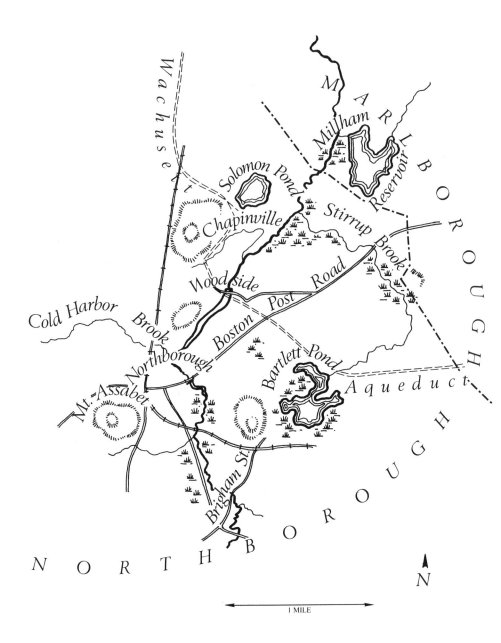

Wachusett

MARLBOROUGH

Millham Reservoir

Solomon Pond

Chapinville

Stirrup Brook

Woodside

Boston Post Road

Cold Harbor

Brook

Northborough

Aqueduct

Bartlett Pond

Mt. Assabet

Brigham St.

NORTH BOROUGH

N

1 MILE

freedom to me. He makes me wish for another world. She makes me content with this.

So it was that while the day's river journey neared its end, Ann and I—two enthusiasts talking of the field of their enthusiasm, two practitioners recalling the labors and satisfactions of their craft—drifted and paddled on toward Sherman's Bridge.

AHZ The energy of the Assabet is not dissipated in wide sweeping curves as the Sudbury's is in the Meadows, and its straighter course with quicker fall provided the waterpower for manufacturing all along its length. Ashland, Wayland, Framingham, Sudbury, Concord—the towns through which the Sudbury runs—have pastoral English-sounding names. On the Assabet, which generally runs right through the center of town rather than on the periphery, the town names commemorate the industrialists who developed them: Maynard, Gleason, Damon. Or someone who contributed money.

Hudson is a town solely created by Assabet waterpower. When the first settlement was still known as "The Mill," Joseph Howe erected one on the Assabet, probably before 1700; his son-in-law, Jeremiah Barstow, inherited his 350 acres on both sides of the Assabet, "including the mill, with all the accomodations and materials," since women were prohibited from inheriting in Colonial times.

A century later the village was called Feltonville, named for Silas Felton, who owned mills there, a respected man who held all the prominent town offices at one time or another. In 1812 there was a small cotton mill on the river that made no cloth, only yarn; there was also a fulling mill and several local tanneries (as late as 1900, some 22,000 gallons of Assabet water per day were used for wool scouring, and 30,000 for washing hides). A distillery made brandy from local apples. But Feltonville remained a small village with a little over a dozen houses, until Felton introduced water-power into the manufacture of shoes in 1820. With it, one machine could do the work of ten women.

Feltonville was renamed Hudson in 1860. Charles Hudson, the local historian, agreed to donate five hundred dollars toward a library if the town was given his name—trusting, I take it, in the immortality of a place name instead of the written word.

That same year the fifteen-foot-high Hudson Dam was com-

141

pleted, for flood control and recreation. Now the dam is owned by the Hudson Power and Light Company. In 1890–91, during the debate over whether the Town of Hudson should buy the then privately owned Hudson Electric Company, the opposition made one of those grandiloquent statements that give those of us blessed with hindsight such amusement: "And, moreover, there is a strong and growing belief that the time is not far distant when there will be no use for light of any kind in manufactories, as the rapid advance of shorter hours of labor will soon dispense with their need entirely."

One spring day Edwin and I make the run from Hudson to Gleasondale. Map spread out on my knees, I look ahead for Orchard Hill, a textbook drumlin around which the Assabet caracoles just above Gleasondale, one of a pair of drumlins rising one hundred feet above the river, oriented south-southeast. One of the pleasures of these days on the Assabet and Sudbury has been learning the vocabulary of glacial evidence missing in my part of the West. Although some of the definitive studies of glacial moraines have been made on the upper Green River in Wyoming, there are none of the gentle glacial surfaces in the West so common in New England; perhaps the molding of the landscape here is one of the reasons New England seems, by contrast, so civilized to me.

I have learned most of my geology in the Southwest, where geological periods are blatantly revealed in bare rock walls. Now as we canoe, I usually keep a USGS quadrangle map open on my knees, a luxury I do not enjoy on less placid western rivers, and when a cluster of egg-shaped contour lines defines a drumlin, I watch for it. I am used to quadrangle maps with forty-foot and sometimes eighty-foot contour lines; when they run close together, one can count on the terrain being precipitous. But with the ten-foot contour lines on the eastern maps, I always expect more than appears.

"Drumlin" is an Irish word, used as a generic term for all kinds of hills; in this country it applies specifically to dozens of smooth rounded glacially formed hills, their long axes paralleling glacial retreat. Unlike prominences in unglaciated terrain, these do not contain and are not formed of bedrock and have, in fact, no obvious relationship at all to the underlying bedrock surface. Shaped by ice moving above them, drumlins must have required long periods to mold them to their final shape—one geologist described them perfectly as an inverted teaspoon bowl. They are rarely more than a mile long, usually less than three hundred feet high, and are composed mostly of older till from a previous glacial retreat, often mantled with the younger till of the most recent withdrawal. In this part of Massachusetts, till may be light gray in color and loose, relatively porous (the younger) or darker and browner. The latter is older, finer and more compact, and also more impervious, known locally as "hardpan."

The other day, scuffing the dirt on a road cut on the side of a drumlin, my boot loosed a heterogeneous assortment of clay, sand, pebbles and rocks. Only the day before that, I had stood in a sand and gravel quarry alongside the Assabet, watching two little boys running up and down the slope, filling their shoes with sand and the seats of their pants with holes. There the rocks and sand were in neatly sorted layers, laid by different velocities of running water as the glacier released seasonal torrents of meltwater. The difference between water-deposited debris and glacier-deposited debris was as clear as a textbook drawing.

The gap north of Orchard Hill was cleared of ice before the one south of it, draining what was left of glacial Lake Assabet and allowing the river to run in its present course. When all the glacial meltwater disappeared, the Assabet dwindled to its present size and began cutting downward into the glacial deposits beneath it, rippling around the boulders and loose rock that are associated with the ends of glaciers. Gleasondale was once known as "Rockbottom," for what seemed an unnecessary amount of boulders in the streambed. Many were glacial erratics, broken off and dragged along from as far away as seven miles.

Today's trip ends at Gleasondale Dam, within sight of the old mill building, which still stands. The mill was erected about 1820 and was originally a cotton mill, later converted to a woolen mill. The milldam was built in 1824. Prudently, we take out well upstream, while below us two fat white ducks ply the water within a wingspan of the lip, oblivious of the sheet of water pouring over, and the standing wave below. Rather than try to put in below the dam, which looks to be a bit difficult, we decide to canoe upstream from Boons Bridge to the Gleasondale Dam on my next trip east.

At the end of July, however, what had looked to be a very

"Huge weeping willows and oaks and swamp maples lean over us as we skirt the shore below Gleasondale. The leaves in the green overhang contrast with the tiny golden and olive-green leaves beneath the water. Eelgrass streamers flutter in the sinuous current. . . . Duckweeds are scattered on the surface like stars on the night sky, glinting as they swirl downstream."

easy trip a few months earlier turns out to be quite a different proposition. After pushing off at Boons Bridge, we are very soon in the midst of sedge islands through which the river works its way, huge tussocks of sedge that must be five or six feet high, languid-leaved, continually blocking our way. We feel as if we are on the set of *The African Queen,* constantly thwarted, taking promising channels that always dead-end. Packed so close together, the sedge tussocks almost become a meadow when the water is this low. Fillets of water rush through tiny channels, but none are deep enough or wide enough to get the canoe through, let alone make a paddle stroke in.

As we turn back short of our goal, I mark the change: going with the current, the Assabet perks along, energetic even if shallow. Huge weeping willows and oaks and swamp maples lean over us as we skirt the shore below Gleasondale. The leaves in the green overhang contrast with the tiny golden and olive-green leaves beneath the water. Eelgrass streamers flutter in the sinuous current. Waterweeds billow like a Lorelei's hair, hissing under the bow, puckering the water, here and there broaching the surface film and making dimples from which small vortices spin.

Two kingbirds accompany us, flitting along through the branches. In this dark-shaded side of the river, the water shines dark but clear. The sun bores like a hundred pin-sized spotlights through the trees. Duckweeds are scattered on the surface like stars on the night sky, glinting as they swirl downstream.

Edwin and I both remark upon a feeling of remoteness here. Edwin quotes me the Appalachian Mountain Club *New England Canoeing Guide* assessment of the Assabet: "Except for its last miles the river is mostly unattractive." "A lot they know about it! We have *been there!*" he huffs. Perhaps it is the high bank which blocks out vistas of houses, and high bushes and trees that muffle other sounds, but in this populated area we paradoxically have a sense of quiet wildness.

That evening, as I draw, the quietude persists. I take up my hand lens to decipher a head of tiny flowers and focus on a small dot—is it the tip of a stamen or a marking on a minute petal? The dot moves under the lens and resolves into an infinitesimal spider, body scarcely bigger than the tip of the pistil itself, a brownish-red creature with red-and-cream-striped stockings, climbing

145

hurriedly up the pistil and spinning out a silk, energized by the warmth of the drawing lamp.

From pistil to pistil to pistil, a triangle, swinging across the abyss between flowers, leaping to another, then up and upside down across a thread to the next anchor, busily spinning out what surely must be one of the finest, most delicate Lilliputian webs ever woven.

7

EWJ   With its current slowed to a lazy crawl, the Sudbury below Heard Pond is largely a silent stream, the course it
follows established long ago. Seeking a downhill way across a
nearly level land, in a blind groping for the lowest and least resist-
ing ground, it has carved out the channel that now contains it.

Always in a river we find impermanence combined with
permanence—the water forever flowing away; the bed, the channel, remaining relatively the same. Riding in a canoe on such a
deliberate stream as carried us along, a stream with its curtain of
drifting sediment veiling the workings of the river, there is always a fascination in trying to deduce what is occurring unseen
beneath the surface. The functioning of fluvial processes, the mechanics of producing the meanders and reaches of a stream, these
form a whole branch of specialized knowledge with its textbooks
on the dynamics of flowing water and its college course on river
morphology.

When the looping bends of a winding stream approach 180
degrees, they are termed meanders. In general, there is a direct
relationship between the size of a meandering river and the size
of its bends. Little rivers make little bends; big rivers make big
bends. At one time it was thought that meandering was always
associated with the old age of a stream. However, it has been

"No two bends, in the whole course of a stream, are ever exactly alike."

found that in certain cases, streams meander from the time of their origin. No two bends, in the whole course of a stream, are ever exactly alike.

What causes meandering? Hypotheses advanced to answer that question have ranged from the rotation of the earth to the theory that as soon as a stream ceases to down-cut it commences to side-cut. As one textbook sums it up: "No one explanation fully satisfies as the cause of meandering."

But the mechanical process by which it is achieved is well known. The current is deflected against first one bank and then the other. Turbulence set up by contact with the streambank on the outside of the curve increases the cutting power of the flowing water. The bank is undermined. It collapses and its material is carried downstream to be deposited as a bar by the slower water on the inside of the succeeding curve. Laboratory tests have revealed that once an initial bend is formed, the sinuosity is transmitted and other bends are formed. The meander system migrates downstream.

The main essential to the production of meandering is bank erosions. The trading of material from banks to bars follows. The rate of this trading depends upon the rate of the bank cutting, and this depends on the material of which the bank is formed and the speed and turbulence of the current. The bars, in their turn, further deflect the current toward the outside of the turns where the cutting occurs. Because bank erosion continues, the meander patterns of streams continually change.

Between these serpentine stretches of a river there are often wide and shallow portions of the stream flowing in a relatively straight line. These are called reaches. They result from two conditions: the channel becomes wide and shoaled because of the ease with which the banks are eroded, and the width of the channel keeps the flow dispersed, preventing the current from being deflected from side to side for a further attack upon the banks. In the middle two-thirds, in some instances nine-tenths, of the river, the rate at which the water flows is uniform. With their velocity reduced and their cutting power lessened, reaches tend to remain almost unchanged for long periods of time.

Somewhere below the Causeway Bridge, as we followed the serpentine of the river on that memorable October 15, the Sedge Meadows on our right and the Sudbury Meadows on our left, we drifted past a narrow bar of stranded flotsam in the middle of the stream. On it were ten or a dozen sandpipers. Late migrants, they seemed very tired, sleeping in the midday. With their black bills and black legs, their chunky little bodies crosshatched with darker gray, white beneath, they resembled a conclave of Quakers, uttering a small soft twittering note, apparently unafraid. One fluttered half a foot or so into the air and alighted again. These were semipalmated sandpipers (semipalmated meaning their feet have only partial webbing between the three toes), the "commonest of the 'peep' in the East." We passed no more than a dozen feet away, floating without paddling.

In this region they go south, usually, between October 1 and 10. The latest sighting recorded by Ludlow Griscom, the famous Harvard field ornithologist, in *Birds of Concord* is October 12. We were three days later than that mark!

A great abundance of this species and of the least sandpiper, with which it often flocks, is described by the early writers. Twelve score of the small birds were taken at "one shoot" by hunters, who often imitated with success the low, rolling "peep" from which their common name derives. They were, by all accounts, delicious eating.

Until well into the twentieth century, small-bird shooting—for food or feathers, for "sport" or "pest control"—was common in the fields and marshes along the Sudbury and the Assabet. Early pioneers classed as vermin crows, doves, grouse and heath hens, along with many seed-eating birds. Grouse so severely damaged the apple orchards that a bounty was offered that was not repealed until the nineteenth century in some towns. (Grouse, heath hen and woodcock were not regarded as game and servants stipulated in contracts that their masters would not give them heath hen more than two or three times a week.) There was then little or no idea of sport in the modern sense, and most of the hunting and shooting for the market was done by what were generally regarded as the town bums and loafers, too lazy or incompetent to do more useful work.

No regulation of any kind existed until 1817, when robins, larks, snipe and woodcocks were protected from March 1 to July 4, grouse and quail from March 1 to September 1. All towns, however, were given the right to suspend these restrictions if they saw fit, and for years Election Day was observed as a sort of holiday when it was customary to have shooting matches, and there was a great deal of indiscriminate shooting of all kinds of birds.

By the second half of the nineteenth century, the situation had worsened. Griscom, in *The Birds of Concord*, wrote:

> The modern generation simply cannot imagine the hunting pressure which existed over the whole country from 1850 to 1906. A greatly increased population were ardent hunters and sportsmen, aided by steadily improving firearms, and means of transportation. Professional gunning for luxury markets reached a scale never previously heard of in the history of the world, and the capacity of the Boston and New York markets to absorb game by the barrel, car and boatload, without any serious break in the price, was simply astounding. Moreover, it must be remembered that all the most destructive methods were legal. Live decoys, baiting, battery shooting, firelighting, netting, and trapping were all freely practiced; only firelighting at night had been stopped in my youth. The original game supply of the northeast was decimated beyond recovery.

[Plume hunting. Birds trapped for cages. Hawks and owls shot on sight. Loons and herons, bitterns, all large birds shot on sight. Small boys acquired skill with their rifles by popping away at flickers, robins, grebes. "Some thoughtless and cruel sportsman has killed twenty-two young partridges not much bigger than robins, against the Laws of Massachusetts and humanity." Thoreau, *Journal*, July 16, 1851.

[Every town supported a taxidermist. Every village four corners had a sporting-goods store. Money paid to boys and men who brought in birds. Price from five cents for small songbird to a dollar for a male wood duck. Part of Victorian taste was to have stuffed bright-colored birds covered with a bell jar. Snowy owls mounted with wings spread on fire screens.]

The last great flight of hawks near Boston was in 1884. One market alone received over a hundred red-tails. "No one living can tell me who bought those Hawks or why, but I am not surprised that the red-tail greatly decreased." Griscom continued:

> Early in the nineteenth century gentlemen could shoot robins and doves near Boston, but this couldn't be done after the middle of the century. However, the lower classes could and did; they broke up the last great robin roosts, and raided the winter flocks of Cedar Waxwings. It was correct for gentlemen to

151

shoot killdeer and small san[d]pipers in the middle of the century, but incorrect after 1880; it was all right for boys to learn by means of these birds, and of course the poor continued to hunt them. In the nineties . . . Italian immigrants began swarming over the countryside, hunting new types of birds for food. Armed with gunnysacks and working in teams, they . . . raided Night Heron rookeries in May for the half-grown young, shot sanderlings and herring gulls on the beaches, and in the fall went to the fresh-water swamps, where they specialized in roosting blackbirds. . . .

With decimation of populations by the end of the century came strong pressures to end the slaughter, followed by protective regulation. Naturalist Thomas Nuttall and Thoreau led the way through their interest in the birds around Boston, fifty years ahead of the rest of the country. The Massachusetts Audubon Society, the oldest society of that type with a continuous existence in America, was founded in 1895, and between 1895 and 1898 the first popular bird books were published. Finally, in 1906, Massachusetts passed a law protecting all song and insectivorous birds, most gulls and terns, the herons and bitterns, doves, the upland plover and the wood duck. In 1906 the waterfowl season was cut to the fall only, from September 15 to January 1. By 1916 the federal government had assumed jurisdiction over all the migratory birds of the continent. Spring shooting had gone forever, and the sale of game and all commercial traffic of any kind in native birds had ceased. "Popular sentiment," noted Griscom, "has changed from callous indifference to real interest."

Today persecution in the direct sense is far less important to changes in small-bird populations than other activities of man— activities which from earliest times have altered habitats. It was, after all, the mowing of meadows, holding the *Calamagrostis* in check, that created a favorable habitat along the Sudbury for marsh birds, notably snipe, shorebirds and rails. Since mowing has ceased, the famous snipe shooting of earlier decades has also ceased, except in years of heavy summer rains, while yellowlegs and pectoral sandpipers have become uncommon to rare. The years between 1860 and 1900 were a boom period for bobolinks, meadowlarks, grasshopper and vesper sparrows—allowing even for the slaughter—because much more general farming than now created a higher percentage of fields and pastures.

We were well past the halfway mark in our journey between the Causeway Bridge and Sherman's Bridge when Ann and I came to the spot I will remember longest, probably, of all we saw on our October 15 adventure. It was long after noon, and we had been looking for a place to land and eat the lunch we had brought. But we were walled in part of the time by buttonball bushes and bordered at other times by wetland, in the midst of a great sedge meadow where the sedges rose to my shoulders.

[Here four or five low willows lean apart. The sedges are trampled down. The boles of the willow awry. We pull the canoe up well on the shelving bank and unload the "Airplane" thermos bottle, which squirts water downward when a handle pressed (so won't spill in air) and the two sandwiches we brought. I have a cup of hot herb tea. Ann has a small can of V-8. She divides sesame seed bars and special cookies she has found good for quick energy on the trail. I sit in great content on my jacket, leaning back against one of the willows. She sits on one of the curved willow trunks. A magic place . . . how far away the world and its frettings. (Will always wish I could go back.) A happy time. Protected from wind. Warmed by sun. The silt-filled river drifting by. A world of great sedges with a slow river flowing through it. Mile after mile of sedges. Broken only by occasional meadows. Sedge Meadows, Sedge World, the Miles of Sedges, Home of the Wrens. I read a *Walk Through the Year* passage on cruelty in nature. Ann disagrees. Weasel is not cruel. But I am talking about whole spirit running through nature.

[I certainly am not blaming the weasel or the hawk or the parasite. It is the "why" behind it all that is the stumbling block. Our human concepts of right and wrong, I realize, have no place in judging acts we see occurring in nature. Our moral principles, our feelings of compassion and concern for the weak, do not apply in nature's activity. Nature functions outside our morality. There is, I know, no "cruelty" involved in the falcon's stoop or the weasel's pounce—that is, so far as the falcon and the weasel are concerned. They are merely following their instincts, merely using the special senses and abilities with which they were born, which they were brought into the world to use. How would the wolf survive if it were born with what we call "compassion"?

[The rattlesnake did not invent them, it inherited its poison sacs. The insect parasite that consumes its living host, saving the vital organs for the last, hatches from the egg with instinctive actions foreordained. It acts not to produce pain but to survive. There is neither "cruelty" nor "enmity" involved when a predator kills its prey.

[But there is terror. And there is suffering.

[Life, wherever it exists, is interrelated. And this is the way it is. And we have to adjust our lives to it. I have never really felt like a predator. Things might be easier if I did. It is not the individual cogs, the weasel and the wolf, that I am at odds with; it is the overall design of the machine, in which neither wolf nor weasel plays a part. Can this be the best of all possible worlds? To wish for another may be just butting our heads against a stone wall. But do we have to call it "the best of all possible worlds" because this is the way it is?

[Still, one of the fringe benefits of our lunch among the sedges and willows is a shift in my thinking about such things as weasels. I have always realized that weasels have to live, but I do not think I really wished them well. Now, little weasel, I wish you well.

[We pack up and start again about 1:45. I leave with regret. How "often hereafter" will I remember those willows set amid the wide meadows under the windy sky. It is easy paddling with a strong wind at our backs—it is the direction of the wind more than the direction of the current that determines the ease or difficulty of the paddle. I have a great feeling of peace with the world, a great enveloping peace through these wide water meadows on this winding stream. A shining experience . . . like a mountaintop in perfect weather.]

AHZ   Edwin and I launch the canoe into the embayment by Boon Road bridge one September morning, heading downstream toward Maynard, the next of the mill towns strung along the Assabet.

Matthew Boone came to the area around 1660 and acquired the pond now known as Boons Pond (without the *e*) as well as a large surrounding area, trading an Indian a jackknife for it. The pond itself is now dammed and therefore larger than in Boone's time, and its runoff enters the Assabet about a third of the way down from Gleasondale on the way to Maynard.

Boone built his homestead close by the pond, on the hillside

154

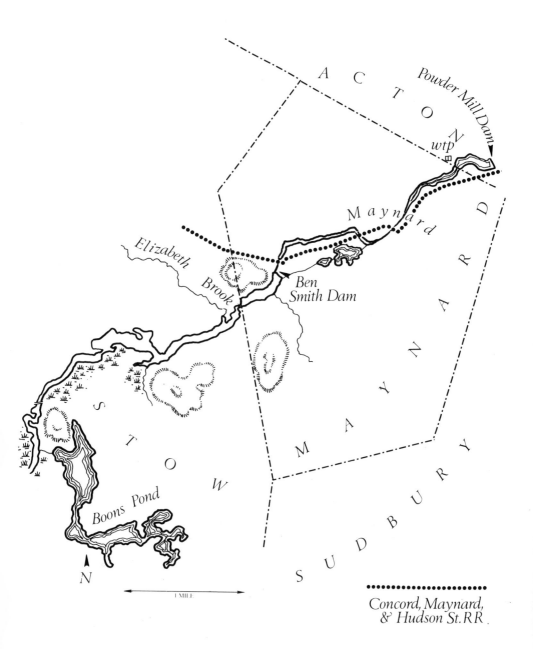

ACTON

Powder Mill Dam

wtp

Maynard

Elizabeth
Brook

Ben
Smith Dam

MAYNARD

S
T
O
W

SUDBURY

Boons Pond

N

1 MILE

Concord, Maynard,
& Hudson St.RR

above the river, and cleared land for planting. Then, in 1675, a chief of the Wampanoags called Philip, who saw clearly that continued English presence would mean the end of the world as the Indian knew it, was able to organize the remnant Indian tribes for what was to be the last major assault on Colonial expansion. A charismatic leader and proud man, he is said to have responded to the governor of Massachusetts' pleas for a peaceful solution: "Your governor is but a subject of King Charles of England. I shall not treat with a subject. I shall treat of peace only with the King, my brother. When he comes I am ready."

What Philip lacked in arms and preparation he made up for in bold strategy and terror tactics. The Indians set fire to unprotected houses at night and shot whoever ran out. A dozen towns were destroyed, six hundred settlers killed, over a half-million dollars lost—it was a short but fearsome war in which scarcely a New England family went unscathed, and which so disrupted Colonial life that all the outlying settlements along the Assabet were abandoned.

So it was that on one mean February day in 1676 Boone packed up his family and took them eastward to Deacon John Haynes's garrison house on the Sudbury, and returned for his household goods. From the scrubby woods where he lived, even though the river is but a few tens of feet away it is invisible, and even though it is late summer when I am here, it is not difficult to imagine it on that winter day, scratchy shadow patterns, flickering light, branches stridulating with the least wind, movements sensed rather than seen or heard, wind gusts masking any alien sounds.

Boone loaded his possessions into his oxcart and, encumbered with his load, started south around the pond. There, beside it, he was ambushed and hacked to pieces. The fragments of his body were found in a pool of blood that seeped into an inlet of the lake, thereafter known as "Red Slough."

But there was little time for grieving, for two months later the Indians attacked again. The settlers of Sudbury, joined by men from Concord, fought it out where the Causeway Bridge crosses the Sudbury and then barricaded themselves in Haynes's garrison house. By withstanding the attack, they preserved the town of Sudbury. Philip was later ambushed and killed, and organized resistance by the local Indians collapsed with his death.

At this time of year, the duckweed looks solid enough to walk on. It spreads across the whole river except for a narrow channel on the right, where current maintains open water. The backwater is studded with islands of pickerelweed and grasses and sedges, and duckweed dots the stems of all of them. Gray dead plants speckle the solid green surface, and where it piles up more thickly the blanket shines more intensely green.

The canoe bow plows it into chunks and leaves it in windows just as if the wind had blown it, diagramming our passage. Sometimes the duckweed blanket heaves slightly, seeming to breathe. Occasionally a gas bubble rises out of the muck, domes up the surface and breaks, and the small disk of open water is immediately gathered over by displaced plants.

At the edge of the channel the blanket frays, resembling the green map of some complex island-bordered peninsula. A little breeze loosens the edges, setting islands to drifting, turning slowly like nebulae, a green galaxy in a black void of space.

An early herbal describes duckweed perfectly and explains its name:

> Ducks meat is as it were a certain green mosse, with very little round leaves of the bignes of Lentils: out of the midst whereof on the nether side grow downe very fine threds like haires, which are to them in stead of roots: it hath neither stalke, floure, nor fruit. . . . Duckes meat is called Ducks herb, because Ducks do feed theron; whereupon it is called Ducks meat: some term it after the Greek, water Lentils.

Lemna minor is the most common species of duckweed on the Sudbury and Assabet, each four-millimeter frond marked with three inconspicuous nerves and keeled on the underside. I fish some up on my paddle; the surface tension of the water glues them to the wood. A tiny root extends from beneath most of them.

Duckweed may rarely send up an infinitesimal flower from a frond margin, but more commonly reproduces vegetatively, fronds proliferating in twos and threes, a new disk emerging from the slotted edge of the original. At frost, minute green scales detach from the fronds and drift to the bottom, where they remain during the winter, rising to the surface in warming weather.

Tiny black insects pepper the duckweed, now also caught in

157

the surface tension of the water on the paddle blade. Some fly and some hop, but not far; some scoot, some run. Whatever they are, they are impossible to catch. Other insects are the same pale green as the duckweed, noticeable only when they move.

Minute as these plants are, they are utilized by even tinier insects, some of which form almost microscopic galls. A fly and a small beetle both lay eggs on top of the frond and the larvae bore into it. Snails graze them, hydras and planarian worms feed off their surface, and one caddis fly larva uses duckweed fronds to form its case. Yet nothing seems to make a dent in the dense swales that clog the stream.

Apparently duckweed was rare here one hundred years ago or so; at least Minot Pratt, one of those fascinating Concordians, of which there were and still are many, found it sufficiently uncommon 1878 to note the presence of a "small floating plant covering the stagnant pools" at the side of the road below Sleepy Hollow Cemetery, and along the brook below.

Pratt, who was the "other grandfather" of Louisa May Alcott's *Little Women* and *Little Men* (his son, John, was the John who married Meg in *Little Women;* and his two grandsons, John's children, were the "little men") made a hobby of introducing plants to Concord. *The Flora of Middlesex County,* written in 1888, says he introduced "within the limits of Concord, plants from all sections of the United States" because he was convinced that many more of the beautiful and useful plants of the world should grow here than did. One of the less useful was the "Chinese chestnut," which became a serious pest. Some took a romantic view of his activities, which began in 1869; botanists were less pleased with his mucking up the native vegetation.

Whether or not one approves of his hobby, he was a sharp observer of what grew around Concord, and the environment in which it grew, and was knowledgeable enough about plants to correspond with Asa Gray, then the leading light in botany at Harvard. His observation that duckweed was scarce in the area can be received as close to gospel.

The tremendous increase in duckweed is blamed, by at least one botanist, on enrichment from sewage. Miles of both the Sudbury and Assabet are highly eutrophic, from the Greek *eutrophos,* which means "well-nourished." For every pound of nitrogen that seeps into the stream ecosystem, over seven hundred pounds of

Water caltrop or water chestnut (*Trapa natans*)

weeds and algae can be produced; phosphorous can generate five hundred times its own weight in vegetation. Plankton production increases on the order of twenty to one. And one human contributes ten pounds of nitrogen and 1.3 pounds of phosphorous via sewage each year.

The density of the duckweed may also be due to runoff from the fertilization of the farmlands and large apple orchards parading over the drumlins that rise along the river. Only about 50 percent of the nitrogen in fertilizers added to farmlands and orchards is taken up by growing crops; the rest is wasted by erosion and leaching—and agricultural runoff, unlike industrial and "human" effluents, which are concentrated in "point sources" and therefore easier to identify and control, disperses along whole stretches of river.

Phosphates do not leach from the soil as quickly as nitrates do, but when they are on the soil surface, they too are exposed to runoff; in springtime when fertilizer is applied and rains are heavy, half the river's yearly dose of phosphate reaches the watercourse. Studies suggest that even were there complete phosphate removal by waste treatment plants that empty into the river,

159

enough would still come into it through overland runoff to make the duckweed thrive.

The duckweed-bespattered river, here straddled by Maynard, forms the northern bound of the "Two-Mile Grant" of 1649. Settlers of Sudbury petitioned the General Court for additional land and were especially covetous of this particular area because of its meadows, rare along the Assabet, which produced opulent crops of grass and sedge. They bought the plot from the original Indian proprietors for twelve pounds—about sixty dollars.

Maynard followed the New England pattern of growing, then budding off from the parent town or towns, and petitioning the General Court for autonomy. The "parents" in this case were Sudbury and Stow, and Sudbury, like many parents, was unwilling to let its "child" go. Petition was made in 1869; Sudbury strongly opposed it because of the anticipated loss of tax and other revenues from Maynard's woolen mills. But eventually, 1,900 acres were taken on the south side of the Assabet, for which Sudbury received almost $21,000 recompense, and 1,300 acres on the north, for which Stow received $6,500, and the town of Maynard was incorporated in April 1871. Among other things, the new town agreed to assume the care of its own indigents, a proviso often listed in New England town charters. Its valuation was set at over one million dollars, and it took the name of Maynard in honor of the man chiefly responsible for its woolen industry for over twenty years. Minutes of the town organizational meeting note that among regular town officials appointed were "Fence Viewers"—a title I rather fancy.

Assabet Village, as the first settlement was known, began with the ubiquitous saw and grist mill, owned by a man named Gibson, whose grandson was the first to fall at the Old North Bridge on April 19, 1775. Gibson's mill passed through many hands as the settlement grew around it. James and William Rice were the first to use its waterpower for manufacturing, in the early 1820s, but as their business expanded they moved away because the Assabet, then free-flowing at this point, did not provide sufficient power for more machinery. Not until Amory Maynard did so was Assabet water dammed here and its power developed for full industrial use.

By 1816 all the processes of cloth manufacture could and were done under one roof; by 1830 good breeding stock of sheep existed in this country. (Merino, the best wool-bearing sheep, were prohibited in Spain from export, but a couple did reach New England; it is told that a colonist on whose farm they grazed, not knowing what they were worth to the woolen industry, ate up decades of progress.) The spinning jenny was in wide use, having been smuggled out of England; looms had been harnessed to waterpower, and hand finishing was replaced by machine finishing. Between 1830 and 1836 the textile industry became prosperous—and clearly this was not lost on young Amory Maynard.

Maynard was fourteen when he left school to help his father with his sawmill and farming; two years later, in 1821, his father died, and Amory took over the business. Twenty-five years later he was well established enough to set about starting a textile mill. He began by buying a corridor of land; the owner, Hamon Smith, was not much impressed by his bearing, and in fact didn't think he'd get paid. But almost as soon as the deed was signed, the mill canal was dug, a dam was built and the pond, still here, filled with water. Maynard acquired a partner, William H. Knight, a carpet manufacturer from nearby Saxonville, who had just sold some of his upstream water rights on both sides of the "Elsibeth River" and had some money to invest; the two continued buying land until they controlled all the available water rights, waterpower, and mill sites in the vicinity.

Maynard and Knight began by manufacturing carpet yarn and carpets. Although carpets may seem an unlikely product in the general context of more necessary goods, they were in great demand: easier to clean than rag rugs, better wearing, a status symbol. The new firm did a good business. Nevertheless, before long, even more profitable flannels and blankets had replaced the carpets.

Generally, the early years of a new mill were very profitable. The power source was nearly free and a new product usually very much in demand. But as time went on and the mill needed to be improved or expanded, profits declined. There was a general paucity of capital for investment, and expansion and improvement had to be made out of profits alone, sometimes severely restricting owners' plans. Probably for this reason, in 1849 Maynard applied for and was granted a charter of incorporation by the General Court.

The labor supply was also a limiting factor, and before long

161

the close-knit paternalistic mill society of the 1830s, largely staffed by American labor, was replaced by imported workers, many of them Irish. But in the 1850s, growth in the woolen industry slowed under heavy competition from Britain—it survived at all only with partial protection from tariffs—and in the panic of 1857 the three wooden buildings that then constituted Maynard's mills had to be sold at auction. In retribution, the town briefly considered changing its name.

Maynard, however, was far from defeated. In 1862 capital for necessary expansion came from large government orders of blankets and flannels for the Civil War. A stock company was formed, the mills were reorganized as the Assabet Manufacturing Company; steam power was added, and production reached 3.5 million pounds of wool per year through the efforts of some 5 hundred employees, most of them women.

At the end of the war, overproduction caused many smaller mills to fail and the larger ones to run on short time, resulting once more in severe depressions in many New England "one-industry" towns, including Maynard. Nevertheless, at Amory Maynard's death in 1890, in spite of the ups and downs, his mills were worth $1.5 million—ten times as much as in 1847, after the first year of operation. But the early 1890s were poor business years, and the Assabet mills went into bankruptcy in 1898. This time, even more disastrous than the loss of jobs was the financial loss to many employees. Before the establishment of a local bank, the company itself banked for its employees and the city. Employees who had deposited their savings with the bankrupt company got back only a little over half.

Receivers kept the mills—by this time the largest woolen manufactory in the United States—running until 1899, when the American Woollen Company bought them for $400,000, about a quarter of what they had been worth less than a decade earlier. The new owners expanded, building most of the structures now standing. They developed new marketing techniques, replaced outdated equipment, and increased plant capacity with an influx of cheap labor, nearly doubling the population of Maynard between 1895 and 1905.

In the early part of the twentieth century, the company generated its own electric power and secured a charter to furnish electricity and streetlights to Maynard and Acton; in 1921 rates were thirteen cents per kilowatt hour. It generated all the town's electricity until well into the 1930s (today Maynard is served by Hudson Light and Power, which originally used run-through Assabet water for cooling), and into the 1960s Assabet waterpower was still utilized to light some of the mill building's indoor lights and the current tenant's Christmas tree.

As the Civil War had, two world wars brought prosperous times to the mills, and they went on a twenty-four-hour, seven-day week. But they shut their doors permanently in 1950, closed by a combination of the decline in the need for wool and the introduction of synthetics. In 1953 ten Worcester businessmen formed Maynard Industries, bought the mill complex, and marketed the space, renting part of it to a small new electronics firm called Digital Equipment.

With completion of the northernmost part of the mill complex, the Assabet was walled into a straight chute along the south side of the stream, and through it, during flood, the river gallops.

I remember the flood of January 1979 boring through Maynard. Edwin, Nellie and I stood fascinated on the Main Street Bridge in the center of town. Upstream from the bridge, the river makes a right-angle turn, speeds under the trestle of the Boston & Maine, and enters the chute—which I had looked forward to running ever since I first saw it. But *not* that day. A marker on the downstream side of the bridge showed the river at almost record height. Water smacked the underneath of the bridge in big insolent waves that built and broke upstream. The skies were ominous. People stood on the sidewalk in uneasy clusters, and cars crossing the bridge proceeded cautiously, as if the drivers were afraid it would not hold. People whose backyards were flooded came to check the marker to assure themselves that it was indeed as bad as they thought it was. As the river lashed at the walls that confined it, it splashed the foundations of the old American Woollen Company, bore by the only USGS gauge on either river above their conjunction, snarled under the old paper mill bridge where handmade paper was produced for the *Boston Journal* in 1840, and discharged into the backwaters of the Powder Mill Dam.

The mill buildings are narrow rectangular brick structures with rows of windows, severe but pleasing. A combination of different decorative elements from various styles was common in mill architecture of the nineteenth century, and the Maynard mills include a Greek Revival clock tower, Lombard corbeling, as well as contemporary Victorian architecture; in its day the compound was judged to be unsurpassed by mill buildings anywhere.

I remember driving from Hudson to Maynard late one June evening. As I passed by the Ben Smith Dam, named after one of Hamon Smith's sons, I suddenly recalled that the excavations for it in 1880 had uncovered a communal grave which held six Indians, and that in the eighteenth century, when this settlement was known as Assabet Peninsula, an itinerant tinker suddenly disappeared here in the middle of making his rounds. Soon after, people skirting the river meadows whispered that they heard odd sounds—those of a tinker at work. When an old lady of the town died, the hollow tappings of the phantom tinker accompanied the funeral procession to her grave. And then were heard no more.

I rounded the curve entering Maynard and ahead of me shone all the lighted windows of the mill, solid and safe. For a moment I had an unanticipated glimpse back into those prosperous times when the mills ran all night. I could almost hear the cheery bell of the little Concord, Maynard & Hudson Street Railway trolley, an interurban that jiggled along between Hudson and Concord, crossing the Assabet no fewer than nine times, and passing close by the mills.

From an economic point of view the CM&H was pure fancy; nevertheless it ran and provided a vital service for more than twenty years. Its rolling stock consisted of a dozen cars, six open and six closed, a couple of snowplows and one work car. It always had less than twenty miles of track and operated without much profit, using rights-of-way occupied by already laid-out streets.

The excursion cars were spiffy—forty-one feet long, a snappy dark blue with spanking white trim. Seats were caned chairs with plush upholstery and there was Brussels carpet on the floor, and woodwork so highly polished a lady could see if her hat was adjusted properly. There were thirty-two electric light bulbs in five different colors, shining through glossy handmade globes.

When it initiated service on August 1, 1901, it took one hour and ten minutes to cover the fifteen miles between Concord and Hudson, and cars left the terminal every thirty-five minutes. During its second month of operation it carried 52,347 passengers in a rural area where the resident population, in 1900, was only some 17,300. Fares were five cents per zone, with a total of twenty cents between end points.

In 1917 it began operating at a loss: a disastrous fire in the power station the following year decimated the rolling stock; on top of this, the "coal famine" resulted in high coal prices and schedules had to be severely curtailed. By this time cars and tracks were run down, overhead wires were frayed and the company defaulted on bond interest payments. Receivers foreclosed at the end of 1922.

But in its heyday it must have been wonderful. CM&H motormen ran errands for people along the tracks, were genial and helpful, enduring with fortitude mischievous boys who pulled the trolley off the wire. They dropped the men off at Summer Street in Maynard, where there was a bar, and took the ladies and children on to town center, left them there to shop. When the men were picked up again, on the way home, they were "in good spirits and their suitcases filled with beer," reads a contemporary account. People still remember how the conductor walked outside on the running board, holding on with one hand and making change with the other.

One Sunday evening in April 1911, a train of the Boston & Maine came chugging around the sharp curve of the river above the Mill Street Bridge, jumped its tracks an ignominious three hundreds yards from the depot. Engine and cars sank into the mud. There were no fatalities, and the CM&H did a land-office business bringing in the sightseers.

And on summer evenings when the moon was full, the CM&H ran open excursion cars with the lights romantically turned down. The young people held hands and sang the songs that were the current rage, and the girls in dotted-swiss dresses with ruffled petticoats, fresh starched, and blue satin ribbon sashes, brought picnic suppers with fried chicken and coleslaw and homemade pickles and devil's food cake, and as they swayed across the moon path on the Assabet on their warm summer evening they must have seen it much as I saw it on my summer evening—ribbons of light from the mills, and a full moon floating upward in the deepening sky.

8

ᎬᏔᏂ   Like barkless tree trunks smoothed and silvered by years
of weathering, the upright timbers of Sherman's Bridge
rose from the water around Ann and me. Among modern spans of
concrete and stone, this last of the river's wooden bridges descends from an earlier time. Its design has remained almost unal-
tered since Colonial days. A car that had just passed a warning
sign on the Lincoln-Sudbury road—"LOAD LIMIT 2½ TONS"—rattled
over the planks above us. Looking up, we noticed that the wooden
supporting columns were encircled by seven distinct rings. Each
band of sediment recorded a different level of the water during
the floodtime of spring.

With the first paddle stroke I feel like a tethered balloon
whose rope has been cut. I am floating free. For Ann it is the
same. Why? Is it the sense of buoyancy, the sense of freedom, the
sense of being one with the canoe? A canoe is graceful, maneuverable, alive. We become part of a canoe in a way we never become
part of a rowboat. Rowing a boat is comparable to clumping along
on the back of a plow horse; paddling a canoe comparable to being in the saddle of a spirited riding horse. In a canoe you have to
maintain your own balance; a rowboat is solidly planted and
maintains it for you.

The tippiness, the instability of the canoe, which appeals to
some, repels others. It represents an element of danger which you
control with your skill. You enjoy a sense of self-reliance, of de-

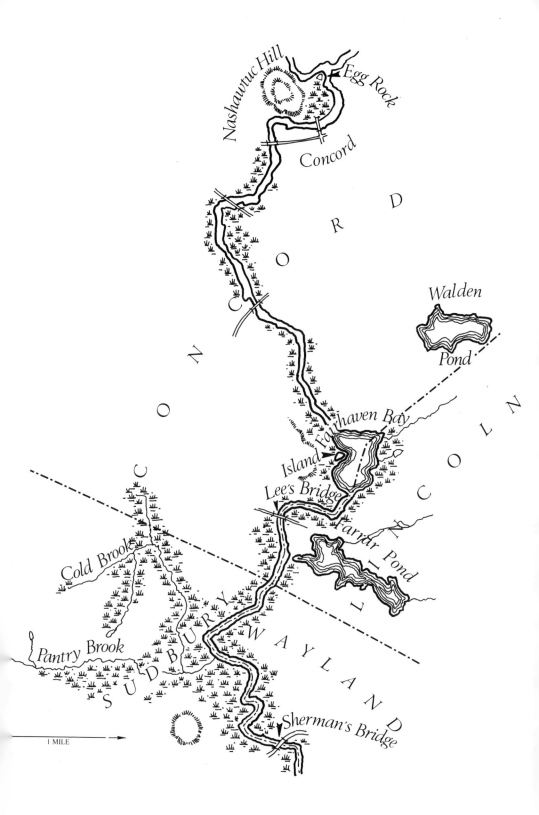

Nashawtuc Hill

Egg Rock

Concord

CONCORD

Walden Pond

C O N C O R D

LINCOLN

Fairhaven Bay

Island

Lee's Bridge

Farrar Pond

Cold Brook

WAYLAND

S U D B U R Y

Pantry Brook

Sherman's Bridge

1 MILE

pending on your strength and skill and experience. You seem more alive in a canoe, in the midst of an adventure. Because we are bipeds, having to balance ourselves on two legs, instead of being solidly planted on four, do we have an instinctive affinity for the unstable, do we instinctively respond to the challenge of maintaining balance in a canoe and derive some deep-seated pleasure from it?

In a canoe you slip through the landscape without disturbing it. You make no noise. You advance with a "silken silence" through the water. You see more. You approach wild creatures more closely, see the wildlife of remote swamps and stretches of streams not visited by any other craft. You can explore unfamiliar places, nose into little bays, penetrate into bogs and marshes and shallows, poke into small side streams. You can enter the "in-between land"—too wet to approach on foot, too shallow to reach in a larger, less maneuverable craft. You can attain places you otherwise could not visit, see things you otherwise could not see. You can drift to watch action and see things in detail. You can come to rest for the close-up view.

The canoe has romantic associations. It is linked with the Indian, the Voyageurs, the first explorers, the pioneer, self-reliant history of America, with adventure stories and daring exploits. Paddling a canoe may be a kind of projecting ourselves into a simpler, more adventurous past. There is an elemental simplicity about guiding a canoe, a getting back to fundamentals like drinking from your hands at a spring. At the first paddle stroke, tenseness begins to fall away. The technique of canoeing is essentially uncomplicated. Your eyes and mind are free to roam, to observe, to enjoy.

Where the river straightens out and leaves Weir Hill behind, drifting into the northwest in a wide straight reach, Pantry Brook emerges from its enclosed lowland valley and joins the larger stream. This valley, leading in from the west, has been famous since the time of the earliest settlers. It, and the area around it, are still known as the Pantry.

In his *History of Sudbury*, Henry Serano Hudson suggests that the original name of Pantry Brook may have been "Pine Tree Brook," that in time, the New England pronunciation, giving it a "Pan Tree" twist, had corrupted it into its present form. And it is true that in early days the area was rich in huge white pines. But it seems logical that the valley, with the brook threading through it, should have been called Pantry from the beginning because of the bountiful supplies it contained for the colonists—waterfowl teeming in migration time, furbearers for the catching, hay in abundance in the meadows, wild cranberries that reddened the wetland in autumn.

Old maps dating back more than a hundred years show, within the watershed of Pantry Brook, small shaded areas. Each is labeled "Iron ore," and they tell the story of a long-gone Colonial industry in which the Sudbury River played its part. They also indicate another source of wealth contributed by the Pantry.

For it was bog ore from eastern Massachusetts that provided the raw material for the first successful production of iron in America. In 1641, a little more than a decade after Boston was established, the son of Governor Winthrop the younger sailed for England to obtain financial backing and skilled workers for an ironworks that would supply the colonists with hammers and nails, axes and plowshares and ships' anchors of their own production. The result was the formation of a joint-share company— the Company of Undertakers of the Iron Works in New England. Financed almost entirely by English capital, it established, on the edge of the wilderness ten miles north of Boston, what became one of the marvels of Colonial times, the pioneer iron works at Saugus. Before the end of the seventeenth century, bog ore was being dug here, on Pantry Brook.

When bog ore, also called limonite, is taken from the ground, it resembles heavy reddish or yellow-brown friable sandstone. Sometimes it occurs in solid masses that have to be broken up with a pick. At other times, it is so soft in composition that it can be removed with a shovel. In early days, when deposits were discovered at the bottom of swamps or in shallow ponds, men in flat-bottomed boats used heavy rakes or long double-handled, tong-like implements called "floating shovels" to gouge out chunks and lift them to the surface.

The creation of bog ore, as Mary Stetson Clarke described it in her definitive *Pioneer Iron Works*, is a process involving many steps. It begins with water seeping or running through accumulated vegetable matter, leaves, grass and wood, and producing carbonic acid, which dissolves and washes away in surface water the mineral iron contained in rocks. The decaying vegetable matter also produces iron compounds through the decomposition of rocks under it. The dissolved iron then collects in swamps, where it is transformed into an oxide by the loss of carbonic acid through evaporation and the subsequent activity of those remarkable microscopic organisms, the *Leptothrix,* commonly called "iron bacteria." A species of what are known as "sheathed" bacteria, *Leptothrix* extract the iron from the water and store it as ferric hydroxide in their infinitesimally small sheaths. Billions upon billions, these invisible creatures live and work and die. The iron oxide their sheaths contain forms a scum on the surface of the swamp water. This sinks to the bottom, and thus, layer by layer, the deposit of bog ore comes into being.

[I drive to the Barton farm at the headwaters of Pantry Brook. His family there from early times. May have received a king's grant of land.

[We drive out across fields along wheel tracks, beside long lines of saplings of some kind, a yard or so high. We stop before a low, boggy place and walk the rest of the way to a place where a ditch is being cleared out. Barton has brought along a long-handled shovel. He gets down in the ditch and digs out shovels of reddish earth filled with lumps, crumbly but heavy.

[The ditch eventually leads into Pantry Brook. The site of the ditch is about three hundred yards from where the beginning Pantry Brook—formed by the juncture of two tributary streams, one of which Barton says is called Lower Slough Run—flows under the single-track railroad that runs north and south.

[Piled up chunks of the excavated material beside the road. They looked like chunks of reddish-brown mud. . . . like jagged rocks but crumbly. But heavier than any ordinary dirt. Granular like sandstone. Wet. Not yet hardened. But heavy. Is this bog iron in an intermediate stage? What will happen when the chunks become thoroughly dry? Now in a state of transition? Barton says help ourselves to any chunks we want.]

In different times and different seasons Pantry Brook appears in different guises. There is a certain quality to its fascination when October encircles the valley with the brilliance of autumn foliage, another when dragonfly wings shimmer in the heat of midsummer days or when the ice of winter locks in the wetland or when the high water of early spring floods the valley from brim to brim. Ann and I first turned aside from the river and

170

"And there is always the encircling rim of the shining silvered maples."

wound among the spreading water trails of the secluded stream on a morning in May. We had the whole valley to ourselves. Cupped within the encircling higher land, it spread out, warm in the sunshine, rich with the primeval scents of the swamp, filled with the reviving life of the spring. Frequently the only sound was the slow swirl of our leisurely paddle strokes as we wound in and out among stands of massed pickerelweed, islands of button-bushes and red osiers, where the sword leaves of the cattails already lifted higher than our heads.

We threaded amid the tussocks of the sedges and low mounds rising above the water and crowned with the unrolling fiddleheads of the royal fern, coming out on little water openings strewn thickly with the outstretched leaves of both white and yellow water lilies—leaves more rounded for the white, more elongated for the yellow. Now and then we paused beside low bushes clad in small new grayish-green foliage, the leaves of the sweet gale, which filled the air with fragrance when we crushed them between our fingers.

Clouds drifted over us and cloud-shadows drifted around us. We were walled in by the shining silver of the branches of the swamp maples that surrounded the expanse of the water—the silver altering to the dullness of lead when the sunshine changed to shadow. Sometimes when I dipped my paddle I felt the blade meet the top of some submerged tussock. We canoed that day where only a week or two later we would have been grounded, ascending all the way to Little Pantry Brook where it joins the valley from the north.

I remember an April day in another spring, when I explored this flooded valley with Robbie Robinson. Beyond the bridge the brown flow of the river continued the wide-sweeping serpentine that had characterized its course through the Sedge Meadows. To advance half a mile down the river valley, we paddled a mile. It was in this remote upper section that an immense bird suddenly shot up ahead of us, a curving band of white shining out on its tail. It was a female Canada goose on her nest at the top of a larger, exposed hummock. She flew fifty or sixty feet away, splashed down behind a thin screen of buttonbushes and swam about, honking over and over again, then flew a hundred yards or so and landed in a larger opening, where her mate was resting silently. They soon lost their concern, stood on their tails and

"We threaded amid the tussocks of the sedges and low mounds rising above the water and crowned with the unrolling fiddleheads of the royal fern. . . ."

"... coming out on little water-openings strewn thickly with the outstretched leaves of both white and yellow waterlilies. . . ."

flapped their wings, swam about or floated, watching but no longer alarmed. How huge the goose had seemed looming up suddenly only twenty-five feet ahead of the canoe!

[From time to time swallows, I think tree swallows, turn and glide, sweeping above us, turn and pass above us again. A little blackish mayfly lands at my feet in the canoe. So far has spring, the belated spring of 1979, advanced. At the highest point a canoe can ascend Pantry Brook, we encounter a stretch of dense sedges— a mini Sedge Meadows. The geese swim in and out of view in the distance as they keep the canoe in sight. On the way back we keep far from the nest on the hummock. Duckweed already among the floating sedges. And always the encircling rim of the shining silvered maples.

[*The perfect day.* Brilliant skies sown with drifting clouds, photogenic clouds. Cool breeze but it eases off toward noon. Already the poplars are fringed with catkins and the red maples are gay with expanding flowers.

[The three things of special beauty on this day: the vivid spring green of the awakening meadow; the shining silver of the swamp maples walling in the river; the shining clouds all across the sky.

[A blue-winged teal takes off and, flying fast, curves away to the left. Then a pair of mallards ahead take wing. Green algae in tents and fans among the decaying grass stems that are just above the water. The sedges are deeper. They are brownish and their algae are brown. The festoons of the algae, green and brown. The algae of spring.

[The new grass is thrusting up six or eight inches high. Sunshine and shadow. Clear pure air. The breeze sweeping up the river and over the meadow. The meandering of the clear little brook. This is our glorious hour, under the shining clouds. The current becomes swifter farther upstream. A few white pines stand out dark among the shining silvery haze of the red maples.

[We can cut "across country" over the islands and peninsulas that thrust out in summer, over hummocks that are dry in August. We push across sunken stands of purple loosestrife, the stems dead and brown, chocolate brown, thrusting up above the water. Red osiers in islands of their own along the normal banks. We paddle past a decaying stub of a tree, a landmark in summer and winter. Here woodpeckers have made their holes.

175

[At one time beavers lived in the valley. In autumn passenger pigeons weighed down the branches of the surrounding trees. And each spring and fall the whistle of waterfowl wings rose to a crescendo. These were known to the Indians long before the colonists came. The valley was a pantry for the red men too. But long gone are the beavers, long gone the passenger pigeon, long gone the clouds of swarming waterfowl. Pantry Brook Meadow, in the early years of the present century, was a center for short-billed marsh wrens. Yet as early as 1949, Ludlow Griscom, found the colony had been reduced to a single pair. (On banks of Sudbury River just below the Causeway bridge sixty or more years ago, there was a famous "colony" of long-billed marsh wrens. The only one known in eastern Massachusetts in grass and not in cattails. Brewster made extensive studies of the colony by canoe in 1890 and 1894. At least 250 pairs. Now none.)

[My paddle touches the hummocks from time to time. All the dense lush growth of the marshy lowland lies now hidden, awaiting its time, below the keel of our canoe. An author who has to stop and take notes gets many a rest from paddling! Hear woodpeckers drumming on dead trees. Everywhere along the flood river signs of spring, the brilliant vivid new green of earlier growth.

[We nose up into little bays and open places. Find some soft new shoots of three-sided sedges rising from the shallow water. Hear again the tones of a wood thrush from the forested shore.

[Much cattail leaf remains where muskrats feeding. It used to be that when the rats were at a peak, you could count 1,000 houses in the Wayland Marshes, between the Wayland Bridge and Sherman's Bridge. That did not mean 1,000 pairs necessarily. Sometimes build two or more houses in addition to feeding platforms. Now population way down. Where many—in Gulf Meadow—in earlier times, now very few. Everywhere now there are fewer muskrats.

[Several times pairs of mallards, and more than once the fast little teal, take off from little patches of open water ahead of us or from one side or the other. Only once did I catch color on the wings of the little teal. That time it was blue. (Eight fly in a compact group once.) The silver screens of the maples are splotched with the patches of the rich red flowers, just opening. Canoeing now where we would be grounded in summer. How many re-

176

membrances I am harvesting on this day of spring, of sunshine and clouds! The waving algae. The mirror of the water filled with reflections. A red-tailed hawk circles in tight turns over the marsh, screaming as it goes. And always the clouds and the shadows of clouds.

[Just above Lee's Bridge, Dunge Hole Brook enters the Sudbury, but this is not shown on present maps. Dunge Hole. This deep swampy depression, the work, no doubt, of the glaciers, as in Fairhaven Bay, is on Route 117, west of Nine-Acre Corner. It is located almost exactly on the Sudbury-Concord line. An acre or less in extent. Some kettleholes are filled with water, some not. It depends on whether their bottoms are above or below the level of the groundwater. Dunge hole not down to water level. "Dunge" may not come from "dungeon" but from Old English spelling of "dung." Dung or manure also originally included mucky soil, not just manure produced by animals. The early New England farmers dug out collected muck, filled with humus, and added it to their sandy soil. Remember in legislative hearing, farmers said muck they used to get was one of the things they should be indemnified for.

[When I got home I looked up "dunge" in the *Shorter Oxford Dictionary* I have in my study. It does *not* include "dunge"—only "dung." I called John McDonald, head librarian at the U. of Connecticut. He had research librarians look it up in the complete multivolumed *Oxford Dictionary*. "Dunge" appears there. But meaning "dungeon," not "dung."

[Moreover, Fuzzy Fenn sent a list of the varied ways she has encountered the early spelling of Dunge Hole. They include: Dungi Hole, Dungie Hole, Dongye Hole, Dungey Hole, Dung Hole, Dung Hool, Dunger Hole, Danger Hole. These all from early town records in Concord. Fuzzy also sent this entry from Thoreau's *Journal*, Vol. XI, p. 172 (September 21, 1858): "Returned by some very deep hollows in Salem (like the Truro ones) called the Dungeons!! as our Dunge Hole."

[That clinches it. Dunge refers to dungeon, not to dung. I had better check up on *everything!*

[I call up Walter Hoyt of the Massachusetts Fish and Wildlife. What happened to all the muskrats? He doesn't know. Raccoons had bad "distemper" epidemic few years ago. Began up Sudbury and seemed to follow the river until it reached the sea.

Raccoons along the way attacked. About same time muskrats seemed decreased. But is there any connection or were the water rats in a periodic cycle of abundance? He suggests Thomas K. Hayes as a source of information. Is head of trapping association and knows the river.

[Meet Tom Hayes, old muskrat trapper. He is a hearty, healthy, hunter-trapper type. Fishes for salmon in Nova Scotia. He has known the Sudbury most of his life. We had much to talk about. And we got along well.

[He says just don't see muskrats this time of year. See occasional remains of feeding and see holes in banks. The houses are largely washed away by the spring high water each year. The muskrats have ten-year cycles of abundance. Were at peak in population two or three years ago. Crash and are building up again. They get some liver disease that cuts them down when reach peak, Hayes say; says in flood some muskrats get up under the ice on solid ground at the edge. He suspects some go up brooks in flood time. What eat? He wonders about that! Suggests I read a book: *A Week on the Concord and Merrimack Rivers* by Henry Thoreau! He has read some of Thoreau's *Journal*—"it tells of muskrat trappers."]

AHZ No one can canoe below Maynard. The whole impounded reach above the Powder Mill Dam is closed by joint action of the Maynard and Acton boards of health (the dam actually is in the very southeast angle of Acton) because of "extreme bacterial concentrations." This particular August day the river smell is nauseating, reeking like an unpumped-out campground outhouse times ten—all the odors that arise from bacterial degradation of proteins and the reduction of sulfates under anaerobic conditions. The scum is so thick on top of the river that beer bottles and cans hang motionless.

It is as if every pollutant ever jettisoned into the Assabet has coalesced and endured here, at this spot, including one of the grisliest from the Maynard paper mill that existed upstream in the 1850s. In 1892 Horace Hosmer remembered:

> The Assabet river was the western boundary of my Grandfathers farm, and also the one my father lived on for 16 years. I knew every rod of it, and thought it the most beautiful river in the world, and do now. There was a Paper Mill up stream which I used to visit occasionally. After the Crimean War 5

tons of soldiers white shirts came to this mill at one time just as they were taken off the dead bodies, matted with blood, and were made into writing paper. I weighed one of my shirts and it weighed ¾ of a pound, so there must have been the blood of 1000 men coloring the waters of our beautiful river. I sometimes thought the cardinal flowers, and the Maple leaves in Autumn were tinged with it.

My evaluation is purely subjective: The river is a mess. Ugly. Repulsive. But there are also objective measurements that give a qualitative picture of the river's health to back up the visual impression. It is the sum of the whole spectrum of tests that determines the uses to which river water may be safely put: drinking, recreation, contact water sports—or some of these or none, as here. The standard tests include measuring quantities of dissolved oxygen, coliform bacteria, nutrients (mostly nitrogen and phosphorus), testing for acidity/alkalinity (or pH), measuring temperature, noting the water's turbidity and color, and the presence of toxic pollutants such as oil, pesticides, etc.

The amount of dissolved oxygen gives an instant picture of water conditions at the moment of testing for it, and registers the amount of oxygen available to aquatic organisms for respiration. A better reading of long-term conditions is obtained by calculating the Biochemical Oxygen Demand, abbreviated to BOD, which is the amount of oxygen needed to decompose the amount of dead organic matter present in the water.

Oxygen for decomposition of organic matter is required in two stages. During the first, carbonaceous matter is oxidized, forming carbon dioxide. This normally takes some seven days, after which the second step begins: nitrogenous substances are broken down, first to ammonia, then to nitrite, finally to nitrate. Total decomposition of organic wastes takes up to thirty days or more. Untreated sewage normally has a BOD some 150 to 200 times that of "unpolluted" water.

Coliform bacteria are present naturally in rivers from soil runoff, decaying vegetation, etc.; some of them come from animal fecal matter, and they are found in all human feces. *Escherichia coli* is the common and easily detected nonpathogenic bacterium that provides a convenient measure of contamination of water by human waste. Although it is not harmful in itself, its presence in large numbers implies the potential presence of toxic bacteria, such as typhoid bacillus, dysentery, cholera. Heavy loads of *Es-*

cherichia coli indicate water unfit for any kind of contact water sports or drinking.

Nitrogen and phosphorus from inadequately treated sewage, certain industrial wastes, agricultural runoff, and malfunctioning and improperly maintained septic tanks may dramatically stimulate the growth of unsavory algae "blooms" like that the Meixsells and I encountered along the Assabet. Such blooms cause more trouble at senescence and death, for their decomposition consumes great amounts of oxygen at the expense of other aquatic life, and their rotting strands drape in reeking windrows upon the shore, and float in foul masses in the water.

Some turbidity in a stream is natural and may be caused by silt in suspension, as in the arid country of the West where the big rivers tend to be continually silt-laden and run like *café au lait*. But in water that has the potential for clarity, turbidity is considered pollution; it can result from effluents, organic debris, or plankton. Turbidity is created by both dissolved and suspended solids; the latter can be removed by filtration but the former remain. Suspended particles, as well as other contaminants, can be harmful to fish eggs, to fish and their food, as well as to plants.

Although massive amounts of industrial wastes were dumped directly into the Assabet in decades past, this kind of pollution is now greatly diminished, regulated by the National Pollution Discharge Elimination System (NPDES) program mandated by the Federal Water Pollution Control Act. There are still problems, however; when industries dispose of their wastes via municipal wastewater treatment plants, their effluents are sometimes "shock loads" that disrupt conventional treatment systems, killing waste-processing microorganisms. And no one knows what contaminants are still contained in sludge deposits from past dumping, although the situation at Maynard gives a clue.

At the end of April 1978, residents of the area near the impoundment above the Powder Mill dam complained of foul odors. The board of health investigated and immediately declared the area a threat to health. Tests of the water showed not only high bacterial counts, but heavy concentrations of industrial pollutants—cadmium, copper, nickel, and zinc, and lesser amounts of arsenic, mercury, chromium and lead—from the sludge the Maynard wastewater treatment plant had been depositing directly into the Assabet until 1975. To clean up the mess, Maynard requested assistance from both the Environmental Protection Agency and the Army Corps of Engineers, but was notified that no funds were available. Since Maynard is the smallest town in the Commonwealth, clean-up expenses loomed dismayingly large, but Maynard has since hired its own consultant and is on its way to solving the problem.

Today serious problems also come from domestic wastes. In the towns of the SuAsCo basin there have been notable increases in population—between 1950 and 1970 the population of Hudson doubled and that of Northborough tripled, and the increase for the whole drainage basin is projected to be 72 percent by 2020. Most of the old wastewater treatment plants were designed for less inflow than they now receive. Several also receive storm-water runoff, which, when combined with an under-capacity plant, causes "hydrological overloading": both treated and untreated sewage may be flushed into the river during heavy storms. Again Maynard is a case in point: The old plant was originally designed to handle 1.3 million gallons per day but had to cope with inflows of from 3 to 3.5 mgpd, and during storms, 5 mgpd, far exceeding the plant's design parameters.

If even untreated sewage is piped into fast-flowing water there is some opportunity for the river to cleanse itself. On the Assabet, however, since wastewater treatment plants empty into the river in either slow or still water shortly upstream from dams, the river has no chance to purify itself. Water in the Assabet is consequently considered almost totally "unsatisfactory" by the Massachusetts Division of Water Pollution Control. It is not worse only because there are no wastewater treatment plants on the river's tributaries, whose inflow improves the Assabet's quality, and because some aeration occurs as its waters splash over its dams. And though all the wastewater treatment plants along the Assabet are in the process of (and some have already accomplished) upgrading their facilities, their discharges, since phosphorus and nitrogen are not to be removed, will continue to create overenriched conditions on the river.

I think of all this as I stand by the Powder Mill Dam looking upstream at the twenty-five acres of flat water that stretch out into an impoundment half a mile long, widening the river to six hundred feet. Somewhere in that unsavory soup, the effluent from the Maynard wastewater treatment plant enters the river.

The ignorance of most of us regarding a primary necessity of urban life is one of the factors that makes it difficult to secure proper public policy in the matter of wastewater treatment. To see a good plant in operation is a real eye-opener, and it is with this in mind that Barbara Mudd, president of the SuAsCo Watershed Association, and Elsie Kennedy, who owns and runs a summer swimming club on a pond tributary to the Assabet, and I have descended on the Maynard WTP. The manager, Don Chisholm, is a young man of enthusiasm who likes his job, takes pride in a well-run plant, and is articulate about explaining its workings.

We stand on the walkway of the primary settling tank, a 45-foot diameter tank holding 95,000 gallons of screened wastewater. Influent is 99 percent water, and screening removes trash and debris, old shoes, what have you, before the water enters the tank. A scraper arm, like a boom, rotates slowly, scraping floating scum off the surface of the water and depositing it at an outlet. The effluent from this primary treatment is pumped through a grit chamber and allowed to stand. The dense suspended grit settles by gravity; fine solids, oils and grease, rise to the top as floc or scum; heavier matter (mostly organic) sinks to the bottom as sludge.

The Maynard WTP uses activated sludge treatment in the secondary stage, which takes out biologically removable contaminants. As we walk toward the two forty-by-forty-foot cement tanks, the roar of the pumps becomes deafening. In the center of each tank a huge pump is suspended, powering spinning impeller blades that spray the water out almost horizontally, such is the force required to aerate the tank's contents, consisting of biologically active sludge, raw sewage from the primary stage, and water.

"Look at that color!" Don Chisholm exclaims with admiration. "It's perfect!" To me the water just looks dull tan, but to Chisholm's practiced eye it indicates proper action is occurring.

In activated sludge treatment, microbes, their growth stimulated by the oxygen in the aerated "water," feed upon the sewage. The rapid turnover of waste is time and space efficient, but close monitoring is needed to control the amounts of air and the length of aeration time. At Maynard, samples are constantly taken: on a slide under the microscope there are blurred tan particles of floc among which flagellates pulse and dart, activated by the heat of the microscope lamp. A rotifer goes wheeling out of the field.

182

These and trillions more of their ilk dwell in the tanks.

Water from the activated sludge treatment next enters two clarifiers, tanks of the same size as the primary settling tanks. Most important, the sludge, once fed into the river, is now trucked out by a private concern. As we walk down the slope to the two clarifying tanks, the three of us remark that the somewhat acrid odors, while not what one could call Chanel No. 5, are nevertheless not as strongly offensive as we had expected.

From the clarifiers the water works through chlorination tanks—open rectangular cement vats with baffles that force the water to take a longer path through the tanks and thus be further aerated—and thence into the river. At the entrance of the tanks there are white pods of foam from phosphates, mostly from detergents ("biodegradable" on the package does not mean that a detergent contains no phosphates, only that the chemicals it contains break down in water).

To remove phosphorus from sewage, tertiary treatment is needed. It produces a high-quality effluent but with concomitantly higher costs, about three times higher than primary treatment. The economics of sewage treatment is the economics of all pollution control: the first increments are relatively inexpensive, but as more complete removal is attained, costs rise almost geometrically. Consequently, there are no tertiary treatment plants planned for the Assabet, and if phosphates are to be kept out of the river system—and the algal blooms they cause eliminated—it will have to be done at the source. For instance, were phosphates eliminated from laundry and dishwashing detergents alone, there would be a 50 percent reduction in the amounts passing through wastewater treatment plants.

From the bottom of the clarifier a small clear stream emerges. We follow it down through the woods at the edge of the river, out onto the sludge apron deposited before 1975; the sludge is springy underfoot, friable, odorless, almost black in color. Very little grows on it since it is usually covered by water (the river is low just now), and because of the heavy metals it contains.

As with all the wastewater treatment plants on the Assabet, improvements are planned here. Plans are for a containment dike which will block off the previously deposited sludge from the river; gravel, three meters thick, will be laid on top to form an impervious layer. In addition, a new runoff pipe from the WTP will be extended to well below the Powder Mill Dam, dropping the treated effluent into a swifter-flowing portion of the river. But for now, the effluent from the WTP corkscrews a little channel a foot or so deep through the apron of sludge upon which we stand, then runs clear over a gravelly bed and disappears into the duck-weed- and scum-covered Assabet. It strikes me as ironic that at this moment the effluent stream is in infinitely better shape than the segment of the river into which it flows.

9

𝓔𝓦𝓙   On a day in late July, the flow of the stream had carried Ann and me unawares over an invisible boundary. Wayland now lay behind us. We had entered Concord. Downstream, Lee's Bridge was mirrored, inverted in the water.

With its two arches of gray stone, one large, one small, Lee's Bridge lifts and carries the South Great Road across the Sudbury River close to Nine-Acre Corner. The bridge is said to have been built according to the specifications of Charles Francis Adams, Sr., who lived in Lincoln, and was a man of wealth and power. Purportedly, Adams agreed to defray the whole expense of building the bridge if the commissioners would pattern it after a famous bridge across the Arno—with a big arch on the Lincoln end and a little bit of an arch on the Concord end.

On either side of the brown river the water was bordered by twin bands of brilliant color, gaudy magenta stripes of wildflowers by the thousand, caught in the water mirror, their stiff, wand-like stems, often four or five feet high, capped as though by large floral torches. To the right, beyond the western bank, the purple tide rolled inland across forty or fifty acres. In an almost unbroken sheet of color, it extended as far as Bound Rock, the glacial boulder where an iron rod implanted in the granite marks the exact meeting point of the boundaries of four towns—Wayland, Lincoln, Concord and Maynard.

We swung toward the western edge of the stream. Three

hard thrusts of our paddles carried us through the band of reflected color and drove the bow of the canoe slicing upward among the matted roots of the forward line of the blooming plants. Climbing out, we pulled the canoe higher up on the land. Then we looked around us. We were standing in a floral jungle, a lush bee pasture where the humming of the insects was the dominant sound.

For centuries where we stood the wild hay of the river meadow, rising dense and high, had dominated the land. Now all the native grasses, almost all of the herbaceous plants that had succeeded them, were gone. In a swift spread, an invading plant, a runaway species from abroad, the purple or spiked loosestrife, had dispossessed indigenous types that over a vast period of time had been adjusting themselves to the conditions of their habitat. We were in the midst of a dramatic botanical takeover. It was all the more dramatic because, according to Richard J. Eaton's *A Flora of Concord*, the first purple loosestrife had been recorded in Concord hardly more than twenty years before—1958.

Now stems beyond counting, flowers unnumbered, producing seeds beyond imagining, the loosestrife spread away. While Ann got out her sketching pad and pencils and became absorbed in recording, in delicate and accurate delineations, the unusual formation of the flowers, I roamed widely, enclosed, pushing my way through the dense stands, walled in by stems almost as high as and sometimes higher than my head. In this country, purple loosestrife, on occasion, attains a height of seven feet.

The first purple loosestrife to reach America arrived sometime before 1860, introduced from Europe, where it is widely distributed and has a long recorded history. There the plant is known by such various names as red sally, purple grass, willow weed, soldiers, killweed, spiked willow herb, rainbow weed and wand loosestrife. Describing Ophelia's tragic death in *Hamlet*, Shakespeare wrote:

> There with fantastic garlands did she come
> Of crow-flowers, nettles, daisies, and long purples

More than nineteen hundred years ago, Dioscorides, the Greek medical man who served in Nero's Roman army and whose *Materia Medica*, describing the medicinal properties of nearly six hundred plants, was widely used all through the Middle Ages,

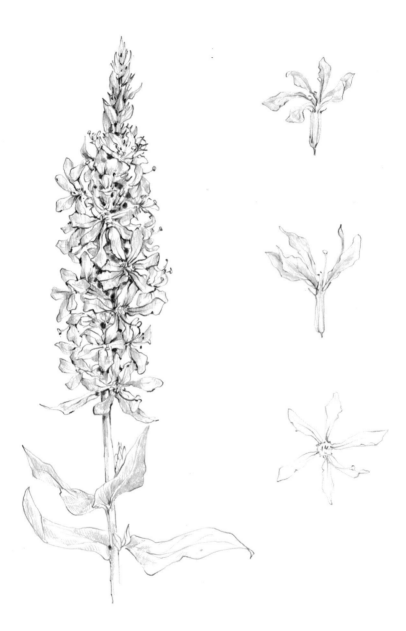

Purple loosestrife (*Lythrum salicaria*)

bestowed the name *lytron* on the purple loosestrife he found growing in the river meadows. The name signified gore or blood flowing from a wound, a reference to the purple-red of the flowers, and has been changed to *Lythrum* in the present scientific name: *Lythrum salicaria*. The specific name, *salicaria*, is derived from the willow-like shape of the stemless leaves. Even the plant's common name, loosestrife, goes far back into ancient times. It had its origin in a mistranslation of *Lysimachos*, a plant named by Greek and Roman authors in honor of Lysimachos, the Greek king, and his successful efforts to "loose"—that is, dissolve or end—strife.

In the years since the initial purple loosestrife bloomed in the New World, the plant has expanded its range until it is now found as far north as Newfoundland, as far south as Virginia, Ohio and Missouri, and as far west as Minnesota. It has invaded western portions of the state of Washington and has been reported in Australia. Some years ago, at an agricultural experiment station in Morden, western Canada, a flower for gardens with large and showy pink blooms was developed from the purple loosestrife. It is known as Morden's Pink.

When I looked around me among the tens of thousands of waving wands, I could see the tops of two or three low willows. They were widely spaced and were my landmarks. Without them, I had the feeling, I could get lost in this magenta jungle. At long intervals I came upon an isolated arrowhead or a clump of smartweed still holding its own amid the engulfing loosestrife, but the soft-stemmed herbaceous plants such as the jewelweed are quickly dispossessed by the aggressive newcomer; only the buttonbush, the bur reed and the broad-leaved cattail, all of which have submerged roots, were thriving along the riverside edge of the purple meadow. Old inhabitants of the area with whom I talked at various times remembered the other wildflowers, particularly the brilliant cardinal flowers, that used to be—but are no longer—a feature of every summer here.

While the loosestrife is limited to areas that are no more than a few feet above the water table, it occupies only dry land, and thus it is that at certain places along the river, as one drifts downstream on midsummer days, one can see along the shore triple bands of color—three different kinds of blooming plants, each occupying its own particular habitat. First, farthest out from shore, runs a band of striking blue, the color of the pickerelweed. Behind it extends a parallel line of white where the water smartweed is in flower, and rising beyond that the wall of the loosestrife flaunting its purple-red.

When I returned for a moment to the canoe, I found Ann still engrossed in drawing details of the flowers. It was such details that fascinated Charles Darwin more than a century ago when he studied the difference in the floral forms of the purple loosestrife, the trimorphism that is inherent in this plant. Its flowers are of three kinds, each growing on a different plant, with styles and stamens of different lengths. One type of bloom with long styles has six medium-length stamens and six short stamens. A second has a medium-length style with six stamens longer than the style, six shorter. The third has short styles with six stamens very long and six stamens of medium length but longer than the style. The color of the pollen also varies, being greenish on the longest of the stamens and pure gold on the other two.

In his experiments, Darwin demonstrated that the pollen from one length of stamen is most effective when carried to a style of similar length. This arrangement, it is believed, increases the efficiency of cross-fertilization, which is carried out entirely by insects: nectar gatherers of various sizes carry the pollen to styles of different lengths. Wherever I went I saw the work of pollen transportation going on around me, and the drone of the black-abdomened bumblebees, the lighter murmuring of the banded honeybees, were with me. The honey made from the nectar of the loosestrife is very dark, the hue of dark brown sugar, but it is rated high both in taste and in sweetness. [Here two competing bumblebees, one closely pursuing the other, whirl around a flower head. Over and over the blur of the wings, the sudden stop, the hurried feeding, the blur again as a bumblebee hoists itself in an aerial jump to the next of the ascending flowers. Climbing a ladder of air!]

Often the honeybees and the bumblebees worked over the flowers almost side by side. And all the while large dragonflies hawked overhead or alighted to ride on the tall wands swaying in the breeze. A small amber-winged dragonfly settled on my shoulder, riding along, basking in the sun. Once I came to a little glade among the loosestrife where half a dozen of the brilliantly red *Sympetrum* dragonflies whirled about in a harvest of minute aerial insects.

Other insects were quiescent. Small ladybird beetles, on that day, were especially numerous. I saw them most often clinging unmoving, head downward, on the stems of the loosestrife. In one place an immature green striped grasshopper had anchored itself to one of the willow-formed leaves, and in another a beautiful creamy white and yellow moth rested on a stem, its wings closed, appearing to be wearing a collar of immaculate white fur. While most of the nectar was being gathered by the bees, other winged creatures, flies and butterflies, shared in the harvest. In one memorable tableau, spotlighted by the noonday sun, a graceful tiger swallowtail butterfly swept down, fluttered for an instant and alighted on a mass of magenta blooms, unrolled its coiled tongue and dabbed it quickly into flower after flower.

At times when I stood still, I could catch the steely sound of small crickets, fragments of a song sparrow's song and the quick "Per-chicory" of goldfinches passing overhead. But when I was in motion, these and all other sounds except one were lost. This was the loud crunching of my feet on the flood wrack, the dry thick carpet of the fallen stems of the loosestrife of another year. The high water of spring had combed them out in parallel lines. Wandering and crisscrossing, dividing and coming together again, what seemed to be animal trails ran in a maze across this carpet of dead stems. But when I looked closely, I saw no evidence of animal travel. Rather the trails were those left by channels of running water, concentrated by the uneven, hummocky nature of the muckland.

Surrounded by a sea of blooming loosestrife, pushing my way among the stems, sending down in my jarring progress a shower of tiny petals so that I advanced as through a fine steady fall of magenta rain, I became aware of a sense of something missing. What was it? Almost a total absense of perfume! Where the air should have been filled with the overpowering fragrance of a million flowers, it was the rank, swampy smell of the river muck that predominated. The main impression made by the loosestrife was one of color, an impression on the eye.

How was it possible for a newcomer, an invader from another continent, to establish itself in so short a time, to take over as completely as the purple loosestrife has taken over throughout these acres?

Several factors seem to be involved. First, of course, is the removal of the plant from the limiting features of its former life: In being transported to a new continent, the loosestrife left behind many of its normal parasites and competitors. Possibly even more important was the fact that in the new land, the plant found a niche it was perfectly fitted to fill. No long period of adjustment was necessary. As Henry A. Gleason and Arthur Cronquist, in speaking of such runaway plants in general in their *The Natural Geography of Plants,* put it: "These plants did not have to wait for changes in the environment before they could arrive."

A letter from Thomas Rawinski, a graduate research assistant at Cornell University who is studying the ecology and management of purple loosestrife, suggests one source of that perfectly fitted environment. Like many other introduced plants, loosestrife thrives where there are disrupted habitats. The plant was in this country before 1850, but it really expanded its range toward the end of the nineteenth century, Rawinski believes as a result of the accelerated development of our waterways for industry and transportation.

The purple loosestrife had other powerful aids in its conquest. A hardy, long-lived, aggressive perennial, it grows rapidly and blooms swiftly. In experiments, loosestrife plants mowed in June resprouted vigorously from roots and stubble and produced flowers within forty-six days. If a low-cut stem is placed vertically in water, it will sprout a new root system, continue its growth and produce flowers. If the stem falls horizontally on water, the leafy portion of the plant will die but the swollen stem will send out new shoots and roots. When a broken stem falls and lies outstretched on muck soil, it sprouts new leaves from the leaf internodes. In fact, all portions of the purple loosestrife rootstock will sprout as long as sufficient moisture is available.

Careful counts have revealed that a flourishing loosestrife plant may lift as many as 2,350 or 3,000 individual flowers in the massed floral spire at the top of its stem. Each fertilized bloom produces a minute seed pod about four millimeters long. Within it are packed approximately 100 tiny seeds. Potentially, a single plant could be the source of as many as 300,000 seeds. Studies of pure stands of purple loosestrife show they may contain 80,000 stalks per acre. This would make approximately four million stalks in the fifty acres of the purple meadow in which I stood. If each stalk in a dense stand reached maximum seed production, the result would be 24 billion seeds to the acre. Of course only a small fraction of this potential is realized; but even so, the number of seeds produced is astronomical.

In his classic *The Dispersal of Plants Throughout the World*, Henry N. Ridley points out a curious feature of these seeds. Although they are produced by a plant essentially riparian and distributed largely by flowing water, they are, at first, not buoyant. At the Royal Botanic Gardens at Kew, in England, the author noticed that they sank immediately. However, he found that they germinated under water in a few days, floated to the surface and were dispersed as tiny seedlings. In another way, an aerial way, swifter and covering greater distances, the spread of the plant has hastened. In mud adhering to the feet or bills or feathers of birds, the minute seeds were carried far and deposited in new locations. Thus the flood of color surrounding me had flowed down the Sudbury or had leaped ahead with flying birds, to overrun lowland acres where for so many years the grasses of river meadows had fallen before the mower's scythe.

Bending down, I grasped one of the stems close to the base and, after considerable tugging, dragged the roots from the ground. The stem was stiff and strong, swollen for an inch or so above the base. The roots extended out, close-packed and wiry. The loosestrife has no taproot. But the shallow, horizontal roots of a stand of these plants interlace into a tough, dense mat overlying the floodplain.

So far as I could see, nothing was eating the loosestrife. No birds have been recorded consuming the seeds. Even muskrats avoid the stiff stems as building material when they are constructing their houses after the first frosts of fall. And though the dense stands prevent erosion and provide cover for wildlife and nesting sites, the invader is replacing valuable food plants, subtracting from the carrying capacity of the wildlife refuge. For this reason various experiments have been conducted to find ways of eliminating or controlling the spread of the plant.

One day, at the headquarters of the Great Meadows National Wildlife Refuge, I worked my way through a bulging folder of reports on the results of such experiments. The sum total of the information gained by the research seemed to be that it can't be done. The report concluded that "cutting even at frequent intervals does not appear to offer a solution in our situation where water-borne seed is continually being deposited from the extensive loosestrife infestations upstream." It ends: "Because of the inefficiency of cutting and pulling, it is recommended that this study be terminated."

When I pushed out to the riverbank again at the end of my third wandering loop of exploration, I found myself upstream from the canoe. Ann had finished her drawings and had packed away her pad and pencils. For a time we sat beside the river eating our noonday sandwiches, noting upstream the lines and patches of arresting color that marked the sites of other conquests of the loosestrife.

What exactly was the color we were seeing? Wildflower guides I have consulted seem oddly undecided. Norman C. Fassett's *A Manual of Aquatic Plants* names it "purple." F. Schuyler Mathews, in his *Field Book of American Wild Flowers,* calls it "purple-magenta." Mrs. William Starr Dana, in *How to Know the Wild Flowers,* declares it is "deep purple-pink," Harold William Rickette, in *The Odyssey Book of Wildflowers,* refers to it as "purplish-red"; Roger Tory Peterson, in *A Field Guide to Wildflowers,* terms it "magenta." Ann, with her artist's eye, agrees.

But magenta, like many other names of colors, brings no precise mental image to the mind of the average person. Thoreau, on a January day in 1852, wrote in his *Journal:* "It is remarkable that no pains is taken to teach children to distinguish colors. I am myself uncertain about the names of many." A course that, so far as I know, has never been offered by any educational institution is one in sensory awareness, offering training in the recognition of colors, the distinguishing of subtle variations in sounds, a refinement of appreciation of delicate scents and fragrances, the enjoyment of touch, the tactile sense. Such a course in sounds and scents and colors and the feel of things would enrich the days of students in a way that would continue through a lifetime.

At last we loaded the canoe and pushed out into the unhurried flow of the stream. We passed under the larger of the two arches of Lee's Bridge and looking back saw for a moment the whole expanse of the loosestrife meadow framed by its curve.

[When I drive past the great field of loosestrife a few days later, I find it dulled. The glory gone. The brilliant color tarnished as though a rust had run across it. In so short a time.]

AHZ   The Powder Mill Dam, but a few feet beyond the footbridge spanning the Assabet below the Maynard WTP, was constructed originally around 1835 by Nathan Pratt, whose powder mill lay in a hollow on the east side of the river. The manufacture of powder was rare in New England, and Pratt's factory was the only one in the area. (Early attempts to manufacture gunpowder in America were not successful, and not until 1675 was it produced in this country at all; stores of powder were one of the most carefully guarded commodities in the Revolutionary War.) By the middle of the nineteenth century it was known as the American Powder Mills, and the Assabet's flow was determined by the requirements of its operation.

The gates of the dam were closed on Saturday night to allow the millpond to fill up again for the week's usage, with the result that the river below the dam was reduced to a mere trickle.

> So completely emasculated and demoralized is our river [wrote Thoreau] that it is even made to observe the Christian Sabbath, and Hosmer tells me that at this season on a Sunday morning (for then the river runs lowest, owing to the factory and mill gates being shut above) little gravelly islands begin to peep out in the channel below. Not only the operatives make the Sunday a day of rest, but the river too, to some extent, so that the very fishes feel the influence (or want of *influence*) of man's religion. The very rivers run with fuller streams on Monday.

The effects were felt up into the Sudbury River and down the Concord, according to an 1860 report.

Powder manufacturing began with cotton being impregnated with nitric acid in a process in which dryness must be assured, since moisture causes explosions. Then the cotton was ground into a powder; at this stage it had to be kept damp since a spark from the grinding wheels could cause it to flash. Accidents were frequent, needless to say. The buildings were constructed with extremely sturdy frames and very lightweight siding so that the walls could blow out easily but the basic structure would remain intact.

Thoreau described the site in his *Journal:*

194

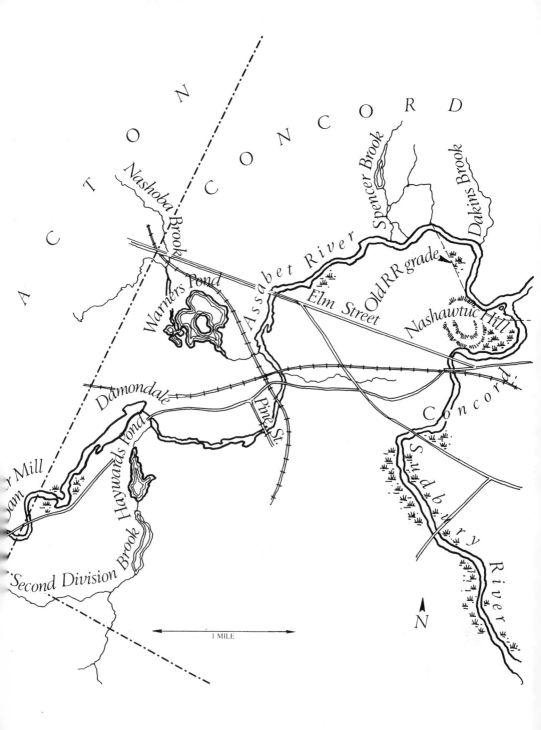

A C T O N

C O N C O R D

Nashoba Brook

Spencer Brook

Dakins Brook

Assabet River

Warners Pond

Old RR grade

Elm Street

Nashawtuc Hill

Damondale

Pine St.

Concord

r Mill

am

Haywards Pond

Sudbury River

Second Division Brook

1 MILE

N

> As you draw near the powder-mills, you see the hill behind
> bestrewn with the fragments of mills which have been blown
> up in past years, —the fragments of the millers having been
> removed, —and the canal is cluttered with the larger ruins.
> The very river makes greater haste past the dry-house, as it
> were for fear of accidents.

The most severe explosions occurred in 1895, when five men were
killed, and in 1915. People here still remember that one, which
was felt for a radius of fifty miles, cracked ceilings and broke windows.

After the powder was ground, the particles were glazed so
that the grains remained separate and therefore pourable. The ad-
monition "Keep your powder dry" referred to the fact that when
damp it would cake and couldn't be poured.

Powder production for the Civil War was exceedingly profitable, and the American Powder Mills paid hefty dividends to its
shareholders until after World War I, when the company went
bankrupt. During World War II the property was owned by
American Cyanamid, which manufactured flashless powder there.
After that war the factory went out of business for good, and
nothing of it now remains but some questionable debris.

The present dam was completed in 1921 for recreation pur-
poses, rebuilt over the original 1880s granite blocks, which were
about six feet high. In 1923, ten-by-ten-inch timbers were added,
forming a cribbed barrier that raised the height of the dam for
power generation. An average of 295,000 kilowatt-hours per year
were generated, and the electricity sold to Boston Edison for $100 a
month. Up into the 1960s the dam was intact, but since then all
kinds of debris—logs, tree trunks, the ubiquitous plastic bottles—
have snagged on the lip, gradually raising the level of the impoundment. The timbers are rotted and water goes through rather
than over. The abutments on both sides leak. The slide gates are
inoperable. The gatehouse's gearing mechanisms are missing parts
and those that remain are rusted useless. The turbine too is frozen
with rust, and its housing vandalized until all that's left is what
couldn't be carried away. Boston Edison reexamined the site in
1978 and estimated that there was a potential capacity of 756,000
kwh per year, but decided that restoration and construction costs
rendered it uneconomical.

Actually this whole stretch of the Assabet has a rather dour

196

history. Here on the footbridge, I pace where the CM&H tracks once ran. Late one Sunday night in November of 1904, George Nelson drifted off to sleep as he was driving his horse and wagon home. His leaderless animal meandered onto the tracks and its hooves caught between the ties. The horse's jerking awoke Nelson, but as he was trying to extricate the animal, the CM&H trolley, bound for Hudson, came whizzing around the corner. Nelson was killed instantly.

From here the river has a run of a little over a mile to its next and last dam, at Damondale. Where the river curves eastward a foundry was established, the second bog-iron smelter in America.

John Josselyn, who was busy selling the virtues of the new country in *New England's Rarities Discovered* in 1672, characterized New England's bog iron ore as being "in abundance, as good bog iron as any in the world"; it was a godsend to settlers who otherwise would have had to import many necessities at considerable cost. Rich deposits (of which the Assabet's was not one) could yield three hundred tons a year, but it was essentially a nonrenewable resource: although bog iron forms rather quickly, it can never reappear in the quantities that centuries of deposition provided for the first colonists.

Deposits along the Assabet were worked as early as 1658. By 1660 the "Iron Farm," a branch of the larger Saugus Iron Works, was established and must have been fairly extensive: a dam, ponds, gate and channel, gears, hammer, several buildings and equipment, forge and furnaces covered 1,668 acres on the south side of the river, nearly three square miles. The town of Concord encouraged the business by granting land for workers' houses and a special permit in 1670 to one Michael Wood "to sell strong liquors to the labourers about the ironworks . . . for their necessary releefe and to no others."

Enormous quantities of wood were needed for the manufacture of charcoal for use in the pudding furnace where ore was processed; along with the bog-iron ore, the seemingly inexhaustible New England forest was the other necessary asset for iron production. In March 1650, the English Parliament ordered all the flourishing ironworks in the Forest of Dean in Gloucestershire to be closed because their rapacious need for charcoal was decimating the historic woodland. John Evelyn, writing in *Sylva*, felt that

" 'Twere better to purchase all our iron out of America than thus to exhaust our woods at home."

The furnace that devoured so much charcoal was a huge stone truncated pyramid, up to forty feet high, with a bottle-shaped interior, opening at the top. A charge of ore, charcoal and flux (which removed impurities from the ore—in Colonial days ground-up seashells often provided the necessary lime) was shoveled inside. A crucible at the bottom caught the molten metal as it flowed downward. The furnace was tapped twice a day to skim off the slag that floated to the top of the crucible and to let the molten iron run out into molds, often simply channels dug in the ground, where it cooled into bars. Finally, forges further refined and improved it, and it was shipped down the Assabet by boat.

After 1685 the ironworks on the Assabet declined, probably as a result of declining ore supplies; the buildings were left unrepaired, workers' houses falling down. Finally abandoned, they have left no trace. The iron works themselves moved westward to Acton and became the foundation for the first settlement there.

Jonathan Herrick and Lot Conant bought the land where the ironworks had been for a farm and gristmill around 1714, and later established a fulling mill. Herrick sold his share to Conant, who deeded it to his son, who ran both farm and mill until the end of the eighteenth century.

Roger Brown bought four acres of the old ironworks property and installed a fulling mill. Tradition (probably apocryphal) says that on April 19, 1775, workmen enlarging Brown's house were interrupted by the news from Concord and work was not resumed until after the war, but according to records, Brown didn't build his house until 1776. His son, John, further developed the fulling mill in partnership with his cousin and they built the first cotton mill on the Assabet (and in the Commonwealth) in 1805—five stories high, one hundred feet long, with a tower facing the road. The development of a factory village followed, with tenements built on the south shore of the Assabet.

In 1824 John Brown sold the whole complex to Caleb Bellows, by which time, an inventory indicates, all the weaving processes there, including finishing, were done under one roof. Because mills were built where waterpower was available, not necessarily where the work force was, early mills offered inducements to secure adequate labor. Wages were high enough to attract good help and mill life had its attractions, in spite of the long hours. There was a closer relationship between employer and employees in such small mills than the larger mills ever knew—for instance, Brown established the first library in the area for his workers. By the 1830s young women working at the mills lived in dormitories provided by their employer. Their leisure hours, what there were of them, were watched over by the company, with emphasis on moral and intellectual life. Nevertheless, accounts of mill girls reciting poetry to the "music of the shuttle" presents an overly romantic picture; hours were long, sanitary conditions not the best, and the life a confined one.

There was help available, if needed, from the ladies of Concord, just downstream. The Concord Female Charitable Society was formed in 1814 for "relieving distress, encouraging industry, and promoting virtue and happiness among the female part of the community." The ladies quickly focused on the new mill "started in the west part of town by John Brown of Framingham, where cotton could be woven."

The mill passed into the hands of Calvin Damon (hence the "Damondale") in 1835, when business was again faltering. Damon did a simple thing: he raised the height of the milldam sixteen inches and installed a larger and more efficient waterwheel. He put in stonework, which remains today along the tailrace and riverbank to contain erosion. A consequence of the increased efficiency was a profit previous owners had not enjoyed; by 1837 he was able to process four times as much cloth as they.

Damon taught his son Edward the business from the ground up. When he was not in school he worked in the mill and in January 1850 wrote:

> I work in the cotton room tending drawing. It is very clean work for the factory. I go to work at seven and work half an hour, then half an hour for breakfast, then work again from eight o'clock and work until half-past twelve. Commence again at one o'clock and work until half-past seven. I like it very well.

If he was paid the same wages as other child card-tenders, he took home $2.50 a week. He took over the mill from his father when he

199

was seventeen, and in 1859 hired Henry Thoreau to check the boundary lines and building placement. Besides surveying, the surveyor noted all that went on around the mill:

> *May 6.* Surveying for [Samuel E., a Damon partner] Willis & Damon at the factory. Hear the *tea-lee* of the white-throat sparrow. It is suddenly very warm and oppressive, especially in the woods with thick clothing. *Viola pedata* begins to be common about white pine woods there. . . .
>
> *May 8.* While surveying this forenoon behind Willis's house on the shore of the mill-pond, I saw remarkable swarms of that little fuzzy gnat *(Tipulidae).* Hot as it was, —oppressively so, — they were collected in the hollows in the meadow, apparently to be out of the way of the little breeze that there was, and in many such places in the meadow, within a rod of the water, the ground was perfectly concealed by them. Nay, much more than that. I saw one shallow hollow some three feet across which was completely filled with them, all in motion but resting one upon another, to the depth, as I found by measurement with a stick, of more than an inch, —a living mass of insect life. There were a hundred of these basins full of them, and I discovered that what I had mistaken for some black dye on the wet shore was the bodies of those that were drowned and washed up, blackening the shore in patches for many feet together like so much mud. We were also troubled by getting them into our mouths and throats and eyes.

Thoreau complained that his assistants, factory workers accustomed to sedentary work, were quite debilitated by the heat. Before going back to Walden Pond he bought a "black sucker" just freshly speared at the factory dam which proved very good eating (it was more likely, according to a Fish and Game specialist, to have been a white sucker, for this is the only species of sucker historically present and still common in the Assabet).

In 1862, the year of Thoreau's death, the wooden mill building he had surveyed burned to the ground. Damon replaced it with a brick mill, and added new housing as business prospered with Civil War orders. Eventually the mill became, in 1917, part of the American Woollen Company of Maynard and suffered the same fate. Today the complex of company stores and post office are gone, but the buildings are used by small businesses—a winery for one—and the dam, albeit breached, still stands.

Jewelweed or spotted touch-me-not (*Impatiens capensis*)

I walk out on the Damondale dam one day early in the fall. A big orange bee works the loosestrife; milkweed pods are green, not yet splitting; red clover and purple thistle, mullein, pale yarrow, light-pink phlox, touch-me-not—still summer in September, with but slight intimations of autumn. A white cabbage butterfly clings to a mustard stalk, abdomen bent, depositing eggs. Two dragonflies, patrolling, nearly bump into each other, break apart, and with a clatter of wings go about their separate business.

I sit, feet dangling, overlooking the breach in the dam. It was broken in the 1968 spring flood when during a three-day period a total of seven inches of rain dumped on eastern Massachusetts. Combining with an abnormally wet spring season and some snow runoff, the booming flow simply ate a chunk out of the dam on the right side, through which the water now pours in a narrow swift tongue. (When the dam was breached the impoundment behind it fell, exposing large areas of odoriferous muck, to the dismay of residents along the river. But within a season vegetation had come in, odors dissipated, and many residents found themselves in possession of some very fertile garden plots for free.)

As I sit here I also remember the water pounding through bank-high during the January 1979 flood, when Edwin, Nellie and I stood on the opposite bank. While we watched I saw a movement, and there was a disconsolate-looking muskrat, not ten feet away, wandering along the bank, back and forth, afraid to enter the fast water and so stressed that our presence was the least of its concerns.

From the dam I have a panoramic view of the old mill. The different colors of the bricks bespeak different clays, different firings, different building periods. Parts have been torn down, parts added, but a sense of the first brick building remains. Two or three rows of brickwork form a curving lintel above each window, though many of the windows are now rendered sightless—some neatly bricked but most shuttered by metal inserts. On the fourth story, only two-thirds of one window is shuttered and a glass pane is out. A white arrow points toward the hole, and painted beneath it are the words "SPARROW HAWK."

As I study the facade, three pigeons wheel overhead, as if conjured by Thoreau, who, when surveying here, noted: "I frequently see pigeons dashing about in small flocks, or three or four

202

"As I sit here I also remember the water pounding through bank-high during the January 1979 flood. . . ."

at a time, over the woods here. Theirs is a peculiarly swift, dashing flight."

The water slides down, black and shiny as obsidian, then wrinkles into creases as it spins around the corner. It pours over a flat rock near the surface, plaiting the attached algae into long streamers. Foam spills over the rock, spins and turns, elongates, shreds, is swallowed by the tiny backwave at the rocks' foot, and then coalesces into platter-sized disks, clustering in the back eddy. Yellow beech leaves tumble into the river at every breeze, landing in the current, sweeping through the breach, riding high, turning and spinning. And always that lovely sound which is like no other, for which there is no one word, a woof and warp of sound, shimmer and sunshine, rock, liquid and light weaving together.

And I see in my mind's eye a canoe, like a beech leaf, hurtling through the break in the Damondale dam on a slick tongue of water. Edwin has written: "Apparently I am accredited for canoeing on gray, green, brown, red or black water—any water except white water. So plans are swarming in my head. Exactly what dates will you and Herman be in Concord? Shall I bring along my Grumman canoe? Will you let me know, when you know, where you will begin and end your white-water run? I want to be sure of the bridges."

I canoe with Paul Huehmer, to whom canoeing the Assabet must be tame after negotiating the white water of the Androscoggin in Maine. Paul is seventeen, six feet tall, with dark hair and a big affable grin. His T-shirt reads "TRUST ME," which is very reassuring because I've seen the bridges we're going under as well as the Damondale Dam and I don't feel much at ease with those tricky currents.

Coming down from the Powder Mill Dam I have half a mile of apprehension. We kneel as the breach in the dam looms closer. Paul has advised me to take a hefty backstroke just before the first haystack in order to raise the bow. I do so just in time to get a washtubful of water right in my lap from the second haystack. We go through so quickly that it hardly seems done. What fun! What great fun!

We skim past the entrance of Second Division Brook, so called because it was in the parcel of land first added to the settlement of Concord—its "second division." The negotiations were evidently lengthy, for "Much weariness about these things" was recorded in town meeting minutes. George Hayward (after whom one of the ponds upstream is named) sold his lot in Concord Center and bought eleven acres here on the Assabet, and he and Lot Conant across the river worked the first farms. Hayward's farm included a peat bog that in later years Thoreau often wandered through and where he found the now rare polygala.

Hayward bought his land in 1669 for eleven pounds, "with the North River over against the forge, the river compasseth it on the North, east, and northeast, George Hayward's mill ditch on the south east, and a line betwixt it and Joseph Hayward's land." There was no bridge and crossings had to be made by boat. In 1671, on the way home from ferrying William Frisell across the river, Hayward drowned.

At one time the area was called Hatshop, because waterpower was used for hatmaking. Before 1800 a young Concord woman made pencils by hand, using elder twigs and removing the pitch with a knitting needle. She pounded the lead to a powder, mixed it with a solution of gum arabic or glue, and worked it into the tube. By 1812 pencils were manufactured on a commercial basis by William Munroe; a cabinetmaker by trade, he devised cedarwood cases by cutting cedar into slabs which were then planed by hand to about an eighth-inch thickness and grooved. The pasty lead was spread in the grooves, dried, then the second layer of cedar glued on top, making a slab of four to ten pencils which were then cut apart. Munroe added a water-powered saw that could cut six grooves at a time, followed by molding and trimming machines, also water-powered, and a press to hold the glued pencils. At one time Thoreau worked at the pencil factory.

The sun is high, the river is fresh, and I'm feeling very set up about running that dam as we go on downriver a mile or so to the Pine Street Bridge in West Concord, where we are to meet Herman, Nellie and Edwin, and end the trip. As we pull in, Herman suggests that since it is early and such a nice day, why don't we go a couple of miles farther downstream? Paul and I talk it over, and why not indeed?

Herman pushes the bow out with his foot and I take a massive backstroke on the starboard side, starting to ask, "Which arch shall we go under?" when I hear Paul say, "oh-*oh!*" and we're in the river.

I have no time to think, only to grab the canoe and get on

the upstream side. We float under the bridge, both of us laughing. (Paul remarked later, in case I was interested, that we took the left arch.) My first thought, after wondering what on earth happened, is to keep my mouth closed and *not* to take a swallow of Assabet River water—which is *very* difficult to do when you're laughing so hard.

Slow as it may appear, the current is incredibly strong, implacable: in 1792 the Assabet was described as "remarkable for its current, which by the eye is scarcely perceivable." It hasn't changed in two hundred years!

Fortunately the water is also surprisingly warm. People stop their cars on the bridge, come bounding down along the shore to help. How ignominious! We assure them we're O.K., still laughing, now slightly sheepishly.

Edwin arrives down the bank, then Herman; both of them of course have been taking pictures as fast as they can snap them. Paul works toward the right bank and stands up. I get up a little farther, get my feet on the ground, haul myself out. We are soaked but somehow I didn't lose my glasses. Together we quick-flip the canoe, which is now spotless from a good washing. I haul out water-soaked seat pads and grab the paddles, which were all trapped beneath. We squish up the bank with sloshy sneaker steps.

What happened? Paul says that he took a big backstroke just as I did, also on the starboard side. There was enough water in the canoe, which is keelless, so that its weight, combined with both of us leaning suddenly to the right, simply rolled us over—an Eskimo roll done in the wrong craft at the wrong place at the wrong time. We shoot a tricky breached dam with no mishap, and then blow it in quiet water—with *lots* of witnesses, especially ones with cameras.

I later come across Edwin's account and have a brief fulfillment of Robert Burns's wish, seeing ourselves as others see us:

> We get to Pine Street and wait to help them with the canoe. Almost smooth water, only a swirl and a race under the bridge. They come in, Ann wet from water shipped at the dam. She persuades Paul to go on to the Elm Street Bridge at Route 2. They push out again, heading back upstream to curve downstream in the right position. Both paddle, logically, on the left side. As they get out in the middle, the current hits the up-

"Seem to be having such a good time I feel like jumping in the river too!"

stream side, the canoe heels over a little that way, the water in it sloshes to that side and heels it over still more, no one has a paddle on the upstream side to counteract the movement, and over they go. Capsized almost in still water! After running the plunging torrent of the dam!

They float downstream in a swift current. Everyone, or at least the two, laughing. A hilarious upset. Seem to be having such a good time I feel like jumping in the river too! Know not too much danger, as the current slows below the bridge. The water is not too cold. But I spring down a path to see if I can hold out a stick or in some way help them make shore. They are swimming, pushing the canoe toward the right bank. Get their footing and I help hold the canoe. Two other men, one with a rake, come to help but are unneeded. Paul empties water from canoe. They paddle across to other bank and we haul the canoe up the steep embankment to the road and get it over Paul's car. Ann gets in beside me in the front seat (and leaves a puddle on the floor that is still there the next day!). All is well!

I don't know about Paul, but *I* wouldn't have missed this unplanned baptism for the world. There's all kinds of ways to know a river, and this certainly is one of them. I find myself chuckling about it for weeks afterward.

I also know that Edwin's well-mannered Sudbury would never do such an outrageous thing.

10

EWJ The building of the bridges are epochs in the life of the river. As Ann and I went under the arch of Lee's Bridge, a running mesh of ripple reflections moved continually across the masonry on the upstream side, shimmering auroras of lines of light thrown up by sun on ripples. Seven half-grown mallards followed a female across the stream and among the buttonbushes as we paddled slowly toward them. Cicadas, in the heat of the day, were shrill in the willows. The bank was lined with double lines of lavender-blue, the massed pickerelweed in bloom and the mirrored image like the reflection and the reality of the loosestrife back upstream.

Following the extremely elongated capital S traced by the river as it approaches Fairhaven Bay, I had the sensation of a photographer watching the image of a print in a developing tray emerge and grow stronger moment by moment. The image was the image of Henry Thoreau. He had rowed and sailed his boat across Fairhaven a thousand times. He had skated over it in winter. He had walked to it through the woods from his hut beside Walden Pond.

"In all my rambles," he wrote in his *Journal*, "I have seen no landscape which can make me forget Fair Haven. I still sit on its Cliff in a new spring day, and look over the awakening woods and the river, and hear the new birds sing, with the same delight as ever."

Thoreau: "In all my rambles I have seen no landscape which can make me forget Fair Haven."

[Small apple trees in bloom at river's edge at the foot of Lee's Meadow. Hear song sparrows singing. Hardly a ripple now. We see the yellow-green clouds of the bankside willows reflected in the still water. Redwings call and cross the stream from willow to willow. Pole Brook comes in on left from Deacon Farrar's Pond beyond the Great South Road. Brook spread out. Push up a way among water smartweed and tangled underwater branches of the buttonbushes. Hear planes most of the time. Constant roar of traffic as it approaches Lee's Bridge. The plastic rings of a six-pack are lodged three feet up in the buttonbushes. Smoke-gray streaks and shoals of shed gnat skins. Blackflies zero in on Ann. A baby muskrat flounders off roots of buttonbushes ahead of us. A monarch butterfly drifts past overhead. A kingfisher flies up the stream, then down the stream, rattling.

[We head straight across Fairhaven Bay, down its length, the ripples spanking on the hull, echoing in the metal craft. Eleven thousand years ago, this widened portion of the Sudbury came into being when a gigantic block of buried ice, left behind by the glaciers, slowly melted away, creating a wide and deep depression. The debris covering it slumped down, leaving a kettle-shaped hole. The size of the buried ice cake determined the size of the hole. (Walden Pond occupies such a kettle hole.) Fairhaven Bay is about seventy acres in extent.

[Bay used to be famous fishing area. About nine years ago got many calls about fish kill here. Effluents brought dense algae, deoxygenation. Even catfish killed. Sudbury cleaner now. Pickerel caught in Fairhaven again. The best crop of fish produced by the Concord.

[Tupelo trees along the shore, with bluets at roots, along path to Wright house. The house and land are going to Concord as a preserve. Great crested flycatcher calls. . . . The little gully below the Wright house where Thoreau and Edward Hoar set fire to the woods. Kingbirds swoop over the glassy water. Tree trunks banded with gray lines—marking the spring's abnormally high water. A jet plane over low, its thunder drowning out all other sounds.

[Paddle up winding path into the buttonbush jungle of Well Meadow. Mourning doves fly over . . . drumming of woodpeckers. "Sweet-so-sweet" of a yellow warbler. Duckweed beginning among the buttonbushes. Dark water. Some bubbles appear drifting into Well Meadow from the bay—reverse current or is this the effect of a breeze that is beginning? I rock the canoe gently and waves sweep across the reflections among the buttonbushes. The "Okalee" of the redwings. The air is fresh—the air of the spring.

[All along this side of the river, the side toward Farrar Pond, is walled with the ramparts of the buttonbushes. We hear no fish snapping under the lily leaves. That may come later in the season? A cuckoo flies over us and alights for a moment, seen in silhouette, in a streamside willow. I catch a single low "Cuk!" Turtle trails run across mud of the shallows. We see a drifting film of swirling oil on the surface of the water from time to time. From motorboats or from drifting vegetation? Bubbles up from decay in the mud. Redwing blackbirds pour out of the buttonbushes with a loud chorus of *chuck*ings.

[Entering the bay again, search for what Thoreau called Purple Utricularia Bay. Seems overgrown. Thousands of buttonbushes are at the height of their blooming. They have a sweet perfume . . . tangled mangrove jungle-like branches close to the surface of the water. How deep water can these bushes root in? I get out my sounding line, which has knots at one-foot intervals, at several places in the general area where the purple utricularia once grew. Thoreau found this the deepest place at Fairhaven Bay—more than twenty-one feet deep. We find it nowhere more than four and a half feet deep.

[For a long time we remain, poked in among a dense expanse of white lilies. The sun has struck them; the blooms are open. We catch the intense perfume. While Ann makes sketches, I watch the events among the lily pads. The blooms appear to tremble in the breeze and to sway with every movement of the water. I see one full-blown flower upright and inverted—where its image is clear in the mirror of the dark water.

[I see elongated white petals scattered over the outspread pads—the petals of a disintegrated lily bloom. A small nymph, perhaps of one of the smaller damselflies, appears on the surface of a submerged lily leaf. When I turn over some of the submerged leaves, I find blobs of gelatinous material. Are they primitive amoeba-like creatures? No. When we examine them through the magnifying glass, we see they are the egg masses of some aquatic creature. All seem anchored along the stems and the veins of the leaves.

[A pleasant breeze. A perfect day. Dragonflies, mostly small amber ones, sweep back and forth and alight on the flat outspread leaves. Dragonfly Landing Fields. Little windows and serpentines have been eaten away in some of the lily leaves. Small damselflies, brilliant metallic blue at front and back, drift around us. One alights on my sleeve and basks in the sun.]

AHZ   The water lilies opened when the sun struck them this morning; they will close late this afternoon. Had it been cloudy we would not have gotten to see them at all. Thoreau sometimes found them still tightly closed long after the sun was up, the hooked tips of the petals caught fast at the top; with one touch of the oar blade he released them, and the flower sprang open. He cut some and brought them inside, where he placed them in a pan of water and noted that they opened and closed with the rhythm of the light until the stamens had all shed their pollen.

In fact, his descriptions of them opening were so lyrical that he even impressed a newcomer in Concord, Nathaniel Hawthorne, who wrote about them in *Mosses from an Old Manse:*

> The pond lily grows abundantly along the margin—that delicious flower, which, as Thoreau tells me, opens its virgin bosom

Fragrant water lily (*Nymphaea odorata*)

213

to the first sunlight and perfects its being through the magic of that genial kiss. He has beheld beds of them unfolding in due succession as the sunrise stole gradually from flower to flower—a sight not to be hoped for unless when a poet adjusts his inward eye to a proper focus with the outward organ.

That sequential opening is something Edwin and I planned to see, getting up before dawn, canoeing down the Concord River, to be there just as the flowers unfolded one by one. Sadly, we never did.

Water lilies, virtually destroyed by pollution, have now returned to grow all along the Assabet and the Sudbury, where there is a thick rich mucky soil in which to root, and quiet waters upon which the large leaves may rest undisturbed. Since they cannot grow in more than five feet of water, they are confined to shallows near the shore. To accommodate to varying water levels, the underwater stems are elastic; each stem has four large canals with smaller ones clustered about them through which air is transmitted to the rootstock encased in the oxygen-poor muck.

Just beneath the surface I can see the developing buds, and a few have risen to the top, almost ready to open but still firmly enclosed in four sepals. One opening flower is almost as big as a saucer, a spectacular creamy white against the dark background of water and leaves. Water lily petals are arranged in a spiral, the outer ones pure creamy white, transitioning to stamens as they progress toward the center, becoming more yellow-tinged at the tip and then finally pure golden stamen. Because of this, water lilies provide insight into plant morphology and how various flower parts may have developed from a common source, and further, what the earliest flowers may have been like. To paraphrase Blake, a history in a wildflower.

An early English herbal lists uses for them never dreamed of today:

> The White Lily has very large and thick dark green leaves lying on the water, sustained by long and thick foot-stalks, that arise from a great, thick, round, and long tuberous black root spongy or loose, with many knobs thereon, green on the outside but as white as snow within . . . encompassing a head with many yellow threads or thrums in the middle where, after they are past, stand round Poppy-like heads, full of broad oily and bitter seed . . . the leaves do cool all inflammations, both out-

214

ward and inward heat of agues; and so doth the flower also, either by the syrup or conserve . . .

Somehow I find it difficult to picture a Colonial housewife with a tableful of water lily flowers, making conserve; perhaps it is because in our day, they are so close to being rare that picking such a quantity seems sinful.

The practical foraging colonists also boiled the leaves for greens, used the roots as a soap substitute, and derived a brown dye from them. The round leaves are veritable apartment houses of small dwellers that take shelter, lay eggs, feed and browse on the underside. Most land plants bear their stomata, through which they breathe, on the protected undersurface of the leaf. Water lilies must bear them on the top side, set into a waxy surface upon which water beads and slides off. In fact, the repulsion of water is so strong that when I poke one under water with my paddle it immediately pops to the surface and is dry within the second.

While we are sitting quietly, nudged into the shore, a hunting osprey patrols overhead. As the osprey hangs over us, it seems dangled on a string, wing-angle changes imperceptible, head turning as if on a gimbal ring. We see this osprey—although of course we cannot be sure it is the same one, and if not, then there are several hunting the same reach of river—several times in our journeys here, and hear from others that there is a nesting pair at Fairhaven Bay and one at Heard Pond, a healthy sign indeed, for a decade ago they seemed on their way to disappearing from the East Coast.

Now, happily, the trend seems to be reversed, and the osprey are again hunting the rivers and shores. As Edwin once said, "Ann cheers for the predator—I tend to cheer for the prey." After I got used to the idea (it has a kind of "nice girls don't" connotation), I realized he's right, of course. There is something magnificent about that keenness of vision, the fleetness, the fierceness of eye and talon, the swift stoop. Sandpipers, twittering in a row, are charming and dear; a hunting osprey, solitary and intent, is nothing short of superb.

EWJ [Baker Farm. We cruise along the shore, stopping, turning in, moving out again. Clematis Brook. The fields that used to be open seem overgrown with small saplings. Bee Tree Hill.

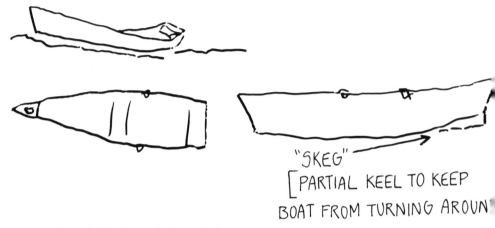

"SKEG"
[PARTIAL KEEL TO KEEP
BOAT FROM TURNING AROUN'

EWT's drawing of Thoreau's boat.

[Spanish Brook, dividing Well Meadow and Baker's Pleasant Meadow (woods). The sound of Spanish Brook falling in its course is a cool sound on a midsummer day. A blue jay calls. We paddle up Spanish Brook. Soon posted . . . Private Land. Massed sensitive ferns along the bank. The chipping of chipmunks.

[Interview with John Quincy Adams, who lives on Fairhaven Bay: I wondered what it would be like to be someone like John Quincy Adams and be *somebody* from the first breath to the last. If you did not disgrace a great name and did not dissipate a great fortune, your life could be considered a success. I asked many questions about Fairhaven Bay. His family has owned much of the east side for generations. When JQA was a small boy, about 1913, Fairhaven Bay was much as it had been in Thoreau's time.

[Adams thought Thoreau's boat must have been flat-bottomed, square-sterned, planked crosswise at the bottom. A dory or skiff, or most like, a catboat. Sometimes such boats were made with a single plank for each side. In the pointed bow, a triangular block, or heavy piece of plank, had a hole in the middle. This held the short mast for the sail, probably a simple leg-o'-mutton, triangular sail. It was not hoisted or furled. The mast was

216

thrust down into the hole in the triangular block and engaged at the bottom of the boat. When the wind died down, or at the end of time of sailing, the mast was just pulled out of the hole and the sail wrapped around it and it was stowed in the bottom of the boat.

[Such a boat had no keel. Flat-bottomed. But often had a partial keel—a "skeg"—at the front. Thoreau in *Journal* speaks of one boat so ill-made it kept turning around. The partial keel kept the boat headed forward.

[Walter Harding and I meet at six at the boathouse. We head upstream in the morning mist, the typical haze before the heat. Our goal is Fairhaven Bay and the island which I wish to explore.

[Under the railroad bridge, a female mallard rests beside a little island of black and brownish or yellowish ducklings huddled into a sleeping mass on the mud. A hundred yards beyond, on the same bank to our right, a young cottontail has come out of the purple loosestrife. It watches the canoe go by with its round baby stare. A silver morning. A silver river. See a waning moon and a rising red ball of a heat-wave sun. All along the way green herons on the mud, flying overhead, perching in trees, changing position. Goldfinches flashing among the riverside bushes. Kingbirds perching on dead tiptop twigs. The sun "comes up like thunder." When my hand dips into the stream I notice how warm the water is. Carp floundering at the river's edge. A mallard and four partly grown young start across the river ahead of us. They try to pass. Give up at the last moment.

[A tufted titmouse, a bird Thoreau never heard in Concord,* calls continually from woods along the eastern bank. Where a bittern is beside the river, a wood duck, female, comes squealing in to splash down only a few feet away. As the canoe draws near, the bittern takes off. A beautiful pale bird, the color of coffee with much rich cream in it. See bullfrogs several times, three or four with bright yellow throats—males—immobile at the water's edge.

[West of the island, through the lowland that separates it from the mainland, there is a wide straight channel, cut for boats. Clotted with green clumps of algae. A turtle and frog haven. The lowland is fringed in triplicate—a wide light-green band of water smartweed, then a wide brilliant band of blooming purple loose-

---

* The tufted titmouse has come north into New England only in the past decade or so.

strife, then the ragged band of the buttonbushes. Song sparrows sing beside the channel. A gray weathered nest in a buttonbush. A cecropia cocoon, a new one, in another buttonbush. Smell an unseen white water lily. A powerful, pervading, intensely sweet scent.

[We land on the southeast side of the island and began following its maze of paths. Mounds of sweet clethra in bloom. A white pine three feet in diameter. We see a long spearhead-like sliver of bark thrust point downward into moss and mold beneath an oak tree. It is eight to ten inches long. Hawks nest high in a slender oak. The lowland seems dense, impenetrable with swamp growths. Grapevine tangle at edge of island here. Large tupelo tree rises above vines.

[Thoreau (Vol. III, p. 176. January 5, 1852): "Sitting on the Cliffs, I see plainly for the first time that the island in Fair Haven is the triangular point of a hill cut off, and forty or fifty rods west, on the mainland, I see the still almost raw and shelving edge of the bank . . . as if the intermediate portion of the hill had sunk and left a cranberry meadow."

[(Vol. III, p. 292. February 9, 1852) "I find that the wood on the Island in Fair Haven Pond has been cut off this winter, but as the young [wood] and underwood is left, I am surprised to see so much witch-hazel there,—more than anywhere else that I know of. It shall be called Witch-Hazel Island."

[(Vol. VII, p. 26. September 8, 1854) ". . . he also called it 'Birch Island.' "

[This morning we find much witch hazel on the island but hardly any birch trees. One American chestnut at the far side of the island, near grape tangle. Somebody has hacked off a limb. A doomed tree, as fungi or blight can enter here. One great mound of sweet clethra twelve feet high. Covered with clots of snow, with the "steepled" flower heads. Find a shotgun shell or two on the island. One flat tombstone found here. A mystery. Inscription: "Ephraim Farrar. Died Jan. 1, 1818. Et. 72."

[On my eightieth birthday Nellie and I decide to make our planned paddle down the Sudbury from Fairhaven Bay to Bittern Cliff to have lunch, as we did together more than thirty years ago when I was getting pictures and material for my edition of *Walden*. With cheeseburgers and Coca-Colas (1979 junk fare), we arrive at the Sam Staples hunting camp.

[With the help of Steady Eddie, get canoe off myself and

launched. Nellie does some paddling in the bow. She wears life jacket because of her back. A stiff wind is sweeping across Fairhaven Bay from the southeast. We ride with it out of the bay and into the more protected Sudbury downstream.

[In July 1859, when Thoreau was surveying the river depth for the litigants in the suit against the Billerica mill owner for flooding the meadows, he found the water in one place off Bittern Cliff was 11 feet deep. This morning, letting down my weighted line with knots a foot apart, I find the following depths: On the opposite side of the river from the cliff: 4 feet. Other places nearer the middle: 6½ and 8½ feet. About a canoe-length and a half out from the cliff, say 20 feet, I record a depth of 10 feet. So little change in a century and a fifth.

[At the upstream side of Bittern Cliff, where the old spring used to be and may still be, we push the bow of the canoe up among sensitive ferns and purple loosestrife and skunk cabbage and eat our lunch, anchored in place by the lush vegetation. A titmouse calls from the cliff above us.]

AHZ The last few miles of the Assabet are its best known, having been written about by no less than Nathaniel Hawthorne, bathed in by Henry David Thoreau, strolled along by Emerson and Margaret Fuller, graced by Ellery Channing and commemorated by George Bartlett, enjoyed by William Brewster and Daniel Chester French, to name only the most famous. And it's easy to understand why: It is, without doubt, the most idyllic reach of the river.

One soft summer morning Edwin and I begin a river day in West Concord, passing under the railroad bridges and a main road bridge within half a mile of our starting point—but somehow the thick surrounding greenness pads the river and preserves it from noise in a way that open meadows and marshes do not. And perhaps it's the knowledge that there is only one more bridge and then open river.

Here the river takes a broad swing to the northwest, eroding the steep bank on the concave side of its meander. The Assabet once flowed where the railroad now goes, through a gap about three hundred feet east of its present course. When glacial retreat unlocked a lower passage farther north, the river shifted, to run as it now does.

The advent of the railroad in 1844 affected everyone: wagon

and stage traffic and all their support systems—inns, harnessmaking, etc.—declined. There was a sudden demand for wood: chestnut for ties, oak and maple for firewood and lumber. Thoreau found himself in demand because of owners' need to know the precise limits of their woodlots for what had suddenly become a very valuable commodity. And from this time dates the influx of businessmen, lawyers, and professors who began to live in Concord and commute to Boston. In 1895 seven trains a day ran back and forth, plus freights.

Within another half mile we pass under the Main Street Bridge, sending pigeons batting out from under the stone arch. Main Street was the Old Union Turnpike, built early in 1804 and going to within half a mile of Factory Village, as Damondale was then known. The Main Street Bridge was called the South Bridge to distinguish it from the more historic one to the north.

Ripple bugs dimple the surface of the water underneath the arch of the bridge. We had no idea what they were, and typically, almost as soon as I was home there was a letter from Edwin:

> Remember the concentrations of those small water insects we encountered on the Assabet? Once they were in such a dense heap they looked like the top of a dark rock projecting above the water. From the way they leaped, exploding in all directions when we approached, I suspected they were some form of small water strider. I checked with Dr. James A. Slater, the hemipterist at the University of Connecticut, and he pinned them down to the genus *Metrobates*. These tiny water striders are between three and five millimeters long. They usually are found near water rippling over stones. Their common name is *ripple bugs*. What we encountered was a mating concentration consisting mainly of adults but, Jim thinks, probably including some nymphs also. Both jump well. In the fall, when I go down to the New York Entomological Society meetings, I will find out all I can about ripple bugs.

As the water deepens, eelgrass streamers billow downstream. On the left bank herbs grow as high as my shoulder, shaded by magnificent oaks. A fresh morning breeze turns the maple leaves silver and waves the big ferns like green feathers. A redwing blackbird chirrs, a song I've come to love and associate with the Assabet—we are lucky if we have one pair on the pond at Constant Friendship. "And the blackbird plays but a boxwood

220

flute,/But I love him best of all," wrote W. E. Henley. Thoreau phoneticized it as *conquere* or *gurgle-ee* (which I think is rather better), which had "clearness and liquidity. They are officers epauletted; the others are rank and file."

A dinner-plate-sized shelf fungus on a dead tree is reflected in the water beneath; otherwise it would be hidden from view by the greenery. A helicopter beats over—it has always seemed to me that there is almost continual air traffic over these two rivers. Today it is less annoying than usual because of the masking sibilance of the leaves. Pondweed leaves flow alongside the canoe, each reflecting light from its varnished surface like a mirror. Catalpa blooms, like small white orchids, float at the edge of the river, swirling in a back eddy.

Fox grape vines festoon every available support; Edwin tells me that from this and another species, the famous Concord grape was developed. Hawthorne wrote of them along the Assabet:

> Grape vines here and there twine themselves around shrub and tree and hang their clusters over the water within reach of the boatman's hand. Oftentimes they unite two trees of alien race in an inextricable twine, marrying the hemlock and the maple against their will, and enriching them with a purple offspring of which neither is the parent. One of these ambitious parasites has climbed into the upper branches of a tall, white pine, and is still ascending from bough to bough, unsatisfied till it shall crown the tree's airy summit with a wreath of its broad foliage and a cluster of its grapes.

I shall always remember this morning as one of the most beautiful canoeing days that Edwin and I spent on the rivers, one of quiet harmony in nature as well as between friends. Everywhere pale-pink morning glories garland the streamside. A song sparrow, perched on a dead branch over the water, carols his version of "God's in his heaven, all's right with the world." He may only be declaiming his territory, nothing more, but to us, his listeners, there is a lilt of joy and summer.

The river fingers into a little backwater on the left, paved with luminescent white water lilies and sweet flag. A green, slightly weedy smell emanates from a thick syrup of waterweeds and duckweed, not an unpleasant smell, just a lush burgeoning smell that billows up on this warming June day, caught and confined.

221

Mingled in with the white are the smaller, rounder heads of yellow water lilies, which Hawthorne, in *Mosses from an Old Manse*, so maligned, making a very Victorian moral comparison between the purity of the white and the low character of the yellow:

> It is a marvel whence this perfect flower derives its loveliness and perfume, springing as it does from the black mud over which the river sleeps, and where lurk the slimy eel, and speckled frog, and the mud turtle, whom continual washing cannot cleanse. It is the very same black mud out of which the yellow lily sucks its obscene life and noisome odor. Thus we see, too, in the world that some persons assimilate only what is ugly and evil from the same moral circumstances which supply good and beautiful results—the fragrance of celestial flowers—to the daily life of others.

The inlet from Warners Pond in West Concord comes in on the left. A kettle pond studded with four islands and surrounded by a rich vegetation, it has been a recreation area for years. Carnivals and water sports and boat races were held at the end of the nineteenth century, and steamboat rides on the *Maude Blake* and picnics and summer camps.

In 1819, when he was not yet twenty, David Loring purchased the water rights on the pond and began the manufacture of lead pipe, later adding sheet lead. Since there was no rail transport to and from Boston, Loring's six-horse wagon was a familiar sight. He was one of the first promoters of the railroad—but after it arrived he had an argument over rates and from that date eschewed rail shipments.

The pond was named after Ralph Warner, who bought out Loring and converted the lead factory to a wooden-pail factory in 1857, employing thirty men and consuming seven hundred cords of wood a year; Thoreau reported floating "pail-stuff" as far as Egg Rock. West Concord was, for a time, called Warnersville. Although he gave land for the grade school and built the community meeting hall, he lost his popularity when he wouldn't let the Concord Junction Religious Society use the meeting hall one Sunday: *Sic transit gloria* Monday. The factory burned in 1894 and two years later Warner sold the remains, the mill and adjoining workers' houses and land, to the Concord Junction Land Company, which intended to develop it for houses. There was some question as to clear title, resolved when the town of Concord acquired the parcel in 1961.

It is a relief, on this beautiful morning, to steer under the last bridge on the Assabet—Thoreau's "One Arch Bridge" now replaced—and to know that ahead is open stream. On shore, day lilies, escaped from cultivation, form big orange-flowered clumps; pickerelweed comes into bloom with huge lavender spears, and nearby three iris fly brilliant cadmium yellow, each color intensifying the other. It was one of Thoreau's favorite bathing places:

> The North River, Assabet, by the old stone bridge, affords the best bathing-place I think of,—a pure sandy, uneven bottom, —with a swift current, a grassy bank, and overhanging maples, with transparent water, deep enough, where you can see every fish in it. Though you stand still, you feel the rippling current about you.

With Teale-like tenacity, Thoreau researched the effect of the new bridge on his part of the river, and recorded in his journal a few days later:

> Abel Hosmer [who lived upstream on the Assabet] says that the Turnpike Company did not fulfill their engagement to build a new bridge over the Assabet in 1807; that the present stone bridge was not built till about the time the Orthodox meeting-house was built. (That was in 1826.) Benjamin says it was built soon after the meeting-house, or perhaps 1827, and was placed some fifty feet higher up-stream than the old wooden one.
>
> Hosmer says that the eddy and wearing away of the bank has been occasioned wholly by the bridge; that there was only the regular bend there before. He had thought that it was in consequence of the bridge being set askew or diagonally with the stream, so that the abutments turned the water and gave it a slant into the banks, thus: I think that this did not create, only increased, the evil. The bank which it has worn away rises some sixteen feet above low water, and, considering the depth of the water, you may say that it has removed the sand to a depth of twenty-five feet over an area of a quarter of an acre, or say to the depth of three feet or a yard over two acres, or 9680 cubic yards or cartloads, which, at twenty-five cents per load, it would have cost $2420 to move in the ordinary manner. . . .

The passage reminds me of Edwin totaling up loosestrife seeds!

Soon Spencer Brook enters from the left; even such a skilled

boater as Thoreau found it difficult to navigate the brook upstream; it could only be ascended a short distance until "tall grasses of the marsh overhang the canoe and the abrupt turns are not
easy." More than a hundred years later, it must look much the
same to us as it did to Thoreau, although a thicket of buttonball
bushes frames the entrance and Edwin and I do not essay to push
through, having tangled with all too many buttonball bushes and
their tough resilient branches.

The brook was named for William Spencer, one of the original proprietors of Concord, who owned the land before James Barrett built a mill there, a mill still in operation in Thoreau's lifetime. With the establishment of Concord, Barrett built both a saw
and a grist mill on Spencer Brook. In 1776 he was made muster
master, a position he held until his death. He also captained a
Concord company appointed to collect, assemble, and deposit military stores at Concord. Thus he maintained a constant guard and
had teams ready to transport stores if need be—musket balls, car-
tridges, cartridge paper, as well as supplies for domestic needs:
axes, wheel spokes, candles, medicines.

On April 18, 1775, marching at night for security, the British
moved toward Concord, not with battle in mind, but simply to
destroy those stores and to arrest Barrett and others whose activities they considered treasonous. Barrett was forewarned by Dawes
and Revere, and had moved many of the stores out of town; some
of his carts had not returned when the alarm was given on
April 19.

As we drift on downstream, not part of that history but still,
somehow, not part of today either, I slip into the self-indulgence
that a summer's day allows. Both of us seem simply content to
register and tabulate the richness of summer about us: turtles in
the pickerelweed, turtles sunning; yellow water lilies in flower;
ribbons of eelgrass under the bow—Edwin's notes record much
the same. The river translates light-blue sky as Wedgwood blue; a
clacking dragonfly flashes metallic-green body and blood-red legs.

We travel a lambent river full of light, unimaginably lovely.
It's the river Renoir painted with picnickers beside it, that Monet
painted with a single pensive figure, that Dufy painted with ban-
ners flying, all light and color and movement. The breeze turns
the leaves underside out, changing their color the way a flight of
pigeons shift color when they veer together.

The river must not have changed much in recent years; William Brewster, the Harvard ornithologist who maintained a cabin just downstream on the Concord, wrote just sixty-six years ago today: "Great sulphurous white clouds floating in a pale blue sky. The foliage of the white maples along the river and the edges of the meadow tossing in the wind, looking thin and dishevelled and showing the whitish under surfaces of the leaves."

On our left is Thoreau's "Shadbush Meadow," an outwash terrace overlying the Assabet River Fault. There one August Thoreau followed a muskrat trail in the grass and recorded seeing a tiercel. It strikes me that Thoreau's worth lies not so much in his philosophy as in the fact that he had the discipline and dedication to write all his observations down. Edwin says that Thoreau had a phrase for everything. But we would never have known had they not been so meticulously recorded.

And so too, I think, for Edwin, whose many notebooks contain the neatly typed, clear and industrious record of his travels, his thoughts, his outlook and his way of life, as faithfully and completely (and to my mind, more gracefully) recorded as Thoreau's.

> The discipline involved in making notes on the spot and doing research afterward enriches instead of diminishing the experience that has seemed transcendent at the time. The preparation in advance of the trip, when a book is involved, enables us to appreciate things in greater depth. And in writing the book, we are, to a large extent, writing it for ourselves. Details fade and blur as time goes on. But if we have written it all in a book, we can experience it again with the intensity of the first encounter.
>
> In the main, these notes are like seeds rather than mature, harvested plants. They will recall memories rather than record complete information.
>
> I have always been putting things down in notebooks and journals. As Thoreau put it, I have felt impelled to "pluck the fruit of the day and store it in my bin." Egotistical? Perhaps. But my experiences, especially with nature, seemed so important to me I wanted to give them what permanence I could. I suppose it is a form of memento-keeping—like some people save wine-bottle corks.

I agree with Edwin. I too find that some thoughts in a journal are, as he says, better expressed there than they will ever be again. The same thing happens in note-taking on the spot; when you are right there, the sense of place sometimes is so strong that words appear on the page by themselves, very much like what drawing is for me—inherent in the page and all I do is rub my hand over the paper in the right way to bring it up.

A small island splits the current, named by Thoreau Willow Island. The island interested him because it was connected with the bridge upstream:

> Jacob Farmer tells me that he remembers that when about twenty-one years old he and Hildreth were bathing in the Assabet at the mouth of the brook above Winn's, and Hildreth swam or waded across to a sandbar (now the island there), but the water was so deep on that bar that he became frightened, and would have been drowned if he had not been dragged out and resuscitated by others. This was directly over where that island is now, and was then only a bar beginning under water. That island, as he said, had been formed within thirty-five years, or since the Eddy Bridge [now Elm Street Bridge] was built; and I suggest that it may have been built mainly of the ruins of that bank. It is the only island in the Assabet for two and a half miles.

We slide around still another Thoreau landmark, Dove Rock, a gray boulder of Nashoba Formation, an old wrinkled pudding-layered rock plunked right in the middle of the stream—a glacial erratic. The dark-gray granitic gneiss is bearded with dried gray moss, so old that there is no agreement among geologists as to *how* old, so metamorphosed that what it was before is lost in eons of pressure and heat—perhaps basalt, perhaps limestone, perhaps sandstone.

As we pass close to shore I lean over and pick up a freshwater clamshell two inches long; clams are the preferred food of muskrats. Thoreau once took home a "handsome little beetle tied up neatly in a clamshell." In midstream, good-sized fish jump, leaving irregular rings of bubbles. Blue jays set up a yattering in a big oak, annoyed with interlopers.

The river hooks sharply south at Dove Rock, pushed by the bedrock outcrop to the northeast, forced to run toward the Sudbury through the more yielding sediments that were once the bed of ancient glacial Lake Sudbury. Alongside, azalea and mountain laurel flower in the shadowed woods, delicate and ethereal.

"We slide around still another Thoreau landmark, Dove Rock, a gray boulder of Nashoba Formation, an old wrinkled pudding-layered rock. . . ."

Here, where it is easy to disembark and unload, bricks for the Hildreth house, barged up the Merrimack and the Concord, were off-loaded.

And now we drift along the bank where grew the hemlocks described by Nathaniel Hawthorne in his journal entry of September 18, 1842, (in his journal Hawthorne occasionally misspelled Thoreau's name):

> On one side, there is a high bank, forming the side of a hill, the Indian name of which I have forgotten, though Mr. Thorow told it to me; and here, in some instances, the trees

Early azalea (*Rhododendron roseum*)

seem ready to precipitate themselves down, and stand leaning over the river, stretching out their arms, as if about to plunge headlong in. On the other side, the bank is almost on a level with the water; and here the quiet congregation of trees stand with their feet in the flood, and fringed with foliage down to its very surface. Vines here and there twine themselves about birches, or aspens, or elder-trees, and hang their clusters, (though scanty and infrequent, this season) over the water, so that I can reach them from my boat. I scarcely remember a scene of more complete and lovely seclusion than the passage of the river through this wood; even an Indian canoe, in olden

Mountain laurel (*Kalmia polifolia*)

229

times, could not have floated onward in more complete solitude than mine did. I have never elsewhere had such an opportunity to observe how much more beautiful reflection is than what we call reality. The sky, and the clustering foliage on either hand, and the effect of sunlight as it found its way through the shade, giving lightsome hues in contrast with the quiet depth of the prevailing tints—all these seemed unsurpassably beautiful, when beheld in upper air. But, on gazing downward, there they were, the same even to the minutest particular, yet arrayed in ideal beauty, which satisfied the spirit incomparably more than the actual scene. I am half convinced that the reflection is indeed the reality—the real thing which Nature imperfectly images to our grosser sense.

At the foot of Nashawtuc Hill, the name Hawthorne couldn't remember, stands a tablet to the memory of George Ripley Bartlett. Journalist, poet of his time, flowing of phrase, often sentimental, he loved the Assabet and loved to organize social events such as "water evenings," when everyone floated together on the river. Lines from a poem called "Floating Hearts," referring to the shape of water lily leaves, describe his Assabet:

> One of Indian summer's most perfect days
> Is dreamily dying in golden haze,
> Fair Assabet blushes in rosy bliss,
> Reflecting the sun's warm good-night kiss.
> Through a fleet of leaf-barques, gold and brown,
> From the radiant maples shaken down,
> By the ancient hemlocks, grim and gray
> Our boat drifts slowly on its way. . . .

He also characterized the perfect size for a boat as the one that had "just nobody in it but you and me."

The Hemlocks was a remarkably handsome stand, according to all reports, and likely a favorite of many. Now they are mostly replaced by willows. A few, descendants of the originals, remain—trunks two feet in diameter, brown and cinnamon, pale-gray knobs where light-starved branches have fallen.

Although it was a sharp chill day in March when Fuzzy Fenn took Edwin and me on a "fluvial walk" along the abandoned railroad right-of-way, and it was windy, the trees damped the wind and close to the river it was almost still. The ground beneath them was brown with needles, covering the hillside, as Thoreau said, "like some wild grain." Upon them green hemlock sprigs and brown oak leaves teetered on masses of haircap moss. Edwin scuffed over some snapping-turtle eggs that had been dug up, probably by a skunk, the leathery shells torn open. The river was high that day but it had been higher; collars of ice hung above the water, giving the trunks a clerical cast. Some, where drops had begun to melt along the edge and frozen, looked like jesters' collars.

An article in The *Concord Freeman* of August 1, 1878, spoke in glowing promotional terms about the extension of the Boston, Lowell & Nashua Railroad (which became the Boston & Maine) on a route across the Sudbury River "and by a bold curve over the neck between the two streams" to the "upper side of the Assabet" and along the Assabet, crossing it slightly above Spencer Brook and thence to Concord Junction. The problem was that the railroad grade, running along the Assabet, infringed upon the seclusion of The Hemlocks.

To try to prevent such a depredation, a "Petition from citizens of Concord against the building of a railroad line through Concord's natural scenery" was sent to the general manager of the railroad:

> We citizens of Concord respectfully and urgently remind you that your contractors are now building the new line through what is to us and to all lovers of nature most precious ground.
>
> The No. Branch of Concord river [Assabet] is our "Central Park" and one of the most beautiful pieces of simple scenery in New England.
>
> We feel it is bad enough to have a railroad at all in that place, but the ruthless destruction of a single tree, or shrub, for firewood or for any purpose not absolutely necessary to building the road will be viewed by us all as barbarism which we hope you can and will prevent.

The first name on the petition is "R. Waldo Emerson," followed by other well-known Concordians, among them A. Bronson Alcott, Daniel C. French, Alfred W. Hosmer—all told, sixty-six petitioners.

But to no avail. The *Concord Freeman* reported that the bridge over the Sudbury was in place on May 1, 1879, that the bridge over the Assabet was expected to be finished by May 15, and both bridges were to be painted on July 3. The "ancient hem-

231

To F. Hosford. Gen'l Man. B & L RR

We citizens of Concord respectfully and urgently remind you that your contractors are now building the new line through what is to us and to all lovers of nature most precious ground.

The No. Branch of Concord river is our "Central Park" and one of the most beautiful pieces of simple scenery in New England.

We feel it is bad enough to have a railroad at all in that place, but the ruthless destruction of a single tree, or shrub, for fire wood or for any purpose not absolutely necessary to building the road will be viewed by us all as barbarism which we hope you can and will prevent

Names	Names
R. Waldo Emerson	C. E. Barrett
A. Bronson Alcott	Elizabeth B. Ripley
F. B. Sanborn	
	Ellen T. Emerson
	Lidian E. Jackson
Dan'l C. French	Martha Bartlett
F. M. Holland	Alicia M. Keyes.

Emerson petition

locks, grim and gray" were partially destroyed. The bridges have been gone for thirty years, as are the boys who swung across the rivers on the bridge supports and walked the ties and found secret places beneath that only small boys find.

Nashawtuc Hill is a 250-foot-high drumlin rising between the two rivers. On its other side, unseen, the Sudbury is making a great loop, drawing up toward the Assabet. Nashawtuc was the dwelling place of Indians who had survived the decimating epidemics of 1617 and 1633; it was an ideal campsite, providing height for surveillance, ample and close water and food. Sometimes they burned sandy hills to allow blueberries to come in, or to clear land for planting corn. They raised pumpkins and beans and had abundant wild game—bear, beaver, otter, muskrat—for food and fur-trading.

Simon Willard was an Indian trader who had bargained for furs with these Indians, and it was he, along with the Reverend Peter Bulkeley, who brought the first families to Concord, then the farthest inland settlement, in 1635. Official purchase took place in 1636, a plantation "six miles of land square," and negotiations were so agreeable that they were commemorated in the name of the settlement: Concord.

For his own land Willard chose Nashawtuc Hill. He accompanied the settlers, served as a military commander in King

Early low blueberry (*Vaccinium angustifolium*)

233

Philip's War, and was later town clerk. He died just one hundred years before the British troops fired on the colonists within half a mile of his hill home. Mary Fenn told Edwin that the mast for the frigate *Constitution* was cut on Nashawtuc Hill.

Nashawtuc rises high, the river runs serene. Waterweeds, solid across the shallows, hiss softly under the bow. Four cedar waxwings dart out of a maple. When I stop to write I rest the paddle across the gunwales in front of me. The water drips off onto my toes and dampens my sneakers and feels pleasantly cool on my feet this warm morning. We let the canoe drift in silence. As it pivots quietly in the current, I turn and look back upstream, remembering the October day when Edwin and I first turned the bow from the Sudbury into the Assabet. My first view of the river was just as Hawthorne had seen it a century earlier, and I was just as enthralled:

A more lovely stream than this, for a mile above its junction with the Concord, has never flowed on earth—nowhere, indeed, except to lave the interior regions of a poet's imagination. It is sheltered from the breeze by woods and a hillside; so that elsewhere there might be a hurricane, and here scarcely a ripple across the shaded water. The current lingers along so gently that the mere force of the boatman's will seems sufficient to propel his craft against it. It comes flowing softly through the mid-most privacy and deepest heart of a wood which whispers it to be quiet; while the stream whispers back again from sedgy borders, as if river and wood were hushing one another to sleep. Yes; the river sleeps along its course and dreams of the sky and of the clustering foliage, amid which fall showers of broken sunlight, imparting specks of vivid cheerfulness, in contrast with the quiet depth of the prevailing tint.

That day when Edwin first showed me the Assabet, we had canoed down the Sudbury through its English-like countryside: opulent trees whose thousands of leaves shot pointillist dots of light as they blew; blowsy clouds fed by ample moisture, ambling across a milky blue sky; thickets along the bank quivering with all kinds of birds. A civilized countryside: houses backed up to the river, skiffs moored here and there, voices and traffic noises carrying on the soft air.

And then, slipping in from the left, came this other gleaming stream, ripples scintillating in the afternoon sunshine. As we turned upstream, the force of the current was just perceptible against the paddle. The river narrowed, closed in a little. No houses were visible. For the first time in this populated countryside I had a hint of untouched river, of wildness. And a whole new vocabulary of gray rock and trees and sunshine weaving it all together.

At that moment on the Assabet there was a golden stillness in the air. Autumnal light filtered through leaves that wafted down in slow rotating helices onto the water. Some, stem and tip turned up like tiny dories, turned quietly, each in its own moment. Others curled like cup-shaped hands, palm up, in gestures of supplication. Older ones slid along just under the water's surface, spinning when caught in the gurgling vortex of the paddle stroke. A round-lobed swamp oak leaf as big as my hand swirled down and settled at my feet. Duckweed shone like flakes of gold leaf. Milkweed seeds sailed in flotillas, white filaments spread out, supporting seeds an inch above the water, keeping them high and dry, each one doubled in reflection. Dappled ripples tapped ever so gently on the bow. And I suppose it was right then, on that day, at that moment, that I was bewitched by the Assabet.

For at that moment I had a sense of unreality, of time out of mind—this clear water, this quiet river—and for that moment the Assabet became the idealized river of imagination, the way I had wished the river I grew up on to be and never was, flowing through an arcade of idealized trees, a river, just as Hawthorne said, to be found only in a poet's imagination—or a child's.

And thus it has remained for me, in spite of the old washing machine and the rusting supermarket basket lying feet up in the middle of the river as it flows through a town, the reeking sewage outflow and the detergent foam that makes the river look rabid, the channelization that denies it freedom. The oxymoronic Assabet: the lovely little Assabet, the dirty filthy little Assabet, the bridged and dammed and polluted little Assabet. And if someone asks me what the Assabet is like, I don't remember the spewing sewer pipe or the stinking algae blooms in besotted backwaters, the endless plastic bottles bobbing downstream like aborted eggs of some misanthropic river monster. I remember that, whenever allowed, it retains lyrical wild reaches where water glints over a clean gravel bottom and blue sky and trees are reflected in its going, and that it runs through my life like a bright silver memory that will not come again.

235

"Now on this June day, we rotate as gently as a leaf and turn downstream toward the confluence and Egg Rock."

All those facets of the river have bound me to it, have taught me something about how other people feel about rivers and how they use them, and what, finally, we owe to a river.

Now on this June day, we rotate as gently as a leaf and turn downstream toward the confluence and Egg Rock. Just as there is pleasure in beginnings, there is poignancy in endings—as Edwin says, "an element of sadness about finishing a book. They record a special portion of our lives that we wish we could hold on to but that we feel is slipping away to the rear. Finishing the book is a kind of rounding out and completing the experience. It is, in a sense, a goodbye. But we have the consolation of having that time in our lives that means so much to us preserved and given a little immortality in the pages of a book."

Ahead the river widens and opens where the Sudbury drifts in from the right, the two rivers kept separate a few feet farther by an islet that lies in the middle of the Y, before losing their identity and becoming the Concord. Once, I remember, we came around this corner and there was a picnic in the Calf Pasture opposite, and the pleasant lilt of voices spun across the water. So must it have sounded when Daniel French had his early-autumn breakfasts here at Egg Rock.

Or I imagine the sound of voices on a fine summer night three-quarters of a century ago, when boaters in crafts large and small would congregate just up from the mouth of the Assabet, and lash their boats, one to the other, until the river was solid boats. Then they would float downstream, drifting with the current, Japanese lanterns swaying, while singers harmonized on songs that everyone knew—a time of harmony and affection that lasted but an evening and then was gone, *morendo*, fading gently as the last notes hung for that imperceptible moment before the final darkness came, the goodbyes were said, and all was over.

We double the point and wedge the bow into shore to read the plaque that marks the joining of the two rivers:

ON THE HILL NASHAWTUCK
AT THE MEETING OF THE RIVERS
AND ALONG THE BANKS
LIVED THE INDIAN OWNERS OF
MUSKETAQUID
BEFORE THE WHITE MAN CAME.

Acknowledgments

Because of the sad circumstances under which this book was completed, I am more indebted than ordinary to the kindness of those who helped and, very simply, without whom it could not have been finished. It is to Nellie Donovan Teale that I owe the deepest debt of gratitude for the most understanding support and encouragement. Her reading of the manuscript was something I shall never forget. She identified and described many of the plants new to me. She provided the wonderful hospitality and quiet of Trail Wood (my appreciation includes Mrs. Anna G. Jurgens and Mrs. Laurian M. Sypher). She also gave generous permission to quote from Dr. Teale's correspondence.

Traveling as far and as often as I did made me very grateful for Mr. and Mrs. W. Clark Stocking's help, and the hospitality of those in and around Concord: Mr. and Mrs. Paul Brooks; Mrs. Edmund Fenn, and her daughter, Mary Gail Fenn; Mr. and Mrs. Perry Hess; Elsie Kennedy and Herbert Grundman; Mr. and Mrs. John McDonald; Mrs. Patricia McFarland; Mr. and Mrs. Lael (Mike) Meixsell; Mr. and Mrs. Merle Mudd; and Mr. and Mrs. Walter Tidman.

John McDonald, of the University of Connecticut Library, where Edwin's papers reside, made facilities at the library available that solved otherwise unsolvable problems.

To Anne B. and Mike Meixsell I owe worthwhile hours on the river, pleasant companionship, and background information about the SuAsCo Watershed Association, of which Mike is executive director. He read and commented on pertinent parts of the manuscript. I also thank Carol Hess for a morning on the Concord and at "Thoreau's Island," complete with a wood thrush chiming in the woods.

Without Paul Huehmer I could not have canoed some parts of the Assabet; with my thanks go apologies for dumping him in the river. His father, Horst Huehmer, Director of Public Utilities for Hudson, supplied historical background, as did William Allen, an unretired retiree of the Hudson Power & Light Company.

William Sullivan showed me around the Damondale mill and talked about its history as well as his hopes for its future. Gilbert Woolley, Sierra Club representative and active member of SuAsCo, gave perspective on current river problems.

Donald E. Chisholm provided an excellent overview of wastewater treatment problems in the area as well as explaining his own particular plant at Maynard. Charles Boika and Robert Minasin also helped in interpreting a subject about which most of us know all too little. I would also like to thank Thomas J. Sheridan, Superintendent of Public Works, Maynard.

Vivian Novis and Lisa Cross gave valuable help on map preparation.

Those to whom Edwin and I are both grateful comprise a long list. At the very top are Mrs. Edmund Fenn and her daughter, Mary Gail. They provided historical background and accompanied us on our journeys in more ways than one. Both Thoreau scholars beyond compare, they gave generously of their knowledge and answered many frantic telephone calls from Colorado with kindness.

Jacqueline Tidman, conservator of the Westborough Public Library, provided us both with access to early Westborough historical documents. Both of us interviewed Mrs. Rachel Dearing, whose father was Dr. Charles Reed, a Westborough historian; fortunately his daughter has inherited his interests and gives to those who know her a rich heritage of remembrances.

Of inestimable help to me was Patricia McFarland, who went over Northborough town records with me; much of it is in unpublished form, and not only made available but brought it to my attention. Both Mrs. Tidman and Mrs. McFarland read portions of the manuscript in which they have expertise, and provided substantiation on quoted material. Needless to say, they may take credit for the accuracy and I for any errors that have slipped through.

Arthur Screpetis, biologist with the Massachusetts Water Pollution Control in Westborough, gave us both technical information and passed on pertinent publications as available. He gave most generously of time and help, and kindly read portions of the manuscript in preparation.

Mr. and Mrs. Eugene Walker gave generous assistance. Mr. Walker, a USGS geologist, counseled on the geology of the region. His wife, Mary, who works with the New England Wildflower Society, made available books to which I otherwise would not have had access. Mary Walker, Ray Angelo, and Jean Baker, botanists with the Harvard-Concord Field Station, checked accuracy of both botanical nomenclature and drawing labels.

Daniel Monihan, Superintendent of the Department of Natural Resources in Concord, provided much technical information about the rivers, as well as suggestions as to where to find more, and was courteous in many ways.

Mrs. William Henry Moss, reference librarian at the Concord Free Public Library, and Miss Joyce Woodman provided tremendous help—working in that library is indeed, as Edwin wrote, a privilege. Miss Woodman did a wonderfully thorough job of checking and xeroxing material.

There were many people with whom Edwin traveled the river and with whom he spent time; if in culling his notes I have omitted anyone, I hope they will forgive me and know that he was eloquent in his praise of all those who helped him in his research. After one particularly pleasant afternoon he wrote: "One of the features of research on this book has been meeting so many people who seemed fine and admirable, as well as helpful."

Roland Wells Robbins spent some memorable days on the river with Edwin; he is recognized in the pages of this book. As is Dr. Walter Harding, with Edwin one of the founders of the Thoreau Society, who made an early-morning canoe trip on the Sudbury every year with Edwin. I am sure he knows of Edwin's devotion to a long-standing friendship and a shared interest.

Mrs. George Emery of Wayland is also part of the text; her research on Stone's Bridge provided Edwin with background information and the chance to make a contribution of his own.

Thomas Goettel, Assistant Manager, Great Meadows Wildlife Refuge, accompanied Edwin when he mowed the "corridor of grass," which was first showed him by Mrs. Richard E. Robinson of Wayland.

Dr. C. Barre Helquist, Department of Biology, Boston State University, identified waterweeds; Dr. James Slater, Department of Zoology, University of Connecticut, identified insects seen along the way.

Edwin spent time on the river with Forest Bradshaw; he ended a day's notes with "We always have such a good time." A nice compliment indeed. He also spent a memorable afternoon with John Quincy Adams, who lives on Fairhaven Bay.

Characteristically, Edwin made a list of those whom he wished to thank. Many of them are mentioned in the text, but there are others for whom I have only names. I'm sure that anyone who spent a few hours with Edwin was profusely thanked in person, but I give the names here, as he listed them, and tender my thanks as well to: Mrs. Leslie O. Anderson, an old and valued friend, a charter member of the Thoreau Society, who shared her remembrances of Concord; Frank Barton, who showed Edwin bog iron at Pantry Brook; Sam Benson, for remembrances of William Brewster; Mrs. K. C. Black; Tom Blanding, who worked on a new edition of Thoreau's *Journals*; Paul Brooks, former Executive Editor of Houghton Mifflin Company, for advice and suggestions; Mrs. Charles D. Childs of Stow, for historical information; Charles Comeau, for information about the powder mills and reminiscences of the Assabet; Alan Cooperman, Water Pollution Control Division, Westborough; Frederick B. Gay, USGS Water Resources Division; Frank Generazio, New England Sand & Gravel Company; Tom Goettel, Assistant Manager, Great Meadows National Wildlife Refuge; Mrs. Louise Grady, Marlborough Historical Society; Elsie Kennedy, for remembrances of the Assabet (and a lively interest in its future); Walter Hoyt, Massachusetts Fish and Wildlife; Tom Hayes, a muskrat trapper whose family has lived along the Concord for many years; Jori Hunken, naturalist at Garden of the Woods, the Framingham wildflower preserve; Markis Kempe, Senior Engineer with the Metropolitan District Commission in Westborough; B. Anthony King, a fine wildlife photographer who, when he canoed the upper Sudbury with Edwin, impressed him with his canoe skills as much as his photographic ones; Mary

McClintok, who lives at Conantum and showed us where Thoreau's bluets once grew; Lee McGlaughlin, Central Wildlife District; Mrs. Thomas McGrath, Curator of the Thoreau Lyceum; Thomas Morehouse, Soil Conservation Service; Mrs. Merle Mudd, President of the SuAsCo Watershed Association; Paul Mugford of the Division of Fisheries and Wildlife, for information on Cedar Swamp; Laurence E. Richardson, who wrote a beautiful book on the Concord River; Mrs. Bobby Robinson, who provided information about SuAsCo and showed Edwin the original grass meadows on the Sudbury; Mr. and Mrs. George Rohan of the Southbridge Boathouse; Steve Rosenthal, our pilot for three trips looking over the rivers; Howard S. Russell, historian of Wayland; Dr. James Slater, Department of Zoology, University of Connecticut, for insect identification and information; Rachel and Juliet Wheeler, John Meyers and Steve Rampley, who provided a convenient launching place at the edge of Fairhaven Bay as well as information about the area; Mr. and Mrs. Russell Wheeler.

And I cannot go without thanking my own personal support system who helped in so many ways: Victoria French, Mrs. Pina Ruiz, Judy Dulla, and Richard Kresge of IBM, and Timilou Rixon who shores up my syntax. And most especially, these friends who gave superb proofreading when time was excruciatingly short: Kate Belden, Stephanie Noyes, Daves Kosley, and Kathryn Redman.

Most of all, I thank M. S. Wyeth, Jr., who shared time on the river with Edwin and me, and Corona Machemer, for superb editorial advice and assistance, and also for encouragement and understanding. I simply could not have completed this book without their guidance. And thanks also to Florence Goldstein and Lisa Pulitzer for many courtesies. Fran Collin gave affectionate professional advice and appreciated support.

And last but first, my appreciation of a husband who printed contact sheets and made final prints of many of Edwin's photographs, and who endured my overextended absences, if not with joy, at least with fortitude, because for obvious reasons this book took many more hours and many more years and many more trips to complete than originally planned.

Ann Zwinger

Constant Friendship
January 12, 1982

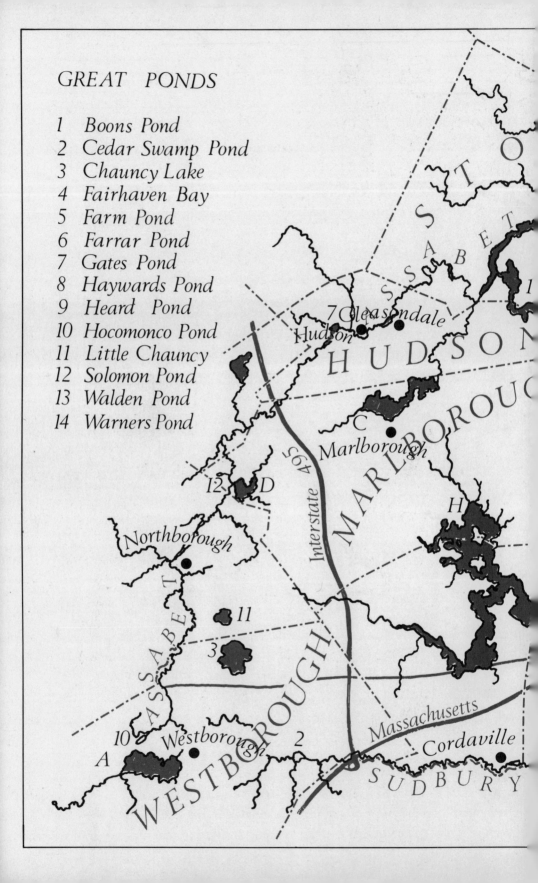

GREAT PONDS

1   Boons Pond
2   Cedar Swamp Pond
3   Chauncy Lake
4   Fairhaven Bay
5   Farm Pond
6   Farrar Pond
7   Gates Pond
8   Haywards Pond
9   Heard Pond
10   Hocomonco Pond
11   Little Chauncy
12   Solomon Pond
13   Walden Pond
14   Warners Pond